Informal Markets, Livelihood and Politics

T0270900

Low industrial growth, the declining agricultural sector and limited expansion of formal sector employment in India have increasingly forced the poor to take recourse to informal sources of livelihoods in the urban economy. Street vending is one such thriving source of self-employment across cities.

This book delves into the sustenance and survival strategies of street vendors across seventeen cities in India and assesses the issues revolving around self-created markets, livelihood and politics that are contested in public space. It also presents a conceptual and theoretical understanding of different socio-economic and policy concerns pertaining to street vending in the country. The study shows how, despite the absence of legal frameworks and institutional support, these urban self-employed informal workers subsist by arranging ad hoc alternatives, creating informal institutions and negotiating with formal and informal actors in the market. It also discusses the Street Vendors (Protection of Livelihood and Regulation of Street Vending) Act, 2014, and examines how inclusive the legal recognition is for these workers of informal economy.

Drawing on exhaustive research and a wealth of primary data, this book will be useful to scholars and researchers in development studies, labour studies, economics and sociology, and those in public policy and urban planning.

Debdulal Saha is Assistant Professor and Programme Coordinator of Labour Studies at Tata Institute of Social Sciences (TISS), Guwahati campus, Assam, India. Prior to joining TISS, he was post-doctoral fellow at the International Center for Development and Decent Work (ICDD), University of Kassel, Germany. His research interests are development economics, labour studies, informal economy and livelihoods. He is co-author of *Financial Inclusion of the Marginalised: Street Vendors in the Urban Economy* (2013) and co-editor of *The Food Crisis: Implications for Labor* (2013).

Informal Markets, Livelihood and Politics

Street vendors in urban India

Debdulal Saha

Routledge
Taylor & Francis Group
LONDON AND NEW YORK

First published 2017 by Routledge

2 Park Square, Milton Park, Abingdon, Oxfordshire OX14 4RN
52 Vanderbilt Avenue, New York, NY 10017

Routledge is an imprint of the Taylor & Francis Group, an informa business

First issued in paperback 2019

British Library Cataloguing-in-Publication Data
A catalogue record for this book is available from the
British Library

Library of Congress Cataloging-in-Publication Data
A catalog record has been requested for this book

ISBN: 978-1-138-68566-6 (hbk)
ISBN: 978-0-367-17726-3 (pbk)

Typeset in Sabon
by Apex CoVantage, LLC

To my loving family . . .

Contents

Tables

Boxes

Foreword

Debdulal Saha's monograph on street vendors is perhaps the first major study on the subject in India. Street vendors as a part of the informal economy have hardly been the focus of research in the sense that there are hardly any monographs on this section, though there have been some articles in print. I can only think of Jonathan Shapiro Anjaria's (2016) work on street vendors in Mumbai as another major study and it is based on one city, namely, Mumbai. Debdulal's research for his doctoral dissertation too was based on Mumbai but at the time of writing his monograph he had done similar studies in other cities and these are integrated along with his basic study. Another difference is that Anjaria Shapiro's study is anthropological, based on thick ethnography and observation, whereas Debdulal, being trained as an economist, has relied more on quantitative data along with qualitative data.

Social scientists in India have only recently begun studying the informal economy. Keith Hart's study on the informal sector in Ghana in 1972 (Hart 1973) was considered a landmark and he coined the term 'informal sector', which was accepted by the International Labour Organisation (ILO). He tried to advocate that it was a sector that was parallel to the formal sector and sooner or later as the developing countries develop on the lines of the developed countries this sector would be absorbed into the formal sector. India rigidly stuck to the approach that the informal sector was transient and that our five-year plans would bring all labour into the fold of formal employment. The planners also felt that informal employment acted as a safety net for employment. This was despite the discussions in the ILO on whether the informal sector could provide a viable alternative. The Director-General's report to the International Labour Conference in 1991 makes this clear. The report weighs the employment potential of informal employment versus minimum labour standards and suggests that employment without minimum labour standards cannot be an alternative (ILO 1991). The planners in India were unfazed by these observations and continued to ignore the informally employed.

It was around the early twenty-first century, when the adverse effects of the liberalisation policies of 1991 were felt on labour, that the government woke up to the fact that something should be done in terms of policy formulations. One of the first steps was of introducing the National Policy on Urban Street Vendors in 2004. For the first time the issue of street vending was taken up and steps were being undertaken to provide these people with legal protection. A decade later, thanks to the consistent campaign of trade unions such as Self-Employed Women's Association (SEWA) and National Association of Street Vendors of India (NASVI), the government passed a law that provides legal protection to street vendors. Debdulal's researches also played a role in pushing for a law.

Debdulal began his research with a study of street vending in Mumbai. This was the focus of his doctoral dissertation. While pursuing his PhD degree he undertook two studies that were related with his work on street vending. The first was a study of street vending in ten cities in India. NASVI had requested me to conduct this study as it could use the findings to put forth the case for legalising street vending. I had asked Debdulal to assist me in conducting the study (see Bhowmik 2010). A couple of years later, when he was planning to submit his dissertation for examination, UNDP, New Delhi, requested me to conduct a study on financial inclusion of street vendors. We wanted to do a study on how street vendors procured financial resources for running their activities. Debdulal had covered this aspect in his doctoral research on Mumbai and I asked him to join me in conducting the research. This time we covered fifteen cities (Bhowmik & Saha 2013). These two research projects plus his intensive study of street vendors in Mumbai have given him a very good understanding of problems of street vending in the country.

After completing his PhD, Debdulal got a teaching position at TISS Guwahati campus. Despite his busy teaching schedule he managed to do two more studies in two cities, namely, Kolkata and Guwahati. This book is an outcome of his researches during the past seven years. It covers the main issues of public policy, governance and the social organisation of street vendors. His researches have given him a deep understanding of the economy of street vending and the urban informal economy. This book provides rich economic and sociological data on the issues. After going through his manuscript I can only comment that this is the most comprehensive study on street vending. The most important part of his findings shows that street vendors are eager to have their profession legalised given the insecurities and harassment they face due to their non-legal status. This issue has been controversial as many researchers feel that legalising of street vending would ruin their trade. I will discuss this issue in the next few paragraphs.

Legalising street vending

Street vending has been discussed by different social scientists. Hernando de Soto has argued that street vendors must be legalised so that they can operate without pressure. He has elaborated in his book (De Soto 1989: 87–90) how street vendors in Lima could successfully organise themselves and force the municipality to provide them space for carrying their activities. They could do this because of the leadership of FEVACEL, a self-defence organisation of the urban poor which was led by the communists. This organisation became central for mobilising street vendors so that they could pressurise the state to prevent harassment.

There are other studies that have emerged as bitter critics of De Soto's views or any theory that talks about legalising street vending. Cross (2000) feels that the so-called illegal activities of street vendors are incorrect. He is critical of Portes's definition that the informal sector uses illegal means to produce/sell legal goods. He engages in a discussion on what is legal and what is not legal. Sale of heroin on the streets is illegal, whereas use of heroin as a pain killer by doctors is legal. Similarly, selling of pirated CDs may be illegal as the original producers and the artists lose royalty. However, for customers who are saved the high costs they are legal as they are recorded on good quality CDs. He argues that the difference between the formal, informal and illegal sectors may never be clear.

Another writer, Neuwirth (2011), who has written a very insightful book on the informal economy, sees the same problem in defining legal and illegal. In the chapter 'Why Not Formalise the Informal' he strongly argues that formalisation (legalisation) of the activities of the informal economy will not help them. Entrepreneurs who operate without seeking licences and thereby do not pay taxes perform well precisely because they can cut down their costs. At the same time, by selling goods cheap they make these affordable for the city's working poor. In this way they contribute to the development of the city. In such circumstances forcing them to go legal would only increase their losses as they cannot compete with big business.

Neuwirth explains that the underground economy would become formal only if it is found beneficial. He shows that the computer firms in Paraguay that operate by smuggling in computers agreed to go legal only if the taxes were reduced. When the government decided to do so, the dealers tried to weigh whether paying taxes was better than paying bribes to the customs officials. Only then did they decide to go legal.

Another book edited by Gordon Mathews, Gustavo Lins Ribeiro and Carlos Alba Vega (2012) more or less follows the path of Neuwirth. This collection deals with how there is a globalising process from below that caters to the less privileged people in the cities in the developed countries. The authors assert that the term 'informal economy' does not capture the meaning of globalisation. Instead they suggest the term 'globalisation from below'. There is a parallel process of globalising in the commodity markets in most cities. Globalisation from above would be the official process. Products could be sourced from different parts of the world: high fashion clothes from Paris, mobile phones, watches, food products and other goods from different parts of the world's finest producers. The products, when marketed in India, would be expensive and only the well-off can afford them. Globalisation from below follows the same practice, namely, importing goods from all parts of the world where they are made cheap but the quality is good. These are accessible to the less well-off sections in the city.

Music and movies are sold in shopping malls and music stores at high prices as these CDs are legitimate. The prices are comparatively high because of the royalties paid to the artists and the profit share of companies. At the same time millions of low-priced but good-quality blank CDs are imported/smuggled from China and on these are recorded songs and films in shady make-shift factories. These are sold at cheap rates to the people through street vendors. This constitutes a huge market and, besides creating employment, it also caters to the needs of the not so well-off.

The authors argue that there is nothing immoral about copying, except in cases that cause harm to human life such as spurious drugs. The plagiarised CDs, clothes or high fashion accessories are illegal because they deprive the producers or artists of royalties and commissions. They argue that a large section of people who buy these goods from the grey sector could not afford to buy them at the regular rates, and hence this does not necessarily deprive the original producers of their rights. This logic is somewhat strange because the authors try to prove that globalisation from below is aimed at providing quality imported goods to the poor whereas globalisation from above is for the rich and famous. This may not necessarily be true because CDs and other duplicates such as clothes and accessories are bought from the streets even by the richer people who can afford to buy them from larger stores or malls.

The more important aspect of legalising street vending arises from the fact that illegality of the trade makes the vendors vulnerable to all types of predators. The vendors pay large amounts of their income as bribes to the municipal officials and the local police in order to stay on the streets. TISS was asked by the Municipal Corporation of Greater Mumbai to conduct a census of hawkers on the corporation's land. One of the findings mentioned that the street vendors paid Rs 385 crore as bribes annually to the police and municipal authorities (Sharma 1998). In Delhi it was found that the authorities collected Rs 50 crore each month from street vendors and cycle rickshaw pullers (Manushi Trust 2001). These figures are old (15 to 18 years). The amount could be at least three times higher at present.

Some researchers may believe that street vendors function best when they operate outside the law. Our researches show just the opposite. Street vendors in India are keen to legalise their activities as they pay a very heavy price both in terms of monetary losses and health. Our studies in ten cities show that street vendors part with 10 to 20 per cent of their earnings to the police and municipal authorities as bribes. The research on financial inclusion showed that they are further squeezed by loan sharks, who charge a minimum interest of 20 per cent per month. They could get loans from banks at much lower rates of interest if they had legal status. Moreover harassment by the authorities through eviction and confiscation of their goods take a heavy toll on the health of these people. The street vendors are always on their guard to see if their goods will be confiscated or when will the moneylender or the corrupt authorities come to take away their earnings. A study conducted by SNDT Women's University and ILO in 2001 in Mumbai showed that 86 per cent of street vendors suffer from diseases related to stress such as hypertension, hyperacidity and migraine.

I feel that Debdulal's work will be of use to academics, researchers and activists besides policymakers. I wish him and his research all success.

Sharit K. Bhowmik
National Fellow, Indian Council of
Social Science Research

References

Anjaria Shapiro, Jonathan. 2016, *The Slow Boil: Street Food, Rights and Public Space in Mumbai*, Stanford: Stanford University Press.

Bhowmik, Sharit K. 2010, 'Street Vending in Ten Cities in India' (mimeograph), New Delhi: National Association of Street Vendors of India (available at www.nasvinet.org, www.streetnet.za, www.wiego.org).

Bhowmik, Sharit K. and Debdulal Saha. 2013, *Financial Inclusion of the Marginalised: A Study of Street Vendors in the Urban Economy*, New Delhi: Springer.

Cross, John. 2000, 'Street Vendors, Modernity and Post-modernity: Conflict and Compromise in the Global Economy', *International Journal of Sociology and Social Policy*, 21(1/2): 29–52.

De Soto, Hernando. 1989, *The Other Path: The Economic Answer to Terrorism*, New York: Basic Books.

Hart, Keith. 1973, 'Informal Income Opportunities and Urban Employment in Ghana', *Journal of Modern African Studies*, 11(1): 61–89.

ILO. 1991, *The Dilemma of the Informal Sector Report of the Director-General*, 78th Session of the International Labour Conference, Geneva: ILO office.

Manushi Nagarik Adhikar Manch. 2001, 'Memorandum Submitted to the Lt. Governor of Delhi on Behalf of Delhi's Street Vendors and Rickshaw Pullers and Owners on 2 October 2001'. Delhi: Manushi Trust.

Neuwirth, Robert. 2011, *Stealth of Nations: The Global Rise of the Informal Economy*, New York: Anchor Books.

Sharma, R. N. 1998, 'Census Survey of Hawkers on BMC Lands', study conducted for Brihan Mumbai Municipal Corporation by TISS and YUVA (mimeo).

SNDT Women's University and ILO. 2001, 'Study of Hawkers in Mumbai' (mimeo).

Preface

This book is based on my doctoral thesis and insights from close association with several researches since 2007. In current development trajectories, nature of work, employment and labour process across the world have been changing, especially in developing nations, including India, in forms of contractualisation, casualisation and informalisation. In India about 92 per cent of the total working population is taking recourse to informal sources of livelihood, of which around 56 per cent are engaged as self-employed. The share of self-employment is way higher than that of regular and casual wage workers among informal sector workers. Street vending is the most visible section of self-employed workers in the urban informal economy. One of the current employment strategies in India is promotion of entrepreneurial skills, which is likely to further enhance future self-employment options. With the passing of the Street Vendors (Protection of Livelihood and Regulation of Street Vending) Act, 2014, the livelihood options through this activity will legally be protected and perhaps street vendors as micro-entrepreneurs may be promoted. The book was planned to be brought out long before but was kept on hold due to passing of the Act. In view of enactment of the Act, field revisit was needed. Some lines of enquiry were changed, field was revisited and some key respondents were re-interrogated. During revisiting the field, I could ask some of the preliminary questions on structural changes of the informal market but it was not possible to conduct an intensive survey as before. Rather, it is too early to expect any changes in existing structure have occurred. This is perhaps beyond the scope of this book or may be the beginning of the next step for further research. In the present context, however, this book would definitely be useful for various stakeholders who are framing laws and different schemes for these vendors.

Much of research interest stems from personal interests and experiences that we encounter in our lives. I belong to a small and growing town, Siliguri in West Bengal. Certain incidents captured my attention, curiosity and imagination during my formative years there. These observations several years later have significantly contributed to form the main thrust of my research work. In 1993, my father passed away. My elder brother dropped out of school to support the family, and took up street vending as an occupation. Back then, questions such as 'is street vending legal or illegal?' and 'is there any dignity in this profession?' did not come to mind. My brother would often recount experiences of running business daily under testing circumstances. He would tell us stories about police harassment and its impact on his income, profits and livelihood. I would eagerly wait for the part of his story where he vividly described how he dealt with the police and civic authorities every day. This tussle was an everyday affair. At the slightest hint of police and civic authorities approaching, he and others like him would fear a possible raid that would invariably result in a confiscation of goods. He was always disturbed and tense about these ubiquitous raids because he constantly feared eviction and harassment. Too young to be aware of the fluidity of my brother's finances, I was simply curious and had many questions which were never answered.

So I assumed that these issues characterised street vending activity. As time passed, my brother managed to obtain a legal trade licence, and started a business in partnership with a few others. This enabled him to become a registered shopkeeper. Not surprisingly, recollections of my brother's life as a street vendor are etched in my memory, and despite the shift in his occupational status, they lay dormant for many years only to resurface several years later.

As a postgraduate student of Economics in the University of North Bengal, I was introduced to concepts of labour markets, their nature and segmentation in developing nations such as India. I also learnt about livelihood options available to those working in the unorganised sector in small unregistered enterprises, self-employed and so on. The NCEUS (2007) report on the unorganised sector played a key role in honing my interest in the informal economy. I was getting increasingly intrigued about exploring the informal economy and its workforce. The watershed moment, however, was when I came across the National Policy on Urban Street Vendors in 2006. It immediately caught my attention because I could relate to the issues of street vendors mentioned in it. I was once again interested in learning why this occupation was full of insecurities. I decided that my doctoral topic would seek answers to the issues raised by this policy as well as my own past experiences through my brother. In starting this journey, I sought answers to the basic questions: why and how does street vending exist in the present context of urbanisation? This laid the foundation for my scientific enquiry, especially for the exploration of dignity (or the lack of it) in the informal sector through the case of urban street vendors. It led me to examine in depth various concepts and theories relating to the informal sector, analytical frameworks and the outlook required towards building holistic policies for street vendors in particular and the urban informal sector in general. It must be clarified here that even though much of my early knowledge about street vending activity came from my brother's lived experience, I have tried to not let that colour or influence the ways in which I conducted my enquiry through the doctoral research and other research projects. In other words, the intention was never to fabricate or exaggerate the issues pertaining to street vending based on my impressions. Rather, I have attempted to portray a realistic representation of this activity and its actors using scientific methods for data collection and analysis.

My initial enquiries started with doctoral research based in Mumbai. Later, I was part of two major projects in 2009–10 (electronically published in 2012) and in 2011–12 (published as a monograph in 2013). The first research was on 'Street Vending in Ten Cities in India' supported by National Association of Street Vendors of India (NASVI) and the second was on 'Financial Accessibility of the Street Vendors in India: Cases of Inclusion and Exclusion' in collaboration with United Nations Development Programme (UNDP) and Ministry of Housing and Urban Poverty Alleviation (MoHUPA). Engaging in these two projects, I could understand the phenomenon of street vending in seventeen cities across the country. These two projects gave me immense scope to raise my own lines of thought. Some cities are progressive towards vending and some are even reluctant to recognise them as workers. Some cases and my own reflection have been drawn from these studies. Through this book I have attempted to bring two sets of lines of enquiry understating street vending as a phenomenon. The first set of questions is straightforward empirical ones which answer why and how does street vending help generate livelihood.

The second set tries to raise theoretical questions, who and what led them to sustain in the urban economy. To evade repetition, I will not be involved in the argument and debate that I raised here as these will be elaborated in detail in ensuing chapters. The aim of this monograph is to provide a holistic picture of street vending in India.

Acknowledgements

Writing this book, I have received countless acts of support, encouragement, generosity and guidance from several individuals and institutions. To start with, I would like to convey my deep gratitude to Sharit Bhowmik, who not only guided my doctoral research but also included me in two major projects supported by National Association of Street Vendors of India (NASVI) in 2009 and United Nations Development Programme (UNDP) and Ministry of Housing and Urban Poverty Alleviation (MoHUPA) in 2011 on street vending. Besides these, I have also drawn insights from my involvement in other short-term projects and consultancies. These have been major learning experiences for me on the subject as they gave me the opportunity to understand various facts associated with the conditions of street vendors across the country. He generously encouraged me to use some of the facts from these projects in the current manuscript. In fact, it is he who constantly inspired me to come up with this monograph. Academically I benefitted immensely from discussions with Jan Breman (University of Amsterdam), Chris Tilly (University of California, Los Angeles), Christoph Scherrer (University of Kassel, Germany), Hansjoerg Herr (Berlin School of Economics and Law, Berlin), Frank Hoffer (ILO, Geneva), Renana Jhabvala (SEWA, Ahmedabad), Edward Webster (University of Witwatersrand, South Africa), Alakh N. Sharma (IHD, New Delhi) and Bino Paul and Mouleshri Vyas (TISS Mumbai). Our faculty colleagues at TISS Guwahati campus have been a source of discussion and stimulus. I would like to thank Virginius Xaxa, deputy director of TISS Guwahati campus for taking out time to read and make comments on the initial drafts of some chapters despite his hectic schedule. I must thank all the students who I teach and guide at post graduate (especially Labour

Studies and Social Protection) and Master's of Philosophy levels at TISS where I bring the debate and discourse on labour markets and informal economy, and received immeasurable feedback which definitely helped shaping my thoughts and ideas. TISS Guwahati campus has also given me enormous support in terms of accessing resources. For financial support, I am thankful to Global Labour University (GLU) and the International Center for Development and Decent Work (ICDD) for supporting me during my doctoral programme. My special thanks to Radha Beteille for copy editing the initial draft of the manuscript. I would like to thank Routledge team, especially Antara Ray Chaudhury from Routledge (India), for providing the steady, clear, professional guidance and support at every stage to see the project through to fruition.

The street vendors who participated in this study have been extremely cooperative and supportive. They were patient, tolerant and provided vital information related to their work. Vendors' names were changed to maintain anonymity and protect their identities in this book. I appreciate the guidance and contribution that I received from different trade union leaders and street vendors in the course of my fieldwork. I truly hope that this book will be helpful to them.

Finally, I am deeply indebted to my mother, Ma, for her relentless support and selfless love. I am blessed with loving brothers and sister, sisters-in law, nieces and nephew for their good wishes, love, support and constant encouragement. I owe a special debt of gratitude to my wife Hemantika, who compromised her own work and time and read every draft of the manuscript and made numerous suggestions and comments. Her unconditional support made the completion of this book possible on time. My sincere apology to all the people, whose names I have not mentioned, but their efforts are not least recognised by me. I would express regret over any mistakes that have been unintentionally made in the book and I must take responsibility for the final product and all its shortcomings.

Abbreviations

AASVA	All Assam Street Vendors' Association
APMC	Agricultural Product Marketing Committee
ASI	Annual Survey of Industries
BHU	Bombay Hawkers' Union
BMC	Brihanmumbai Municipal Corporation
BNMC	Bidhan Nagar Municipal Corporation
CBO	community-based organisations
CITU	Centre of Indian Trade Unions
CSO	Central Statistical Organisation
DGET	Directorate General of Employment and Training
GIC	General Insurance Corporation
GMC	Guwahati Municipal Corporation
GOI	Government of India
HSC	Hawkers' Sangram Committee
ILO	International Labour Organisation
JBY	Janshree Bima Yojana
KMC	Kolkata Municipal Corporation
KSHU	Kolkata Street Hawkers' Union
LDEs	less-developed economies
LIC	Life Insurance Corporation of India
MBO	membership-based organisation
MCGM	Municipal Corporation of Greater Mumbai
MFIs	micro-finance institutions
MGNREGA	Mahatma Gandhi National Rural Employment Guarantee Act
MMRDA	Mumbai Metropolitan Regional Development Authority
MoHUPA	Ministry of Housing and Urban Poverty Alleviation
NASVI	National Association of Street Vendors of India

NCEUS	National Commission for Enterprises in the Unorganised Sector
NCL	National Commission on Labour
NDP	net domestic product
NGO	non-governmental organisation
NHFI	National Hawkers Federation in India
NSSO	National Sample Survey Office
OBCs	Other Backward Classes
PMO	Prime Minister's Office
RIL	Reliance Industries Limited
SBI	State Bank of India
SC	Scheduled Caste
SEWA	Self-Employed Women's Association
SHG	self-help group
SNA	System of National Accounts
SPO	superintendent of police
sSTEP	Society for Social Transformation and Environment Protection
ST	Scheduled Tribe
TISS	Tata Institute of Social Sciences
TVC	town vending committee
ULB	urban local body
UNDP	United Nations Development Programme
UPA	United Progressive Alliance
YUVA	Youth for Unity and Voluntary Action
ZVC	zone vending committee

Introduction
Street vending in informal economy

The nature of work and employment across the world has been changing, especially over the last four decades. While workers in developing countries, including India, have been facing consequences of globalisation and international restructuring of the global labour market in forms of sub-contraction, casualisation and contractualisation, poor models of social protection make employment even more vulnerable to market fluctuation across the globe. With low industrial growth, declining agriculture sector and limited expansion of formal sector employment, the poor have increasingly been taking recourse to informal sources of earning livelihoods and creating their own markets in urban economy. Street vending is one of them and is flourishing as an occupation all over the world. This occupation provides an opportunity to fathom the dynamics in the lives of the world's working poor. This book is an attempt to show the current situation of the vending activity and discuss the issues related to this occupation through various cases from different cities across India. The main thrust of the book is on the strategies of survival and sustenance of the vendors in the urban informal economy. The monograph is based on my doctoral thesis, and insights from my close association with several studies carried out between 2009 and 2014. Analysis and description are mainly drawn from primary data. We have tried our best to provide the macro picture of street vending in India through micro views of the activity.

The following simple narration of a 45-year-old male street vendor staying in Mumbai describes how informal street markets operate and also shows the way in which various layers of informality and illegality exist: '. . . I came to Mumbai in search of better-paid job because there is limited earning opportunity in my village but ended up vending on the streets. I began the activity by helping my uncle in his vending stall and then I took over his stall on rent. While helping him, I developed contacts with different people such as police, BMC officials, moneylenders, and wholesalers and other street vendors from this locality . . . this activity has become more challenging and sustenance in this city has become even more difficult because rates of interest on loans, rates of bribes and competition have increased tremendously'. This person migrated from Uttar Pradesh during the late 1980s and since then has been a vendor in Dadar, Mumbai. He is one of thousands of street vendors operating on the streets in various cities across India. This is one of the first narrations of respondents during my fieldwork in Mumbai which reveals the various channels of entry to this occupation, sustenance and daily struggle and consequences. Mumbai formed the first entry point in the study which paved way for conducting research on street vendors across India. The cases of Mumbai outlined the methodology to be followed for other research that had been undertaken during 2009 and 2014 and also helped to identify the issues to be covered. This is mainly because the basic issues related to the activity are found to be similar across cities; only the degrees differ.

Informal economy: origin and debates

The debate over existence of informal sector could be traced back to the fault-ridden growth models adopted by the nations of the global south especially post–World War II. This consisted of import substituting industrialisation by building up capital-intensive industries, saving precious foreign exchange and reducing dependency on import from the north. These strategies were seemed to be promoting economic growth, which in turn would automatically take care of employment. Dual-sector models of economic development propounded by Lewis (1954) and Ranis and Fei (1961) explains the growth of a developing economy in terms of transition of surplus labour from a traditional rural subsistence sector to a modern urban industrial/capitalist sector. Wage rate being higher in the modern sector, workers from rural traditional sectors would be drawn into modern urban sector. The modern sector was characterised by self-sustaining growth which was brought by output expansion and reinvestment of profits leading to higher labour demand. This labour transfer would continue until all labour is absorbed in the modern sector. However, less developed economies (LDEs) were confronted with unprecedented levels of unemployment/

underemployment coupled with large-scale rural-urban migration which was direct contradiction of what was proposed by the afore-mentioned models.

Harris and Todaro (1970), in their study, explained that this migration was in response to rural-urban differences in expected incomes. Migration took place after calculation of costs and benefits from migration decisions. While some migrants (having skills and education) would manage to join formal jobs, others would remain unemployed or find some employment in the sectors which were not modern, continuing with the job search. Unemployment or employment in these non-modern sectors was perceived to be a temporary phenomenon. However, this phenomenon was contested with ever-expanding employment in the non-modern sector, which showed no sign of slowdown.

The International Labour Organisation (ILO) became increasingly concerned with such puzzling nature of employment in the urban settings of LDEs in the late 1960s and constituted the World Employment Programme, under which several country and city missions were set up to understand the state of labour markets and structural factors behind growing employment and unemployment problems. In all these country and city studies, structural imbalances (especially absorbing capacity of modern sector is different than the traditional sector) in employment opportunities between rural and urban areas and modern and traditional sectors was the reason behind these problems. Consequently these imbalances led to the urban informal sector which absorbed migrants who were in search of job in the modern sector. The Kenya Mission, which was one of the most comprehensive of the city and country missions led by the ILO, tried to conceptualise the phenomenon of the informal sector and highlighted the dualistic nature of labour market. This was the first compendious employment mission to Africa which studied the relationship between the informal and formal sectors. It also identified characteristics of the informal sector. These were: reliance of indigenous resources, small scale of operation, unregulated and competitive market and family ownership of enterprises. Throughout the mission, the ILO found that informal sector is very efficient and profit making. It also suggests that the informal sector is capable of providing necessary commodities and services to a large section of consumers. Thus giving importance to the informal sector will help solving the unemployment problem not only in Kenya but also across the world.

Nevertheless, Keith Hart – an anthropologist who was a part of ILO missions – coined the term 'informal sector' which challenged the traditional development theories developed by Lewis, Fei and Ranis, and Harris-Todaro which laid greater stress on industrial growth to achieve full employment and economic growth. Hart explained that informal sector is an outcome of dualistic tendency of urban labour market. The traditional development theories failed to explain why and how industrial development was not able to absorb rising number of job seekers. The temporary phenomenon 'informal sector' was becoming an ever-expanding permanent feature of urban labour markets in developing countries, assuming proportions of 'economy'. Hart's study was based on the migration of the group named 'Frafras' from North Ghana to South Ghana in search of job opportunities in the modern sector. However, the people who were coming from rural areas to urban areas in search of better jobs could not find it due to lack of skills and job opportunities in the urban economy. Industrial growth being limited was not able to absorb a growing number of migrants. Many of them were forced to generate alternative means of livelihood (self-employment or wage employment in non-modern jobs) in the urban labour market till they find job as industrial wage workers. The reason as to why people took recourse to informal occupations was that these migrants could not afford to stay unemployed because of substantial costs of living in cities and hence ended up taking wage or self-employment in small-scale units. Their job status existed somewhere between open unemployment and formal sector employment. Notwithstanding, migration was not the only factor responsible for growing and persisting informal sector in any economy.

Hart illustrated a range of activities based on income opportunities within the informal sector and tried to show diverse groups of informal workers. He classified the two categories based on the legitimacy of activities – informal income opportunities based on legitimate or law-abiding occupations and informal income opportunities based on illegitimate/illegal occupations. The legitimate informal activities in the informal sector were further classified into five categories. These are: primary and secondary activities, tertiary enterprises with relatively large capital inputs, small-scale distribution, other services and private transfer payments. Primary activities comprised farming and other related activities. Secondary activities include the work of building contractors, self-employed artisans, shoemakers, tailors and beer and spirits manufacturers. The informal sector also comprised tertiary enterprises with relatively large capital inputs, such as housing, transport and commodity speculation. In small-scale distribution work, Hart differentiated the market operatives such as petty traders, street hawkers, food and drink caterers, bar attendants, commission agents and dealers, and called their activities informal activities. In the other services, Hart gave the examples of musicians, launderers, shoe-shiners and barbers. On the other hand, gifts and similar flow of money and goods between persons, borrowing and begging are categorised in the private transfer payment. Hustlers, receivers of the stolen goods, usury, drug pushing, prostitution, smuggling, bribery and so on are examples of illegitimate informal services. On the other hand, petty theft, larceny, speculation, money doublers and gambling are examples of transfers within illegitimate informal occupations. However, Hart's conceptualisation of the informal sector was too simplistic way to look into informal sector. His argument was mainly based on 'income opportunities' rather than 'sector', and he had considered mostly 'self-employment' into consideration to define informality.

Later Victor Tokman studied the apprehension of Keith Hart whether the reserve army of unemployment and underemployment really constitutes a passive, exploited majority or whether their informal economic activities pose some autonomous capacity for generating growth in the incomes of the poor. Tokman described the interrelationship between the formal economy and the rest of the economy. The research conducted in Latin America and Caribbean nations highlighted that purchasing and selling took place in the same sector. Tokman has interestingly pointed out two approaches – benign approach and subordinated approach. In benign approach, Tokman described the autonomous informal sector as economically efficient which has a comparative advantage in relation to similar activities in the formal sector. Tokman opined that the informal labour force will survive as an autonomous segment even though the market is competitive. In subordinated approach, he explained that there is exclusion of informal labour in the formal sector. Labour force in the formal sector is without any formal privileges in cases of contractual employment or underemployment. He defined this as informal labour within the formal employment which is subordinated forms of labour in the formal sector. He found out that the informal economy was restricted in growth because of the market competition despite being autonomous.

In the late 1970s, Moser (1978), based upon her research on petty commodity production, analysed the inter-dependencies between formal and informal sectors. Later, in the late 1980s, Castells and Portes (1989) supported Moser's view. Both these approaches were based on structure of both the sectors. According to them, the formal and informal sectors are interrelated, connected and interdependent in terms of both capital and labour. Workers have been pushed out from the formal sector – where they had once enjoyed job security – to the informal sector, where there is no security. This is because firms try to reduce input and labour costs, to increase competitiveness and maximise profits (Moser 1978; Castells & Portes 1989). These studies have further focused increasingly on the informal sector as a mechanism to explain the survival strategies of the poor excluded regular employment in the modern sector and the strategies by firms in the latter to bypass regulatory constraints and reduce their labour costs. The reasons for this structural imbalance are large-scale rural to urban migration in search of jobs, together with an inadequate number of jobs resulting from capital-intensive, foreign-owned manufacturing companies, which entertained only skilled workforce, forcing most workers to join the informal sector. This sector, however, was not unproductive and stagnant but competitive and labour-intensive developing its own skills and technology using family labour and/or local resources (Moser 1978).

Peruvian economist Hernando de Soto viewed informality as the key to survival, with workers purposively ignoring unreasonable official rules and regulations in order to make a living. His discussion and exhaustive work is on street vendors, para-transit operators and others. Soto supports these forms of production and reproduction because he sees them as a part of economic development. In contrast, Peruvian elites criticised this occupation, noting that its manifestation leads to underdevelopment and has to be eradicated for economic development. Despite bureaucracy and mercantilism, he argues that most of the population shows tremendous initiative and entrepreneurial dynamism by finding informal means of production and reproduction. De Soto depicts that in capitalist countries legalism (legal cost, bad laws and state intervention) and excessive regulatory control by the state should be relaxed so that entrepreneurship and free market can flourish. Administrative delays by the state and long processing delays lead to considerable personal and financial cost. De Soto further highlights that excess bureaucratic structure plays as a dysfunctional problem of underdevelopment. De Soto defined informality from institutional point of view illustrating its legal and extra-legal characteristics. He idealised creating an image of plucky entrepreneurs desperately struggling to make a living in face of stifling government regulations and horrific mismanagement of public enterprises. By mobilising grass-roots entrepreneurship and harnessing the potential of intermediate technologies, development can be achieved. De Soto recommended a reduction in public sector investment and involvement, deregulation, debureaucratisation and privatisation of public enterprises so as to remove unfair competition. In policy terms there were fundamental differences on the role of state, with the ILO recommending an increased role and De Soto recommending a reduced one.

De Soto portrayed the informal traders as courageous people who struggled against bureaucracy and the harsh conditions of the open streets just to make a living. De Soto formed a political movement call Movimiento Libertad to embody free market, entrepreneurial and anti-bureaucratic philosophy. He called for mass legislation and small enterprises, squatter holdings and reforms of agrarian cooperatives. His new radicalism has been manifested by providing moral support and advice to the new president and simplified registration procedure for squatter holders, i.e. thereby reducing bureaucratic and administrative hurdles to a large extent. His framework of informal sector development is directly related to deregulations, debureacratisation and privatisation which emphasises reduction in role of government and protecting private property so that power of market plays to accelerate economic development. However, one can argue that how far are debureacratisation, deregulation and privatisation effective in the context of informality across the world, especially developing nations. He states that informality exists when people or businesses choose to operate outside formal law. Does this assumption hold true? Do people really choose or are forced to do so? De Soto further stated that people choose informality because the costs of acquiring these benefits are easy while the time and expense of becoming formal is exacting or even inconceivable at times. This might be true. One common supposition is that individuals choose to live and operate outside the law because they want to avoid paying taxes. More important, however, are the delays caused by layers of bureaucratic machinery. De Soto suggested that the government could promote through market forces the rapid diffusion of property rights not only for enhanced economic growth but also for political stability in most parts of the developing world.

Informal/unorganised sector debate in India

The exact definition of informal sector has eluded academics and institutions for over four decades. From the theoretical standpoints, the sector has expanded to include nature of enterprise as well as employment characteristics of the people occupied in these activities. Nevertheless, the employment-based definition of informality is a relatively a new concept which embraces both the nature of employment and characteristics of the informal enterprises. This is in a way broader and more inclusive since it includes employment without formal contracts and worker benefits and without social protection both within and outside informal enterprises (Chen 2007). Across the developing countries, the informal sector continues to expand in absolute and relative terms (Charmes 1998). Perpetuation and growth of informal sector have been mainly due to unavailability of formal sector jobs, weak capacity of the formal sector to generate adequate employment and incomes, illiteracy, high labour force and population growth rates, and rural-urban migration among others (Sethuraman 1976; Charmes 1998).

Considering the case of India, the terms 'informal sector'[1] and 'unorganised sector' are used interchangeably. High rates of employment and output growth in this sector attracted attention of the government. However, a concise definition of the sector was missing for a long time. In fact, the Government of India, through its first National Commission on Labour (NCL) set up in 1966, had tried to define the unorganised sector from the view point of its peculiar features and nature of work. According to the first NCL (1966–69), the sector was identified as unorganised which included those who have not been able to organise themselves in pursuit of their common interest due to certain constraints like casual nature of employment, ignorance and illiteracy and small and scattered size of establishments. Almost three decades later, in the second NCL (set up in 2002) unorganised sector was reconceptualised more explicitly, explaining the constraints, characteristics of the sector and categorising the workers who are engaged in it. The second NCL has defined this sector as a high incidence of casual labour mostly doing intermittent jobs at extremely low wages or doing their own-account work at very uneconomical returns. There is a total lack of job security and social security benefits. The areas of exploitation are high, resulting in long hours, unsatisfactory work conditions and occupational health hazards. The second NCL is considered as an important step forward which does not only define informal sector but also highlights the importance of social and economic security for this sector.

The second NCL has also explained the constraints such as (a) casual nature of employment, (b) ignorance and illiteracy, (c) small size of establishments with low capital investment per person employed, (d) scattered nature of establishments and (e) superior strength of the employer operating singly or in combination. In addition, the commission identified characteristics of unorganised sector which are: (i) low scale of organisation, (ii) operation of labour relations on a casual basis, or on the basis of kinship or personal relations, (iii) small own-account (household) or family-owned enterprises or micro-enterprises, (iv) ownership of fixed and other assets by self, (v) risking of finance capital by self, (vi) involvement of family labourers, (vii) production expenditure indistinguishable from household expenditures and use of capital goods, (viii) easy entry and exit, (ix) free mobility within the sector, (x) use of indigenous resources and technology, (xi) unregulated or unprotected nature, (xii) absence of fixed working hours, (xiii) lack of security of employment and other social security benefits, (xiv) use of labour-intensive technology and (xv) lack of support from the government. It must be noted that these characteristics were not newly invented in the global economy. These were similar to what ILO's Kenya Mission and Keith Hart had pointed out while defining and explaining informal sector. The report of the NCL (2002) was an important attempt by the Government of India at recognising and documenting the varied nature of enterprises and workers in this sector.

However, not only conceptualising the sector is difficult; measuring the sector and the number of workers in the informal economy is a more difficult task. The Government of India through its different offices has been trying to conceptualise the sector more coherently and comprehensively. In India, the National Sample Survey Organisation, renamed as National Sample Survey Office (NSSO), which has been conducting surveys of unorganised enterprises at periodical intervals, adopted the following criteria for the identification of unorganised sector:

a   In the case of manufacturing industries, the enterprises not covered under the Annual Survey of Industries (ASI) are taken to constitute the unorganised sector.

b   In the case of service industries, all enterprises, except those run by the government (central, state and local body) and in the corporate sector, were regarded as unorganised.

The NSSO conducts a separate survey round for the informal/ unorganised sector. All non-agricultural enterprises, excluding those covered under the ASI, with type of ownership as either proprietary or partnership were treated as informal non-agricultural enterprises for the purpose of the survey.

Notably, the definition of informal sector proposed by the National Commission for Enterprises in the Unorganised Sector (NCEUS) set up by Planning Commission in 2007 under the chairmanship of (late) Prof. Arjun Sengupta is considered more comprehensive so far. The definition of the informal sector has been brought to the level of enterprises. It is explained that the enterprises can be of ownership categories of (a) proprietary, (b) partnership, (c) registered under the Companies Act as companies, (d) cooperative societies registered under the Societies Registration Act and (e) government or public sector undertakings. Out of these ownership categories, enterprises operated on proprietary and partnership basis do not constitute as separate legal entities independent of their owners; that is, the liabilities of the enterprises fall entirely on the owners. Non-registration under specific forms of national legislation is another characteristic which can be used for identifying informal enterprises as per international guidelines. However, in India, there is no unique form of registration which can be used for such identification, though there are several voluntary and mandatory registration systems for specific segments of industrial units.

The non-maintenance of complete accounts that would permit a financial separation of production activities of the enterprise is generally satisfied in the case of proprietary and partnership enterprises employing less than ten workers as those enterprises are not under any legal obligation to maintain separate accounts. In view of the above, the following definition of unorganised/informal sector has been recommended by NCEUS: 'the informal sector consists of all unincorporated private enterprises owned by individuals or households engaged in the sale and production of goods and services operated on a proprietary or partnership basis and with less than ten total workers'.

The word 'enterprise' in the above definition has the same meaning as defined in the System of National Accounts (SNA) in 1993 and refers to an institutional unit in its capacity as a producer of goods and services. An enterprise is classified as proprietary if an individual is its sole owner and as partnership if there are two or more owners on a partnership basis with or without formal registration. It excludes all corporate entities, registered cooperatives, trusts and other legal entities. Though the above definition does not make any distinction between agricultural and non-agricultural enterprises, the concept of enterprise is so far being used in India only in the context of non-agricultural sector. The use of such a restrictive meaning of enterprise would lead to the exclusion of a large number of workers in the agricultural sector, unless a corresponding unit of enterprise in agriculture is specified and used. NCEUS, therefore, recommended that each operational holding in the crop production, plantation, forestry, animal husbandry and fishing activities may be considered as an enterprise for the purpose of applying the definition of informal sector. In the absence of identification of operational holdings in agriculture as enterprises and collection of the relevant details in the labour force surveys in India, it has not been possible to apply the above definition of informal sector in the field of agriculture.

Therefore, considering these definitions and conceptualisation by different organisations one can distinguish between the informal and unorganised sectors in terms of sector and employment. While the informal sector is a more sector-specific concept and is based on the 'nature of enterprises', the unorganised sector is based on 'workers' or 'nature of employment' (Kannan 2009). Nonetheless, both these concepts lack in conceptual clarity and uniformity across the sub-sectors of the economy. NCEUS (2007) has explained the lack of clarity using two examples. First, the Central Statistical Organisation (CSO) uses the term 'organised enterprise' as small units with ten or more workers with power or twenty or more workers without power for the manufacturing sector. Second, employment in the unorganised sector has hitherto been derived as a residual of the total workers minus workers in the organised sector as reported by the Directorate General of Employment and Training (DGET). The DGET figures, however, fail to capture the informal/unorganised employment in the formal/organised sector – a phenomenon which is becoming increasingly significant in the Indian economy. Therefore as far as definition of informal sector by NCEUS is concerned, it has been broadly described as consisting of units (unincorporated enterprises owned by households) engaged in the household production of goods and services in order to generate employment and incomes (NCEUS 2007). Production units in the informal sector are not constituted as separate legal entities independently of the household. The owners of the production units have to raise finance at their own risk and are personally liable, without limit, for any debts or obligations incurred in the production process (NCEUS 2007).

Dimensions of informal sector

Informal sector in developing nations is conspicuous by the presence of certain inherent characteristics. In view of informal sector being heterogeneous in nature, let us discuss multidimensional aspects, namely, economic, social, gender, legal, cultural, and institutional of this sector.

Economic

The most important dimension associated with informal economy is economic aspect. A significant portion of workforce across the developing economies is engaged in the informal economy. The economic dimensions are reflected in contributions to gross domestic product (GDP) and employment of developing countries. In India, about 92 per cent of total labour force is deriving their livelihood from this sector. It is labour-intensive and the majority of informal sector workers are low skilled or unskilled across the world. Formal education levels tend to be lower than in the formal sector. A large share of informal sector participants has not received any formal education; of those who have, the vast majority have obtained only some basic or primary education. The informal sector provides livelihood options to the people who are left out by the formal sector. As industrial growth and employment elasticity of industrial output are limited in a country like India, opportunities are not sufficient to absorb the ever-increasing number of job entrants every year. For instance, due to low wages in the tea plantation industry, workers are moving out from the sector and searching for jobs in urban settings in India. Also, skill deficit among Indian educated youth results in limited job options in so-called formal labour market and hence such youth are engaged in informal sector. Some of the ex-mill workers who have lost their job and engaged in street vending in Mumbai can also be taken as an example. The informal sector is as a cushion in these situations and provides a means of livelihood.

Wages tend to be very low in this sector, typically markedly below those offered in the formal sector, and often below legislated minimum wage levels (Tokman 1992). Notwithstanding, the earnings profiles of informal sector participants differ both considerably and systematically by occupational status. Generally, self-employed persons have the highest earnings followed, in descending order, by regular wage earners, casual wage earners and, lastly, apprentices. Moreover, there is a significant gap in earnings of the self-employed compared to wage earners in the informal sector, as a result of which many self-employed workers eventually become entrepreneurs.

Mode and means of operation of informal sector are flexible. Actors in the informal sector, especially in the developing or underdeveloped countries, prefer to operate with relative autonomy, flexibility and freedom compared to their formal counterparts. In other words, they have the freedom of operating their own business. In addition, they have the flexibility to determine their working hours or days of operation and the power to make decisions in the absence of formal rules and regulations (Chen 2007). The informal sector is the only sector which enables competition with other actors involved in the same activity without any formal training and education. Hence, it provides a fair chance to survive in this sector. Castells and Portes (1989) and ILO (1972) noted that ease of survival is one of the strong reasons for the existence and expansion of the informal sector as far as the developing countries are concerned. In order to survive in the informal sector, workers follow alternative strategy which sometimes leads to another level of informality.

Migration is one of the important characteristics of the informal sector which is implicitly linked to the urban economy. This sector has general tendency of absorbing migrant labourers, especially in the urban economy. People from rural areas come to the urban economy in order to search better paid job or for better opportunities. Hart's study in Ghana had also shown that due to lack of formal sector or skilled job in the urban economy, migrant labourers get involved in the urban informal sector and this tendency has continued to persist. Linkages between the formal and informal sectors can often be quite dense and extensive, particularly in the urban areas.

Social

As far as developing countries are concerned, vast segments of the workforce are less educated and lack requisite capital to start a livelihood. It is relatively easy for them to enter the informal economy. Since the informal sector is characterised by the conspicuous absence of any formal agreements, written and legally recognised contracts or even a proper employer–employee relationship, social contact or network is one of the most important means by which they enter and exist in this sector. It is the interplay of trust and norms of social conduct that determines their entry and sustenance in this sector. Hart (1973) and Breman (1980) pointed out that one of the main features of the informal sector is its 'ease of entry' which, however, largely depends upon social networks. Workers generate and exercise social capital to exist in the informal sector. Studies by Harriss-White (2003) and Chen (2007) show that labour relations, where they exist, are based on casual employment, kinship or personal or social relations rather than contractual arrangements with formal guarantees.

Gender

Informalisation accompanies increased feminisation of work. The participation of women in the informal sector has been increasing over the years and in most cases the working conditions of the women are far worse than those of men in the informal sector (Chen 2007). The process of labour feminisation is associated with increased female participation in the workforce, enhancement of work hours, falling standards of living, as well as gender discrimination within the workplace as reflected in lower hourly pay received by women workers compared to their male counterparts (Vanamala 2001). It has been remarked that casualisation of women's employment is a distinctive feature of globalisation (RoyChowdhury 2005). Although new work opportunities have emerged for female workers in export-processing zones, this employment is usually informal in nature (Vanamala 2001). Standing (1989) said that 'the deregulation of labour markets (Informalisation) necessitated by global production systems would favour women in terms of cost effectiveness resulting in feminisation of jobs' (Neetha 2009: 22).Women tend to get involved in different types of activities, associated with different levels of earning than that of men. A majority of female workers in developing countries are in the informal sector. This is true for sub-Saharan Africa and South Asia (Sethuraman 1998). It is also evident that female workers depend more on the informal sector than their male counterparts. But women's participation in terms of their share of informal sector employment is more mixed. While women are over-represented in the informal sector in developing countries, they are under-represented in formal sector employment (ibid.). In terms of occupational distribution within the informal sector, women are more likely to be employed in manufacturing, trade and services than in construction and transport as marginal workers. Women tend to dominate trade and, depending on the country, are sometimes employed even in manufacturing and services. For example, in the informal manufacturing sub-sector of Southeast Asia, there are more women than men in the garment and leather manufacturing sector (Lubell 1991). Furthermore, female workers tend to earn less than male workers. This gender disparity in earnings prevails often markedly and widely.

Legal and institutional

Informal sector enterprises are free from institutional and regulatory framework. However, this notion does not hold true uniformly. This is evident from different parts of the developing world that a significant share of informal sector enterprises really operates on the margins of legality. Informal sector in cities are more likely to comply with various regulations than those in smaller towns or rural areas (Tokman & Klein 1996). The degree of enforcement rigour by authorities also affects the degree of compliance – in particular the capacity for law enforcement tends to be concentrated in cities, which is a clear sign of duality. The legal and illegal connotations of the informal sector were highlighted by researchers like Hernando de Soto (1989, 2000) and William Maloney (2004). Studies found that the informal sector is an outcome of failure of legal framework and government regulations (De Soto 1989, 2000; Feige 1997; Maloney 2004).

Cultural

The cultural dimension of the informal sector cannot be ignored. The evolution of informal sector is rooted in history and its ability to generate surplus constitutes one of the most primitive forms of capital accumulation. The nature of informal sector activities also changes across geographic locations. For instance, important locations of cities in India (Delhi, Kolkata, Mumbai and Hyderabad) are also recognised because of their street food junctions and local street markets.

Workers in the informal sector: types and composition

Defining workers within the informal sector is becoming even more challenging as the nature of occupation within this sector is extremely heterogeneous in nature, especially in terms of condition of work between employer and employees, working hours, social relation and so on. Informal workers, however, can be broadly classified into three categories. First, wage workers in informal enterprises or persons employed against remuneration as informal workers, directly by employers or through agencies or contractors, are called wage workers. Wage workers include casual and temporary workers, migrant workers; domestic workers employed in households and also include regular workers in the informal sector. Second, self-employed or persons who run farm or non-farm enterprises or are engaged in a profession or trade, either on own account including unpaid family workers, individually or with partners or as home-based workers. Third, the unprotected wage workers in the formal sector or the workers in the categories of regular, casual and contract workers who, though engaged in the formal sector, come under the informal sector because they are unprotected and informally employed in the formal sector.

Taking the nature of expansion of the informal sector and its pervasiveness in different forms across developed and developing nations into consideration, one can understand how the concept of the informal sector expanded into the concept of the informal economy. In nations of North America and Europe, production was gradually becoming more decentralised with flexible employment relationships (Chen 2007). Thus jobs in these activities were becoming 'atypical' and 'non-standard', having hourly wages but no attached benefits, through the introduction of piece rates and subcontracting of the production process to smaller-scale informal units and industrial homeworkers or outworkers (ibid.).

As far as workers in the informal sector in context of India are concerned, definition provided by NCEUS is more comprehensive and coherent. The definition follows as: 'unorganised or informal workers consist of those working in the informal sector or households, excluding regular workers with social security benefits provided by employers and the workers in the formal sector without any employment or social security benefits provided by the employers' (NCEUS 2007: 4). It is 'employment-based' definition of informality which is found to be more contextual in India. In the informal sector (as defined by the sector-specific definition), a significant section of the labour force may be employed as informal workers, with their conditions of work being equally precarious to those of the workers employed in the unorganised sector (ibid.).

In many developing countries, informal sector is the primary source of employment for workers, particularly for those who are relatively disadvantaged in the labour market (e.g. unskilled, semi-skilled or low-skilled women, physically challenged and older workers). For instance, in 1990–94, informal non-agricultural employment in sub-Saharan Africa was 60–80 per cent, whereas it was 73.7 per cent in India, 77.9 per cent in Indonesia, 67.1 per cent in Pakistan, 66.9 per cent in the Philippines and 51.4 per cent in Thailand (ILO 2000; Charmes 2012). In comparison, the informal sectors in Latin America and North Africa appear to be somewhat smaller, which is between 30 and 60 per cent of non-agricultural employment (Charmes 2012). The informal sector is important in terms of its contribution to GDP. This is because if a large section of any country's labour force depends on the informal sector, their contribution to their GDP would be high. For instance, Charmes (2000) determines that in sub-Saharan Africa (excluding South Africa), the informal sector contributes between 20 and 50 per cent of non-agricultural GDP. His estimates for a few countries in South and Southeast Asia and Latin America mostly fall within the same range of 20–50 per cent. According to Jacques Charmes's (2012) extensive analysis based on percentage share of employment in the informal economy in total non-farm employment by five-year period and by country and region shows that non-farm informal sector ranges from 32.7 per cent in South Africa to 77 per cent in the Democratic Republic of Congo, 84 per cent in Cameroon and 87.2 per cent in Mozambique in 2005–10. During the same period, the increasing trend of employment in the informal economy was similar in Latin America. It increased from 54.2 per cent in 1995–99 to 57.7 per cent in 2005–10 (ibid.). Shares in non-agricultural employment ranged from 42.2 per cent in Brazil, 42.8 per cent in Uruguay to 71.3 per cent in Peru, 75.1 per cent in Bolivia and 75.2 per cent in Honduras. Except Argentina, Brazil and Mexico, shares in non-agricultural in almost all countries in Latin America increased between 1995–99 and 2005–10. In South and Southeast Asia, employment in the informal economy is stabilised around 70 per cent of non-agricultural employment, ranging from 41.1 per cent in Thailand to 84.2 per cent in India and 86.4 per cent in Nepal (ibid.).

Composition of workers in India

According to NSSO (2004–05), the contribution of the informal sector to net domestic product (NDP) at current prices in India has been over 60 per cent (NCEUS 2007: 5). Thus, the informal sector has a crucial role in Indian economy in terms of employment and its contribution to the NDP, savings and capital formation. In India, a large portion of the workforce is dependent on the informal sector for their livelihoods. From the data issued by NSSO 61st and 55th rounds, it was seen that although the total employment had increased from 396.8 million to 457.5 million from 1999–2000 to 2004–05, the number of formal workers in formal enterprises had actually registered a decline. On the other hand, there had been an increase in the number of informal workers in formal enterprises. At the same time, the percentage of informal workers in informal enterprises has remained constant. Hence the rise in employment over this period has mainly been informal in nature (NCEUS 2007). In 2004–05, the informal sector workforce in India was estimated at about 426 million workers, representing nearly 92.7 per cent of the total workforce (see Table I.1). Interestingly, the informal sector directly accounts for 398 million, comprising 87 per cent of the total workers, while 7.3 per cent of this huge labour force employed formally comprising both organised sector and unorganised sector. In 2011–12, about 435 million workers employed informally, comprising 91.9 per cent of total employment. Comparing the 61st and 68th rounds of NSSO data, the trend impressively indicates a marginal drop in the informal employment categories, whereas the number of persons employed in the formal sector has increased marginally. But the percentage share of formally employed workers in the organised sector has declined from 52 per cent to 45.4 per cent.

Table I.2 shows interesting trends in sectoral distribution of formal and informal employment between the 61st and 68th rounds of NSSO. Not surprising, employment in the agricultural sector holds

Table I.I Comparison of formal-informal employment across organised-unorganised sectors between 2004–05 and 2011–12 (in millions)

	2004–05			2011–12		
	Organised	Unorganised	Total	Organised	Unorganised	Total
Formal	32.06 (52)	1.35 (0.3)	33.41 (7.3)	37.18 (45.4)	1.39 (0.4)	38.56 (8.1)
Informal	29.54 (48)	396 (99.7)	426.20 (92.7)	44.74 (54.6)	390.92 (99.6)	435.66 (91.9)
Total	61.61 (13)	398.01 (87)	459.61 (100)	81.92 (17.3)	392.31 (82.7)	474.23 (100)

Source: CII 2014: 41, based on the 61st and 68th rounds of NSSO. Note: Figures within parenthesis indicate percentage in share.

Table I.2 Comparison of sectoral distribution of formal and informal employment between 2004–05 and 2011–12 (percentage in share)

2004–05	Organised sector		Unorganised sector		Total
	Formal	Informal	Formal	Informal	
Agriculture	0.76	0.99	0.00	56.75	58.50
Manufacturing	1.21	2.10	1.10	8.33	11.73
Non-manufacturing	0.53	1.45	0.00	4.42	6.41
Services	4.48	1.89	0.19	16.80	23.36
Total	6.98	6.43	0.29	86.30	100.00
2011–12	Organised Sector		Unorganised Sector		Total
	Formal	Informal	Formal	Informal	
Agriculture	0.06	0.16	0.00	48.69	48.90
Manufacturing	1.48	2.79	0.06	8.28	12.60
Non-manufacturing	0.69	3.77	0.01	7.18	11.65
Services	5.62	2.72	0.22	18.29	26.84
Total	7.84	9.43	0.29	82.43	100.00

Source: CII 2014: 42, based on the 61st and 68th Rounds of NSSO.

significant share in informal employment as compared to manufacturing and service sectors. However, comparing the 61st and 68th rounds of NSSO, informal employment in the agricultural sector is shrinking, whereas informally employed workers in the service sector have been increasing from 2004 to 2005. Within the service sector, informally employed workers are the predominant category in the workforce. In 2004–05, 4.48 per cent of the workers employed formally in the service sector, while 16.8 per cent of the workers were engaged informally in the service sector. Similar trend is seen for 2011–12.

Of the 395 million informal sector workers, agricultural sector accounted for 253 million and the remaining 142 million are employed in the non-agricultural sector. The agricultural sector consists of entirely informal workers, those who are mainly self-employed, comprising 65 per cent and the casual workers (35 per cent). Around 63 per cent workers are mainly self-employed in non-agricultural informal sector and the rest of the labour force (37 per cent) in the non-agricultural informal sector (NCEUS 2007). Looking at survey data on employment and unemployment of both the 61st and 68th rounds of NSSO (see Table I.3), self-employment is the dominant category among different groups of workers within the informal sector. In 2004–05 about 60 per cent of total employment in the informal sector was self-employment, whereas 56 per cent of workers derived their livelihood from self-employment in 2011–12. On one hand, shares of self-employment in the total informal employment have declined. On the other hand, shares of regular/salaried and casual wage workers within informal sector have increased from 2004–05 to 2011–12 (see Table I.3).

Table I.3 Comparison of status of the informally employed workforce between 2004–05 and 2011–12 (in millions)

Status	2004–05	2011–12
Self-employed	257.16 (60.34)	244.97 (56.22)
Regular wage/salaried	36.19 (8.49)	48.79 (11.19)
Casual workers	132.81 (31.16)	141.91 (32.57)
Total informal workers	426.16 (92.73)	435.66 (91.78)

Source: CII 2014: 4, based on unit level data of NSSO. Note: Figures within parenthesis indicate percentage in share.

It is evident not only in India but also in developing countries in Latin America, Africa and Asia that self-employment has always assumed centre stage in the informal sector. The trend is similar since the 1970s. The informal sector is highly heterogeneous in terms of the types of activities and encompasses a range of sub-sectors including manufacturing, trade, services, construction and transport (ILO 1972). The relative distribution of these activities shows a wide variation between countries, but by and large, trade and services tend to dominate followed by manufacturing. Construction and transport are less prevalent. Informal sector enterprises are small scale and labour-intensive. Informal sector participants also face a variety of constraints including limited or lack of access to resources and markets as well as to land and physical infrastructure (Tokman & Klein 1996; Sethuraman 1998).

Charmes (1998) shows that non-wage employment in the form of self-employment, family labour and apprenticeships accounted for more than 80 per cent of informal sector employment in urban areas in sub-Saharan Africa, while wage employment accounted for only about 10 per cent. Sethuraman (1998) shows that two-thirds or more of informal sector enterprises are either single-person (i.e. self-employed) or family operations. Wage labour appears to be more common in manufacturing, transport and construction activities; in larger informal sector enterprises; and in urban areas across the world. While regular wage worker is typical, casual wage labour is substantial. Working and workplace conditions in the informal sector are also often a cause for concern all over the world as legislated standards and regulations are not applied.

Street vendors in urban economy

Street and roadside trade is an important economic activity that sustains a significant percentage of rural and urban dwellers, especially in the developing countries. They are the most visible self-employed group of workers in the informal sector. The number of street vendors has been growing extensively not only in India but throughout the world, but especially in cities in the developing countries of Asia, Latin America and Africa. Empirical evidence indicates that street vendors are the most visible and symbolic insofar as informal trade and other services in the informal economy in the developing cities across the world are concerned (Nattrass 1987; Cross 1998a; Skinner 1999; Bhowmik 2005; Brown 2006).

It is also considered as one of the important and vibrant segments of the urban informal economy. Since the early 1970s researchers and institutions (Hart 1970; ILO 1972; McGee 1973; Bromley 1978; Moser 1978; Tokman 1978; Nattrass 1987; De Soto 1989; Fields 1990) have become increasingly concerned with the phenomenon of a growing urban working section which could not be termed 'modern'. In these studies, street vending was taken to be one of the activities as an example to define, describe and theorise the peculiar and heterogeneous features of the informal sector. If we see the historical evolution of the informal sector, Keith Hart (1973) – who introduced the term 'informal sector' in the academia – took roadside small traders/street vendors whom he defined as 'micro-entrepreneurs' and described their capacity to be able to make a living and survive in hostile circumstances.

Workers in the informal sector have been categorised according to their visibility, and street vendors can be classified as the 'most visible' workers in the urban space. There are a number of issues related to the activity that are highlighted in studies conducted in Latin America, Africa and Asia. A majority of the street vendors across the globe are migrants from rural areas, where poverty as well as lack of opportunities for gainful employment has pushed them to look for better opportunities in the cities. Cross-country migration has also been noticeably growing among street vendors. For the rural poor, street vending is the most important and the easiest means of earning a livelihood, because it requires low financial input and relatively low skills compared to other occupations. The cities have witnessed rapid growth in their numbers due to urbanisation accompanied by rural joblessness, rural-urban migration, economic crisis and shrinkage in formal job opportunities, coupled with the burgeoning population in the last few decades. Again, due to lack of skills or capital, many among these people failed to procure formal jobs. The only option left to many was self-employment in the informal sector. The growth and expansion of this sector indicates that vending is a profitable venture and that it has both demand and supply. Besides, one can also argue that the inability of the government to provide employment to this growing workforce has led to the creation of this informal sector. The combination of urbanisation, migration, financial crisis, natural disasters, limited education and skills, search for economic opportunity and income, strategic nature of street vending, family influence in the form of support from a family member, entrepreneurship, lack of finance for larger business, evasion of taxes, orphanhood, widowhood, poverty and lack of opportunities in formal job and economic development trends have led to a rapid increase in the number of street traders operating on the streets of developing countries around the world (Skinner 1999; Donovan 2002; Mitullah 2004; Bhowmik 2005; Brown 2006; Kusakabe 2006; Roever 2006; Saha 2011a; Bhowmik & Saha 2012, 2013). These studies showed that vendors do not have public health-care access, career training, safety at workplace, basic amenities such as sanitation facilities and childcare facilities at the workplace, access to institutional credit availability and social and economic securities. In addition, the government is apathetic to these workers in the urban economy and they face frequent harassment by local authorities and police. Another important issue that has come up is poor unionisation among these vendors.

In view of characteristics and nature of street vending across cities in the Global South, the features of street vending in India are by and large similar. According to NCEUS (2007), a substantial portion of such employment opportunities is generated in the urban areas and a majority of this workforce is economically marginalised. In the era of globalisation, in India, after agriculture retail is the fastest emerging sector for providing employment opportunities (Gaiha & Thapa 2007). This sector contributes to about 10 per cent of India's GDP (ibid.). The retail sector has been broadly categorised into two parts: (a) organised or formal retail sector undertaken by registered, licenced retailers; and (b) traditional low-cost retail undertaken by the unorganised or informal retailers. The latter are low-capital intensive (Guruswamy et al. 2005). However, in recent times, global retail chains such as Walmart, Tesco and Carrefour too are planning to enter the Indian market due to economic liberalisation. Domestic retail chains like Reliance Retail, Aditya Birla Group, S Kumar's and Shoppers' Stop are contributing to the expansion of the organised retail sector. Besides this sector, small-scale retailers, largely a part of the unorganised retail market, such as the local 'kirana shop', grocery vendors and stationary and mobile vendors, are also growing in the Indian labour market.

In India, street vendors have been in existence since ancient times. In all civilisations, ancient and medieval, one reads accounts of travelling merchants who not only sold their wares in the town by going from house to house but also traded in neighbouring countries. However, in modern times, we still witness their counterparts, although in lesser conditions of life and living. Recently the Government of India has granted constitutional recognition for street vending. A street vendor, in India, is defined as 'a person engaged in vending of articles, goods, wares, food items or merchandise of everyday use or offering services to the general public, in a street, lane, side walk, footpath, pavement, public park or any other public place or private area, from a temporary built up structure or by moving from place to place and includes hawker, peddler, squatter and all other synonymous terms which may be local or region specific' (GOI 2014: 1–2). By definition, the activity is heterogeneous and complex in nature, thus making it diverse. From the definition given above, we can also deduce that they are firstly considered to be self-employed workers in the urban economy. The definition highlights their working places, where they are operating in the absence of a permanent built-up structure. As the vendors' place of work is defined to be 'non-permanent' and 'without a built-up structure', it would also be interesting to understand the issues pertaining to the access and use of streets or public places, and, in this regard, the role played by the state and its agencies.

Street vendors have been grouped into three categories in the Street Vendors (Protection of Livelihood and Regulation of Street Vending) Act, 2014. This categorisation is based upon their time, place of operation and visibility in the marketplace. In the first category, there are vendors who carry out their vending on a regular basis at a specific location on the street or public place (ibid.). In the second, there are those vendors who do not carry out vending on a regular basis but are seen at some place in the street or public place at some time during the day or week. In this category are those vendors who sell goods in weekly bazaars (ibid.). The third type are mobile street vendors who move from one place to another carrying their wares on pushcarts, in cycles or baskets over their heads or even in buses, trains and so forth (ibid.). In the present study we have considered street vendors who are stationary in the sense that they function at a specified location all-round the year and mobile vendors. Street trade is undertaken by both men and women and their workplaces include street pavements, street corners, sidewalks, neighbourhood sidewalks and even in main transport nodes such as railway stations, bus stops and construction sites and around sports complexes.

As mentioned earlier, street vending plays a significant role in the urban informal economy by providing employment and generating income for the urban poor. It is estimated that around 30 per cent of Mumbai's workforce buys at least one meal a day from vendors (Bhowmik 2001). Vendors sell different kinds of goods such as clothes and hosiery, leather-made products, moulded plastic products and different varieties of household goods in India. Most of these goods are manufactured in micro, small-scale or home-based industries which employ a large number of workers (ibid.). The manufacturers themselves could have hardly marketed their products on their own. In addition to non-agricultural products, street vendors also sell perishable items such as vegetables, fruits and cooked food. Hence, they provide the market for home-based manufacturing products as well as agricultural products and support micro, small-scale and home-based workers. It can therefore be argued that there are several sectors that are linked with street vendors in terms of the products they sell.

Besides the employment context, street vendors also support urban rich as well as urban poor. They prop up the urban rich by providing them with their daily requirements at their doorsteps (Tiwari 2000; Saha 2011a). On the other hand, lower-income groups also benefit because they spend a higher portion of their income on purchases from street vendors because the vendors' goods are cheap and affordable. The urban youth also prefer to purchase clothes and other accessories from them because products sold by them are typically cheaper than those found in formal retail shops (Bhowmik 2001; Bhowmik & Saha 2012).

NCEUS (2007) has categorised workers in the unorganised sector/informal sector based on their levels of income. Interestingly, NCEUS has found that around 75 per cent of the self-employed workers belong to the poor and vulnerable groups in the unorganised sector in India and only around 25 per cent belong to the high-income group (see Table I.4). It has also categorised different types of workers within the self-employed workers based on income. Street vendors, according to NCEUS, belong to the self-employed low-income group of workers (see Table I.5). They are poor and vulnerable. There is a deep-rooted and persistent relation between working in the informal sector and being poor. However, this relation is not a simple one and is determined by the employment status within the informal sector itself.

Table 1.4 Percentage distribution of income among informal sector workers

Status	Total	Self-employed	Regular wage workers	Casual workers
Poor and vulnerable	78.7	74.7	66.7	90
Higher income	21.3	25.3	33.3	10
Total	100	100	100	100

Source: NCEUS 2007: 8

Table 1.5 Distinction of self-employed workers by income

Low-income self-employed who are closer to or marginally above casual workers	High-income self-employed who are closer to or higher than regular workers
1 Handloom weavers (mostly women)	1 Independent professionals (such as doctors, lawyers, artists and accountants)
2 Chikan workers (mostly women)	2 Shop owners in urban areas
3 Street vendors	3 Rice mill owners
4 Food processors	4 Workshop owners
5 Rickshaw pullers	5 Commission agents
6 Rag pickers	6 Brokers of real estate, housing and others
7 Beedi rollers (home-based workers)	7 Owners of small hotels and restaurants
8 Agarbatti makers (mostly women)	
9 Potters	
10 Bamboo product makers	

Source: NCEUS 2007: 51

Street vending and issues of legality in India: current debate

The fact that vendors operate in public spaces raises issues of legality/illegality. As self-employed workers in urban economy, they have the right to carry out trade or business as mentioned under Article 19 (1) (g) of the Indian Constitution, which is subject to reasonable restrictions. As far as use of public spaces is concerned, in the Indian Constitution, under Clause 6 of Article 19, it is mentioned that 'public streets are primarily meant for passing or re-passing without any unreasonable obstructions' (Basu 1989). However, it is also stated that before determining what actually constitutes 'public nuisances' or 'illegitimate encroachments' and 'unreasonable obstructions', planners need to ascertain relevant details such as the size of the street, number of vehicles and commuters on the street and the nature of additional uses to be made of the public streets (ibid.). The Supreme Court judgement on the PIL (*Sodhan Singh vs Delhi Municipal Corporation*) clearly mentions that hawkers play a definite role in 'modern urban society' and their activity must be sufficiently regulated so that it does not become an obstruction and adds to public comfort and utility.

As mentioned earlier, street vendors have a tendency to assemble in certain public places, finding 'natural markets' as customers find it convenient to purchase their product. The problem arises as local authorities – police and municipal authorities – often prevent street vendors from using these public places for carrying out trade. These natural markets are viewed as 'encroachments upon public space' leading to overcrowdings, traffic jams and road accidents. In the past, violent agitations had broken out between the BMC and the Bombay Hawkers' Union (BHU) during the 1980s when the BMC tried to demolish several hawking stalls on the charge that they were causing obstruction and undue congestion (Anjaria 2006).

The United Progressive Alliance (UPA) government came to power in 2004 and, in its National Common Minimum Programme, expressed its commitment to protect unorganised/informal sector workers and accordingly, NCEUS was set up under the chairmanship of (late) Dr Arjun Sengupta in September 2004. While the NCEUS was engaged in identifying the problems faced by small- and micro-enterprises, the Prime Minister's Office (PMO) emphasised the importance of looking into the concerns of urban street vendors as they constituted a significant section of urban working poor. The National Policy on Urban Street Vendors was drafted in 2004. The policy was formulated in 2006 where the street vendors were recognised as urban service providers. It stated: town vending committees (TVCs) should be made responsible for the allocation of space to street vendors and other aspects such as registration; issuance of identity cards; monitoring the facilities; identifying areas for vending with no restriction; setting the terms and conditions for hawking; taking corrective action against defaulters; and collecting revenue. The new policy differed from the earlier one in the mode of operation of TVCs. The policy of 2006 stated that TVCs were to be constructed on a ward-wise basis and changes were introduced in its composition as well.

However, subsequently in 2009, the policy was revised (GOI 2009) which contained specific recommendations. Nevertheless, both the initial and revised ones are more or less same. The policy recommended the formation of TVCs at the city/town level. The model law on street vending in 2009 also highlighted that given the limitation on the total commercial vending space, it was not possible to provide each vendor the right to a permanent vending location (ibid.). Thus, the vendors could be given the right to use the commercial space for income-generating purposes for a particular period during the day. Committees may decide the amount to be charged from vendors after considering the local conditions. The functions of TVCs were expanded to include monitoring the quality of products sold by vendors, maintaining health and hygiene and safety conditions at the vending sites and so forth.

The model act is supposed to provide guidelines for the states for framing and enforcing laws on street vending. Some of the state governments (such as Odisha, Andhra Pradesh and Chhattisgarh) framed laws for street vending, and one could see the success stories of Bhubaneswar (capital of Odisha) and Vijayawada in Andhra Pradesh. On the other hand, there were many states and state capitals (e.g. Maharashtra and Delhi) that had not done anything concrete. Some of the municipal corporations such as Bhubaneswar had taken the mentioned laws very seriously and implemented them in their city plans.

However, the need for framing a central law on street vending was felt by the Ministry of Housing and Urban Poverty Alleviation (MoHUPA) and several national consultations were held in different parts of the country. Notably, MoHUPA had proposed to launch a new scheme for urban street vendors in the 12th Five Year Plan in consultation with academic institutions, NGOs, membership-based organisations (MBOs) and different trade union activists. Finally, the watershed moment for street vendors came in 2014. The Street Vendors (Protection of Livelihood and Regulation of Street Vending) Bill 2014 was passed by both houses of the parliament and become an Act. This Act is for protection of livelihood rights, social security and regulation of urban street vending. It took a lot of time, sincere efforts and attempts by various individuals and organisations in the process. To name a few, Self-Employed Women's Association (SEWA), National Association of Street Vendors of India (NASVI),

Manushi, and National Hawkers Federation in India (NHFI) were actively involved in fighting for the cause of street vendors not only in the capital of India but across different states. In view of the current situation of street vendors, the provisions of the Act and the way in which it would be enacted in light of the ground realities shall be critically discussed in the concluding section.

Extra-legality, state and politics: study context

De Soto argued that the state is responsible for creating bureaucratic and legal obstacles to legitimate enterprise and ownership of property. He emphasised debureaucratisation, decentralisation and deregulation, and reduced government role in production which would lead to free interplay of market forces. By debureaucratisation he meant simplification of laws by which unnecessary laws can be eliminated and functioning of legal institutions can be optimised. While decentralisation is achieved by transferring legislative and administrative responsibilities from the central government to local and regional governments, deregulation allows increasing responsibilities and opportunities of the private individuals. De Soto emphasised that power structure should be reframed. Power should be concentrated in the hands of local governments. Street vending is believed to operate in extra-legal framework which implies non-compliance with the state laws. The question is whether the vendors do prefer or are forced to operate the activity outside the formal regulatory environment. In the process of operating the activity, they enter into political nexus with various agencies in sustaining at the market. While De Soto (1989, 2000) has highlighted how the state is responsible for the emergence of informal arrangements, Marjit et al. (2006), RoyChowdhury (2007) and Marjit and Kar (2009) pointed out political rationale on the part of the state for perpetuating informal arrangements. The idea of informality discussed by them is from the views of state's failure in economic management. On one hand, due to the high incidence of poverty and absence of a social welfare system, a democratic state uses the informal sector as a buffer for the poor people. On the other hand, the extra-legal occupations work as substitutes for social security and emerge as an innovative and effective re-distributive strategy (Marjit & Kar 2009). The extra-legality of street vending can be attributed to hierarchical bureaucratic structure of the state, its agencies and involvement of different actors. Close coordination (or absolute coordination failure) between actors or agents regulating the activity is leading to wastage of resources which is dead capital in De Soto's view. Hernando de Soto further explained that the other path of development depends on active involvement of individuals themselves via collective organisation. On the other hand, Portes (1994) argues that the state's intervention is necessary for development. Alenjandro Portes (1994) emphasised well-coordinated rules and regulations between the state and beneficiaries to be occurred for better functioning at the market. In other words, Portes (1994) stressed a stronger government.

The nature of street vending is characterised by extremes of informality and illegality. The case given at the beginning of the chapter points out several interrelated aspects of a vendor's work and life, factors that drive several thousands of young, uneducated, unskilled and capital-less rural men and women to this occupation. It has been argued that street vendors are the political actors who utilise their agencies to negotiate over individual interest, bonding social relationship and business (Sanyal 1991; Cross 1998a). Although vendors are aware of the exploitative nature of relationship, they do not mobilise to protect self-interest or even class interest. Rather, they coordinate in sustaining social relationship and their overall working life. In the absence of laws and policies, different labour market institutions (Saint-Paul 2000), including formal (organisations and agency) and informal (rents in forms of bribes), are formed which help them to sustain at the market. Now the Act that clearly outlines the rules of the activity is a formal institution which shall govern street vending. Therefore, at this outset, there are four questions: first, do street vendors choose to operate outside the formal state machinery and administrative set-up or do they actually suffer because of the state's incapacity to give them their due recognition and support in perpetuation of livelihood? Second, what and how do politics of market institutions interplay for street vending in existence as extra-legal activity? Third, whether and how will these labour market institutions lead to better functioning of this segment of informal sector? And lastly, will the informal market institutions of rents perpetuate even in the presence of the legal labour market institutions (the Act)? This monograph will try to capture and address the myriad and often contradictory aspects of street vendors' life and work.

Due to the informal nature of street vending activity, vendors face difficulties in conducting their business: their tussles with the civic authorities and the daily struggle for occupying public space. There are also other issues that they encounter, including access to finance. Since street vending is a trade characterised by transactions on a daily basis, they need access to capital (more specifically cash) every day, even for accessing wholesale markets and so on. In the absence of a proper legal framework governing street vending activity, they find themselves unable to access sources of institutional credit. Despite all odds, it is a fact that most street vendors are able to conduct their business, survive in the market, sustain livelihood in the informal set-up and provide alternative markets in the urban economy. In view of the passing of the Street Vendors (Protection of Livelihood and Regulation of Street Vending) Act, 2014, it can be said that it is indeed a victory of continuous struggle from below. The Act has successfully addressed many issues concerning vendors' livelihood and conferring legality to their activity. Having said these, the following questions have been framed to understand the occupation:

1 Why is street vending so important in the present context of urbanisation?
2 What constraints do street vendors face while operating their business?
3 How do vendors manage to conduct business in the market despite facing different constraints?
4 What changes have occurred in the activity and lives of street vendors after passing of the Act?

My primary investigation had started with my doctoral work back in 2007. The field was in Mumbai. The first field visit in Mumbai revealed that street vending has many layers of informality. The challenge with informal sector research is its ambiguous nature of data. The questionnaire developed for fieldwork was comprehensive. It was interesting to closely observe the vendors' day-to-day activity and the way in which business was being carried out. I observed how vendors sold their wares, negotiated with the authorities over bribes, negotiated and persuaded moneylenders over the rates of interest and studied the way in which they connected with their customers. I realised the importance of incorporating 'cases' into the study in order to elucidate each of these themes by providing a context-rich description. This also made me look for 'deviant or extreme cases', which helped to give a holistic understanding of various themes in one case. Frequent visits to meet the same vendors helped to build a rapport, thereby facilitating data collection. It is noteworthy that the methodology and data collection strategies did not guide the field visits. In fact, it was the other way around. Pilot field visits helped to reformulate the objectives based on the emerging themes and these in turn created a need for a flexible approach to the selection of methodology and data collection methods.

Entry to the field was in three stages. The first was when I visited alone. It yielded no results and I was mistaken to be someone from Brihanmumbai Municipal Corporation (BMC) office or a person from the local police station. The reason for this mistake was because I had started asking them about their income, including what proportion of their income was given as bribe, and various questions related to public space. Later, I realised that trade unions mobilising street vendors could help in facilitating my data collection process. Therefore, I approached a few trade union leaders who seemed to know a number of vendors in each location, the nature of working hours (discussed in detail later) and other facets of their trade. The moment I was introduced in the field by these union leaders, I was welcomed. However, the vendors to whom I was introduced by the union leaders were repetitive and biased. Beyond a point, I stopped asking any questions because the responses seemed heavily tutored. Having said this, I must admit that the trade union helped in relieving entry barriers to the field. I stopped collecting data with my structured questionnaire and started visiting the field to and observe the street vendors' day-to-day activities. This was also when I realised that it was not so simple for anyone to enter and operate in this market, even though it might appear that way.

Different themes (discussed in subsequent chapters) have emerged from the field data and experiences. One such instance is from my first day in the field when I came across an elderly female vendor, Vandana (name changed). Meeting her helped me to reconceptualise my research design. Here is how it happened. Vandana could not tell me her exact age. Her fellow vendors said she was nearly 70. I started to interview her. She soon moved away from my present questions and began narrating her 'life history'. She gave extensive details on when and how she entered the vending occupation, how she pursued it in the midst of insecurity, that she was beaten up and jailed by police and civic authorities several times; how she failed to give her son a proper education due to lack of money and so on. I put my questionnaire and field diary away and kept listening to her. Vandana also recounted stories of raids and how unions interfered with her vending activities. She critiqued the role played by some unions and the way in which they operate. Vandana was the first person who raised questions about the role of the state in the lives of street vendors like her and of the state's duty to protect the vendors' livelihoods. To say the least, talking to her helped me identify and look for a number of themes in my study. All the interviews that took place after Vandana's, therefore, imbibed crucial aspects of a street vendor's work and life. These would later go on to rearticulate the entire tone and tenor of my research. Vandana's case was an eye-opener for me at a number of levels. But more fundamentally, it helped me to realise that contrary to my belief and training, statistical and quantitative techniques were not enough to capture the myriad aspects of a vendor's work and life. We often face difficulty to adopt an appropriate research methodology to address issues pertaining to labour. Though NSSO data provide macro-level data on informal sector, we need to depend on primary sources to get employment- or sector-specific micro-level data. Thus, a combination of quantitative and qualitative methodology has been used in the study.

The same research methodology was adopted in subsequent studies. Research undertaken in 2009–10 supported by NASVI (National Association of Street Vendors of India) considered street vending in ten cities in India and the report was submitted in 2012. The cities were: Bengaluru, Bhubaneswar, Delhi, Hyderabad, Imphal, Indore, Jaipur, Lucknow, Mumbai and Patna. Later, a research supported by UNDP (United Nations Development Programme) and MoHUPA (Ministry of Housing and Urban Poverty Alleviation) was undertaken on financial inclusion of street vendors in fifteen cities – Ahmedabad, Lucknow, Kanpur, Bengaluru, Bhubaneswar, Bhopal, Delhi, Guwahati, Hyderabad, Jaipur, Kolkata, Mumbai, Patna, Ranchi and Vijayawada. This study was conducted in 2011–12. Issues pertaining to the activity are similar. Since the line of enquiry is similar, the same questionnaire was administered in other cities. Nevertheless, a pilot study was conducted at every city to test the questionnaire. Field was revisited in Mumbai, Kolkata, Delhi and Guwahati in 2014–15 in order to know the current situation of street vendors especially post Act. Data were mainly drawn from my doctoral research and research projects undertaken during 2009–15. Post-Act situation has also been captured based on data gathered from Mumbai, Kolkata, Delhi and Guwahati. This book includes descriptive data from ten cities, namely, Bengaluru, Bhubaneswar, Delhi, Hyderabad, Imphal, Indore, Jaipur, Lucknow, Mumbai and Patna. Deviant cases have also been drawn from these cities. In addition, some case studies have been considered from other cities like Ahmedabad, Bhopal, Guwahati, Kanpur, Kolkata, Ranchi and Vijayawada.

Outline of the book

The book attempts to address issues and features of street vending and living and working conditions of street vendors in the informal economy in India. Due to ever-increasing importance within the informal sector and the complex nature of vendors' problems, they often attract the attention of academicians and policymakers. Inherent characteristics of street vending are by and large similar to the multidimensional characteristics of the informal sector. Characteristics and structure of the informal street market and issues related to street vending are discussed throughout the chapters. The book consists of introduction and six chapters, beginning with the debate and growth of so-called informal economy in the developing countries, including India. Notably, important studies done by several authors (ILO 1972; Hart 1973; McGee 1973; Bromley 1978; Moser 1978; Tokman 1978; Nattrass 1987; De Soto 1989; Fields 1990) considered street vending as one of the examples which could define, describe and theorise the peculiar and heterogeneous features of the informal sector. There are mainly three theoretical approaches to the informal economy – dualist (ILO 1972; Hart 1973; Tokman 1978), structuralist/interdependency (Moser 1978; Castells & Portes 1989) and legalist (De Soto 1989) – discussed. These approaches have been contextualised within street vending in the present milieu in India. A description of study locations, field experiences which significantly shaped the research questions and the choice of methodology are provided in this section. These in turn determined the methods of data collection that eventually have been used.

Features and structure of street markets are presented in Chapters 1 and 2. Chapter 1 illustrates the profile of street vendors in India. It begins with a brief description of socio-demographic profiles of street vendors in urban India. This chapter addresses the basic questions of who are the street vendors, where do they come from, what are their family background and other details.

This is because socio-demographic factors do not determine only the product they sell but also the level of income that they earn. Work-related characteristics and how prices are being set mutually are illuminated in Chapter 2. How the informal market operates and ways and means by which vendors provide goods and services to urban dwellers have been discussed here. The main factors for vendors taking up this occupation are the force of circumstances – poverty especially to support their families, widowhood, low level of education and childcare including money for their children's education. This activity has both 'push' and 'pull' factors. The lack of jobs in the formal sector for persons with inadequate education and skills pushes them towards this profession because it requires minimal education, skill and investment. In the absence of non-farm employment in rural areas, people migrate to cities in search of better job opportunities. The presence of relatives in cities or towns facilitates their entry to this occupation. It is the aspiration of a better life and the dream of finding their children better opportunities that attracts them to cities. In the absence of a proper legal framework for street vending, social contacts, social network and cohesion play a decisive role in the market, which are elaborated in Chapter 2. Kinship, ethnicity, religion and localism are found to have an impact on vendors' lives, especially at the places where they ply their trade. Vendors also relate to others based on the place of birth or origin. Sharing the same local origin and language makes it easier for a person to enter and exist in the market. The number of years of business, language and origin of the vendors are factors that play a key role in building the two dimensions of 'trust' and 'reputation', even for those who borrow money at high rates of interest. Economic linkages with formal and informal sectors are seen as important roles in this activity. They help many micro-enterprises to flourish because the products sold by these small enterprises are marketed and sold by the vendors. These linkages have been illustrated in Chapter 2. This occupation has prosperity and scope for upward mobility within the trade and flexibility in the occupation. The prospect of rising up the income ladder by engaging in vending of items that fetch higher returns is perhaps another significant factor attracting many workers. However, this mobility and flexibility take place within the vending occupation, implying that only vertical mobility (within the activity) is possible, not horizontal (not occupational shift). Due to the informal nature of this economy, vendors do not have accessibility to formal institutional credit. As a result, vendors depend on moneylenders, who in turn take advantage of their vulnerability and charge exorbitant rates of interest. Street vendors are financially vulnerable and they need to borrow money for various purposes. Some of these are directly related to their business and some are not. The main purposes of borrowing are related to social security, business and payment of bribes, which often lands them in a debt trap situation.

Despite the growth of street vendors, their work is uncertain and insecure. Before explaining the uncertainty and insecurity, the issues relating to public space have been taken into account in Chapter 3. This chapter discusses why public space is a contested issue in the urban economy. The main reason for the denial of dignity is due to occupying public space. The existing rules and policies over public space for street vendors are discussed. This chapter also contains an elaborative discussion on the alternative arrangements vendors make to survive in the market. The attitude of civic authorities and citizens towards the use of public space has been highlighted to show the actual conditions of work. Therefore the main argument in this chapter is surrounding rights at work of the street vendors. Despite having a number of factors working against them, not the least of which is the absence of a legal framework and institutional support, vendors manage to survive in the market. How does this happen? The 'alternative arrangement' made available to them is the payment of bribes. This chapter portrays in detail the ways in which the bribe cycle works as far as street vending is concerned. Bribe payments are demand driven. Therefore, the demand for and supply of bribe payments are explored. This includes the amount of bribes paid, the frequency of these payments, the various actors involved and the proportion of a vendor's income that goes towards bribe payments. In short, street vendors' survival strategy is paying *bribe*. Their survival amidst challenging conditions and ever-changing environment exhibits their flexibility and adaptability. Street vendors manage to conduct their businesses by negotiating mainly with the police and municipal authorities. This understanding is, however, solely based upon the payment of bribes or a certain portion of their daily incomes as 'rents' to the authorities. This has, in fact, become the norm for these vendors, without which the police would evict them summarily from their marketplaces. Studies have revealed that those who do not pay rents are disturbed and harassed regularly. This interferes with their 'right to work with dignity'. The bribe paid to the municipal authorities is greater than that paid to the police. The available data show that in the case of most vendors, nearly 5–10 per cent of their daily incomes are usurped by the civic authorities. These issues have been addressed in this chapter.

Chapter 4 describes the nature of insecurity and uncertainty of the markets where these vendors operate, the uncertain nature of their work, the different forms of uncertainty and insecurity that they experience. Competition at the marketplace and prolonged working hours are a result of this insecurity and uncertainty. Social relations and contacts at the workplace and how these help them to overcome any odd situation have been illuminated. My original presumption was that street vendors' borrowing is mainly for business purposes, but a significant portion of street vendors also borrow for social security such as education and health care. As a result they find themselves stuck in multiple and chronic debt traps and are also exposed to various degrees of harassment. Unfortunately, the bribe payments do not ensure a hassle-free work environment in which a street vendor can conduct his business. Impoverishment and uncertainty due to high and regular bribe payments characterise a street vendor's work life. These issues have been elaborated in this chapter.

Despite low unionisation among street vendors, MBOs, especially trade unions, have a big role to play in organising vendors against various forms of harassment. Unions mainly play a role in securing the trade of the vendors by ensuring their right to public space utilisation. Chapter 5 discusses the freedom of association in a street vendor's life. The questions that I ask are: how does collective bargaining influence the negotiations regarding harassment and eviction issues faced by vendors with a special focus on the utilisation of public space? What factors influence the decision of joining a union? Do social networks play a role? Does being part of a union guarantee the street vendor access to institutional credit and social security? What are the successes and failures of unionising for street vendors? Chapter 5 provides some answers to these questions based on an analysis from field responses.

Chapter 5 also intends to address the struggle of street vendors and organisations culminating in passing of the Act. Also, the responses received from state administration at different levels and reasons for these responses have been discussed. Different states have their own political ideologies and have followed different strategies to address the issues. These issues have been discussed in detail through different case studies drawn from different cities. Some unions follow a participatory mechanism through which vendors try to find solutions to their problems. Unions mainly focus on negotiating with the civic authorities, forming cooperatives for accessing working capital and providing social security and awareness training programmes. The most common form of harassment faced by vendors arises from the rent-seeking activities of the authorities, some intermediate bribe collectors and local leaders.

Whether De Soto's assumptions on debureacratisation, decentralisation and deregulation of the state are the solution or whether the state's intervention is required more for development are the key arguments here and have been examined and challenged in the context of informal street market in India in Chapter 6. Many layers of informality are existing in the activity. One of them is through informal payment of high interest rates on credit from moneylenders. Several vendors have reported that the number of moneylenders was limited previously. Not only has there been an increase in the number of moneylenders, but also in the number of loan schemes designed and introduced to attract vendors. Schemes of loan are tailor-made according to the demand from vendors and there is an increase in competition among vendors as well as among moneylenders. The lack of formal institutional credit leads to another form of informality. It can be argued that informal credit transactions are leading to a rise in the circulation of usurious capital. This happens because the amount borrowed from the moneylenders is paid back at high interest rates and this amount is circulated again in the form of usurious capital. Along with this practice, vendors also survive by paying bribes to the civic authorities, which is unrecorded and unregistered. Such forms of illegality are associated with informality. After the Act was passed in 2014, the question is: whether will the Act provide a new direction to the informal market while implementing it? If so, how? Post Act, some basic characteristics of this informal market have undergone structural changes. The Act is about protecting the existing street vendors, not promoting any employment opportunity to the new entrants. This leads to further questions: is there any restriction in the market for new entrants or will the entry take place in a different mode altogether? While implementing the Act, changes in attitudes among civic authorities, grass-roots level organisations and street vendors seem to have occurred. These changes are manifested in the transformation of informal market – demand-driven to supply-led.

This leaves us further with following questions: shall the Act lead to different layers of informality at the micro level or lead to more urban unemployment by restricting the entry at macro level or will vendors continue sustaining in extra-legal frame? This chapter answers these questions. Lastly, how significant the concept of decent work is for street vendors especially post Act? The concept of decent work devised by the ILO has been of relevance for analysing the roles and responses of various stakeholders in the street vending activity. The chapter not only examines how inclusive the Act is from decent work perspective but also highlights the scope and challenges to achieve it.

Note

1 Informal sector has been used throughout the monograph.

Chapter 1

Street vendors in urban India

An overview

This book aims to present a holistic picture of street vending and the way in which this occupation is carried out in urban India. It is evident that street vending is a growing phenomenon not only in India but also across the world. Urban working poor find street vending as one of the easiest means of livelihood generation. However, their entry to this occupation is subject to various factors. From the views of different parameters such as economic, legal, institutional, social and cultural that are associated with the activity; one can say that this occupation is multidimensional. Notwithstanding, it is important to know who these vendors are, where they have come from, what their previous occupations were and their educational background, their social backgrounds and the age bracket. This chapter discusses descriptive statistics of socio-demographic profile of street vendors in urban India. The chapter is based on descriptive data collected on street vending considering major cities in India, namely, Bengaluru, Bhubaneswar, Delhi, Hyderabad, Imphal, Indore, Jaipur, Lucknow, Mumbai and Patna.

According to the Government of India (GOI), there are around 10 million vendors in India (NCEUS 2006). It was found that the number of street vendors has been rising across all major urban agglomerations (Bhowmik & Saha 2013). Estimating the number of street vendors in India is not easy because of the informal nature of their occupation. Moreover the number of vendors is continuously increasing, which also makes enumeration difficult. These numbers depend on time of day or the season of the year when they take to vending. Field experiences have shown that some vendors only sell in the morning or the afternoon, or in the evening, while some sell only on weekends and others sell only

during certain seasons. Data on the total number of street vendors have been drawn from various trade unions, associations and
municipal corporations in each city. However, these data are only
an approximation because very few Indian cities in the country
have accurate data on the actual number of the street vendors.
Notwithstanding, the calculation shows (see Table 1.1) that the
proportion of street vendors to the total population in seventeen
major Indian cities has been increasing and the percentage of the
population working as street vendors has been increasing significantly along with urbanisation and city development.

Table 1.1 Proportion of street vendors to the urban population in selected cities in India

Name of the city	Total population	Total street vendors	Proportion of street vendors (percentage)
Ahmedabad	5.57	0.10	1.80
Bengaluru	8.43	0.10	1.19
Bhopal	1.80	0.01	0.78
Bhubaneswar	0.84	0.03	3.58
Delhi	11.26	0.30	2.66
Guwahati	0.96	0.02	1.56
Hyderabad	6.81	0.10	1.47
Imphal	0.26	0.01	1.89
Indore	1.96	0.04	2.04
Jaipur	3.07	0.40	1.30
Kanpur	2.88	0.10	3.48
Kolkata	4.49	0.10	2.23
Lucknow	2.82	0.10	3.55
Mumbai	12.48	0.25	2.00
Patna	1.68	0.05	2.97
Ranchi	1.07	0.04	3.26
Vijayawada	1.05	0.01	0.74

Source: Computed by the author based on Census 2011 and various documents from
trade unions. Note: Population under municipal corporation area has been considered in
each city. Total population and total number of street vendors are presented in millions,
and street vendors' proportion to population has been calculated in percentage.

Socio-demographic and economic profile of vendors

Gender composition

While looking at the sex ratio of street vendors in different cities, it is found that vending is a male-dominated occupation (see Table 1.2). Females constitute 28 per cent in all the cities taken together. The sole exception is that of Imphal, where an overwhelming majority (88.5 per cent) are females, while males constitute 11.5 per cent. The predominance of females in Imphal is not an isolated case, because if we look at other cities in the Northeast such as Shillong, Dimapur and Aizawl, we would find the same trend. Guwahati and Agartala may show slightly different trends. Each of the cities shows a different feature of male and female composition. In some, the percentage of females is very low and in others, it is slightly higher. For instance, more than 80 per cent of vendors are males in cities like Bhubaneswar (91.5 per cent), Hyderabad (84.0 per cent), Lucknow (96.5 per cent) and Patna (81.0 per cent). In metro cities of Bengaluru, Delhi and Mumbai,

Table 1.2 Gender composition

City	Gender		Total
	Male	Female	
Bengaluru	140 (70.0)	60 (30.0)	200 (100.0)
Bhubaneswar	183 (91.5)	17 (8.5)	200 (100.0)
Delhi	140 (70.0)	60 (30.0)	200 (100.0)
Hyderabad	168 (84.0)	32 (16.0)	200 (100.0)
Imphal	23 (11.5)	177 (88.5)	200 (100.0)
Indore	146 (73.0)	54 (27.0)	200 (100.0)
Jaipur	139 (69.5)	61 (30.5)	200 (100.0)
Lucknow	193 (96.5)	7 (3.5)	200 (100.0)
Mumbai	145 (72.5)	55 (27.5)	200 (100.0)
Patna	162 (81.0)	38 (19.0)	200 (100.0)
Total	1,439 (72.0)	561 (28.0)	2,000 (100.0)

Source: Computed by author, based on field survey conducted in 2009–10.

Note: Figures within parenthesis indicate percentage in share.

female participation in street vending is comparatively higher (about 30 per cent). In growing cities like Indore and Jaipur, female vendors are found to be higher in numbers which are 27 per cent and 30.5 per cent, respectively. Supporting children's education is the main reason for women to be engaged in the activity especially in these cities. Difficulty to sustain with one income earner in metro cities (especially in case of Bengaluru, Delhi and Mumbai) is seen to be another reason for female vendors to join this occupation. Lucknow has the worst sex ratio with only 3.5 per cent female vendors.

Religion

On examining the data on religion, we find that an overwhelming majority (over 80 per cent) belong to the Hindu community (see Table 1.3). In Bhubaneswar, Imphal and Jaipur, the vendors who belong to Hindu account for 90 per cent. In the other cities, the proportion of Hindu vendors lies between 70 per cent and 80 per cent. These include Bengaluru (72.5 per cent), Delhi (83.5 per cent), Indore (84 per cent), Lucknow (78.5 per cent), Mumbai (87 per

Table 1.3 Religion

City	Religion				Total
	Hindu	Muslim	Sikh	Christian	
Bengaluru	145 (72.50)	40 (20.0)	4 (2.0)	11 (5.5)	200 (100.0)
Bhubaneswar	194 (97.0)	6 (3.0)	0 (0)	0 (0)	200 (100.0)
Delhi	167 (83.5)	29 (14.5)	4 (2.0)	0 (0)	200 (100.0)
Hyderabad	110 (55.0)	80 (40.0)	1 (0.5)	9 (4.5)	200 (100.0)
Imphal	185 (92.59)	11 (5.5)	0 (0)	4 (2.0)	200 (100.0)
Indore	168 (84.0)	31 (15.5)	0 (0)	1 (0.5)	200 (100.0)
Jaipur	189 (94.5)	9 (4.5)	1 (0.5)	1 (0.5)	200 (100.0)
Lucknow	158 (79.0)	41 (20.5)	0 (0)	1 (0.5)	200 (100.0)
Mumbai	175 (87.5)	24 (12.0)	0 (0)	1 (0.5)	200 (100.0)
Patna	172 (86.0)	22 (11.0)	4 (2.0)	2 (1.0)	200 (100.0)
Total	1,663 (83.15)	293 (14.65)	14 (0.7)	30 (1.5)	2,000 (100.0)

Source: Computed by the author, based on field survey conducted in 2009–10.

Note: Figures within parenthesis indicate percentage in share.

cent) and Patna (86 per cent). On the other hand, Hyderabad contains 55 per cent of Hindu vendors which is the lowest among all cities. When compared with other cities, Hyderabad has relatively higher proportion of Muslim vendors (40 per cent). In Lucknow and Bengaluru, about 20 per cent of the total vendors are found belonging to the Muslim community. In Mumbai, it is 12 per cent, Patna has 11 per cent, Indore has 15.5 per cent and Delhi has 14.5 per cent. Bhubaneswar and Jaipur have less than 5 per cent Muslim vendors. Among the other religious communities, Christians and Sikhs form very small proportions (less than 5 per cent). Sikhs, however, come to around 1 per cent or less. In cities such as Imphal, Jaipur and Bhubaneswar we did not come across any Sikhs. Christians form only 1 per cent in Lucknow, Mumbai, Patna and Indore, whereas Bengaluru has 5.5 per cent, Hyderabad has 4.5 per cent and Imphal has 2 per cent. Jaipur has only 0.5 per cent of street vendors from the Christian community.

Social group

Across cities, vendors falling under general category are high with 33.1 per cent of the total sampled population, followed by OBC constituting 29.5 per cent. Mumbai contains 47.5 per cent general caste vendors. Cities like Imphal and Bhubaneswar have the highest proportion of general category vendors with 97 per cent and 77.5 per cent, respectively, whereas cities like Patna (62.5 per cent), Indore (50 per cent), Lucknow (53.5 per cent) and Bengaluru (31.5 per cent) have relatively higher number of vendors who fall under OBC category. Relatively higher numbers belonging to SC category are found in Hyderabad, Jaipur and Indore (see Table 1.4). Interestingly 38.5 per cent of vendors in Delhi, 28 per cent in Bengaluru, 18 per cent in Lucknow, 14.5 per cent in Mumbai and 11 per cent in Patna could not report their caste identity or may have chosen to remain silent on the issue. Notwithstanding, vendors in almost across the cities reported that their caste identity neither has any relation with the types of products that they sell nor has any impact on their daily sale. The ST population is more or less absent in street vending. In Bhubaneswar, Delhi, Imphal, Indore, Lucknow and Patna, they constitute less than 1 per cent of the street vendors. Jaipur is an exception, with around 15.5 per cent STs involved in street vending. Being a capital, Jaipur attracts a significant number of ST population from nearly villages even some of them are from Udaipur.

Table 1.4 Social group

City	Social group					Total
	General	SC	ST	OBC	Not reported	
Bengaluru	31 (15.5)	31 (15.5)	19 (9.5)	63 (31.5)	56 (28.0)	200 (100)
Bhubaneswar	155 (77.5)	22 (11.0)	1 (0.5)	22 (11.0)	0 (0)	200 (100)
Delhi	29 (14.5)	55 (27.5)	2 (1.0)	37 (18.5)	77 (38.5)	200 (100)
Hyderabad	52 (26.0)	88 (44.0)	15 (7.5)	45 (22.5)	0 (0)	200 (100)
Imphal	194 (97.0)	0 (0)	4 (2.0)	2 (1.0)	0 (0)	200 (100)
Indore	26 (13.0)	71 (35.5)	3 (1.5)	100 (50.0)	0 (0)	200 (100)
Jaipur	38 (19.0)	81 (40.5)	31 (15.5)	47 (23.5)	3 (1.5)	200 (100)
Lucknow	23 (11.5)	33 (16.5)	1 (0.5)	107 (53.5)	36 (18.0)	200 (100)
Mumbai	95 (47.5)	24 (12.0)	10 (5.0)	42 (21.0)	29 (14.5)	200 (100)
Patna	19 (9.5)	34 (17.0)	0 (0)	125 (62.5)	22 (11.0)	200 (100)
Total	662 (33.1)	439 (22.0)	86 (4.3)	590 (29.5)	223 (11.2)	2,000 (100)

Source: Computed by the author, based on field survey conducted in 2009–10.

Note: Figures within parenthesis indicate percentage in share.

Marital status

Table 1.5 shows that most of the street vendors are married. In fact we can divide the cities in groups of percentages of married vendors. Bhubaneswar (80 per cent), Delhi (73 per cent), Indore (77 per cent), Lucknow (76 per cent), Mumbai (70 per cent) and Patna (82.5 per cent) are cities where more than 70 per cent of street vendors are married. The other cities – Bengaluru (66 per cent) and Hyderabad (67 per cent) – have between 65 and 70 per cent married vendors. In Jaipur only 57 per cent are married and relatively higher proportion of vendors is found unmarried (34 per cent).

We can take the case of Imphal separately because of the pre-dominance of female vendors. The marital status of women shows that 65 per cent are married. This is low compared to other cities, comprising mainly male vendors. The breakup shows that only 10 per cent are unmarried; at the same time, 22 per cent are widowed. This indicates that widowhood could be a cause for taking to street vending as women do not have social support. In fact we have not collected data on the marital status of women separately in the

Table 1.5 Marital status

City	Marital status					Total
	Unmarried	Married	Widowed	Separated	Divorced	
Bengaluru	37 (18.5)	132 (66.0)	18 (9.0)	12 (6.0)	1 (0.5)	200 (100)
Bhubaneswar	40 (20.0)	160 (80.0)	0 (0)	0 (0)	0 (0)	200 (100)
Delhi	17 (8.5)	146 (73.0)	28 (14.0)	7 (3.5)	2 (1.0)	200 (100)
Hyderabad	57 (28.5)	134 (67.0)	6 (3.0)	3 (1.5)	0 (0)	200 (100)
Imphal	20 (10.0)	130 (65.0)	44 (22.0)	1 (0.5)	5 (2.5)	200 (100)
Indore	25 (12.5)	154 (77.0)	21 (10.5)	0 (0)	0 (0)	200 (100)
Jaipur	68 (34.0)	114 (57.0)	14 (7.0)	3 (1.5)	1 (0.5)	200 (100)
Lucknow	41 (20.5)	152 (76.0)	3 (1.5)	4 (2.0)	0 (0)	200 (100)
Mumbai	39 (19.5)	141 (70.5)	20 (10.0)	0 (0)	0 (0)	200 (100)
Patna	24 (12.0)	165 (82.5)	11 (5.5)	0 (0)	0 (0)	200 (100)
Total	368 (18.4)	1,428 (71.4)	165 (8.2)	30 (1.5)	9 (0.4)	2,000 (100)

Source: Computed by the author, based on field survey conducted in 2009–10.

Note: Figures within parenthesis indicate percentage in share.

other cities but it could be a fair guess that most of them would be married and/or widowed or destitute.

Age distribution

Age is an important component of the demographic profile and in this occupation. It is seen to be dispersed in the range of 10–85 years (see Table 1.6). There are incidences of child labour in this activity as in the sample thirty-seven vendors were found to be below 18 years of age. Hyderabad had thirteen child vendors followed by Indore (nine child vendors). However, considering the high rate of married status of the vendors, most of them should be in the 20-plus age group. In Bengaluru, 82 per cent of the street vendors were in the age group of 25–46. One finds that in Bhubaneswar, 80 per cent were between the age group of 25 and 46. Delhi had 27 per cent in the age group of 25–32. In Hyderabad, the largest number of vendors (65.5 per cent) was in the age group of 25–46. In Imphal, the age group was slightly

Table 1.6 Age distribution

City	Age distribution (in years)							Total
	10–18	18–25	25–32	32–39	39–46	46–60	60–85	
Bengaluru	1	4	36	54	75	29	1	200
	(0.5)	(2.0)	(18.0)	(27.0)	(37.5)	(14.5)	(0.5)	(100)
Bhubaneswar	1	19	61	59	39	18	3	200
	(0.5)	(9.5)	(30.5)	(29.5)	(19.5)	(9.0)	(1.5)	(100)
Delhi	0	20	55	35	39	39	12	200
	(0)	(10.0)	(27.5)	(17.5)	(19.5)	(19.5)	(6.0)	(100)
Hyderabad	13	29	46	44	41	25	2	200
	(6.5)	(14.0)	(23.0)	(22.0)	(20.5)	(12.5)	(1.0)	(100)
Imphal	4	5	10	26	41	99	15	200
	(2.0)	(2.5)	(5.0)	(13.0)	(20.5)	(49.5)	(7.5)	(100)
Indore	9	27	31	30	55	40	8	200
	(4.5)	(13.5)	(15.5)	(15.0)	(17.5)	(20.0)	(4.0)	(100)
Jaipur	3	37	66	61	33	0	0	200
	(1.5)	(18.5)	(33.0)	(30.5)	(16.5)	(0)	(0)	(100)
Lucknow	1	46	34	47	39	27	6	200
	(0.5)	(23.0)	(17.0)	(23.5)	(19.5)	(13.5)	(3.0)	(100)
Mumbai	2	20	42	49	42	35	10	200
	(1.0)	(10.0)	(21.0)	(24.5)	(21.0)	(17.5)	(5.0)	(100)
Patna	3	30	32	31	61	36	7	200
	(1.5)	(15.0)	(16.0)	(15.5)	(30.5)	(18.0)	(3.5)	(100)
Total	37	237	413	436	465	348	64	2,000
	(1.8)	(11.8)	(16.0)	(21.8)	(23.2)	(17.4)	(3.5)	(100)

Source: Computed by the author, based on field survey conducted in 2009–10.

Note: Figures within parenthesis indicate percentage in share.

higher, as 49 per cent were between 46 and 60 years. In Indore, the age distribution of vendors is found to be rather uniform with 44 per cent in the age group of 18–39 and 37.5 per cent in the age group of 39–60. It has also relatively higher proportion of child vendors (4.5 per cent). In Jaipur, 80 per cent were in the age group of 18–39. In other words, an overwhelming majority lay in early age group. Interestingly, our sample did not cover anyone above 45 years of age in this city, as there were just a handful of them. In Lucknow too, 23 per cent were in the young age group of

18–25. In Mumbai, a majority (66 per cent) lay in the age group of 25–46; another 17 per cent were in the age group of 47–60. In Patna, relatively large percentage (30 per cent) is found in the age group of 39–46.

By looking at the average age group, one can see that the bulk of street vendors in all the ten cities were in the productive age group of 25–55. This also indicates why there is a high proportion of married vendors. On the other hand, there is less number of street vendors in the higher age groups. Delhi comparatively has a higher percentage of older street vendors with 6 per cent being in the age group of 61–80. Imphal, like Delhi, has 7.5 per cent in the older age group. The other cities such as Indore has 4 per cent above 60 years and Lucknow has 3 per cent above 60 years. In Mumbai, 5 per cent of vendors are above 60 years.

Migration

Migration results in a large influx of population and most of these people find employment as street vending. This is mainly because of the low cost of set-up and ease of entry into this occupation. In this study, a few number of street vendors were found to be migrants. Street vending had both the 'push' factor and 'pull' factor. The lack of jobs in the formal sector for persons with inadequate education and skills pushes them towards this profession because it requires minimal education, skill and investment. In the absence of non-farm employment, people migrate to cities in search of better job opportunities. The presence of relatives in cities or towns facilitates their entry to this occupation. It is the aspiration of a better life and the dream of finding their children better opportunities that attracts them to cities. These are the 'pull' factors towards the activity. However, the primary reason for migration for males is for work and income opportunities whereas for females, it is marriage.

Vendors were found to be migrated from all parts of the country such as West Bengal, Bihar, Odisha and Assam in East and Northeast India; Uttar Pradesh, Punjab, and Rajasthan in North India; Gujarat and villages of Maharashtra in western India and Karnataka, Kerala and Tamil Nadu in South India. In the sample 72 per cent are found to be not-migrated while 28 per cent are migrated. In Delhi most vendors are migrated (91 per cent) while in Mumbai 78 per cent are migrated. This is because these two cities attract people from all over the country offering employment options to the urban poor. At the other extreme is that of Lucknow, where none of the vendors were migrated (see Table 1.7).

Delving deeper into the cases and pattern of migration of these vendors into the cities in the study, we can see that nature of migration does not show any exceptional features. Except Delhi and Mumbai, other cities show dismal proportion of migrants among vendors. This can be explained. Bihar and Uttar Pradesh (UP) are the states which are pushing a large number of migrants to the cities. As in these cities language is not a barrier and they are mainly Hindi-speaking population, migrants find Delhi and Mumbai as their destinations. This is not the case with Bengaluru or Bhubaneswar. These cities attract migrants either only from nearby rural areas or neighbouring states of Karnataka, Tamil Nadu (in case of Bengaluru) or Andhra Pradesh (in case of Bhubaneswar) or rural inter-district migrants. Thus cities having Hindi-speaking population pull migrants mainly from North India. However, in

Table 1.7 Composition of migrants/non-migrants

City	Migration status		Total
	Migrated	*Not migrated*	
Bengaluru	76 (38.0)	124 (62.0)	200 (100)
Bhubaneswar	58 (29.0)	142 (71.0)	200 (100)
Delhi	182 (91.0)	18 (9.0)	200 (100)
Hyderabad	24 (12.0)	176 (88.0)	200 (100)
Imphal	16 (8.0)	184 (92.0)	200 (100)
Indore	13 (6.5)	187 (93.5)	200 (100)
Jaipur	30 (15.0)	170 (85.0)	200 (100)
Lucknow	0 (0)	200 (100.0)	200 (100)
Mumbai	156 (78.0)	44 (22.0)	200 (100)
Patna	4 (2.0)	196 (98.0)	200 (100)
Total	559 (28.0)	1,441 (72.0)	2,000 (100)

Source: Computed by the author, based on field survey conducted in 2009–10.

Note: Figures within parenthesis indicate percentage in share.

non-Hindi-speaking cities, one would find intra-state and inter-state (neighbouring) migrants in large numbers.

Cities like Lucknow and Patna show very small number of migrants among the sampled vendors. The reasons may be that these vendors are second or third generation of migrant population who came to these urban hubs from rural counterparts in search of livelihood. If we look at the structure of parental occupation of these vendors, almost 28 per cent of them had their parents working as either small farmers or agricultural workers. Notably, on the other hand, the proportion of migrants is also 28 per cent. This implies that a substantial portion of migrants had parents engaged in the agricultural sector that moved to urban areas and chose the vending occupation.

Interestingly we found six Nepali vendors operating in Delhi, Hyderabad, Imphal and Mumbai. One case can be discussed here. This was captured in Mumbai. The vendor came to Kolkata from a rural area of Nepal with the help of his friend. He set up business and settled there. However his income was not high as per his expectation. He also faced constant harassments and evictions. He was aspirant, decided to move to a bigger city and so came to Delhi. His friend in Kolkata helped him to get contacts in Delhi. However, it was at the time of Supreme Court case of *Sodhan Singh vs Delhi Municipal Corporation* in 1989 when there were large-scale evictions, protests and outbursts. He finally decided to move out from Delhi and settled down in Mumbai in search of better future for his children. He settled in Mumbai in 1990s and since then has been plying his trade in the Chembur area of Mumbai. Notwithstanding, he regrets leaving Delhi because sustaining in Mumbai is more difficult than in Kolkata and Delhi. Similarly vendors migrated from Bangladesh can be seen in cities like Kolkata and Guwahati. The above-mentioned case shows that metro cities in India are pulling migrants not only from rural states of India but also from neighbouring countries and providing vending occupation as one of the livelihood options to the working poor.

Previous occupation

As the number of street vendors has been increasing over time, it is important to understand the 'pull' and 'push' factors towards this activity. In other words, why does a large section of the urban working poor take up 'street vending' for livelihood generation instead of other available opportunities in the urban informal economy is the important question that one must address. Vendors' previous occupation is an important factor to explore in order to understand what leads them to eventually take up vending. Table 1.8 shows that out of 2,000 vendors, around 26 per cent were unemployed before taking up vending. Only 4 per cent were agricultural wage workers. Interestingly, the largest proportion – almost 52 per cent – of the total vendors were engaged as regular wage workers before becoming owners of stalls, while 5 per cent were casual wage workers in some formal retail outlets and became self-employed street vendors. A small number (eleven in total sample) were students, who entered this profession due to lack of formal sector job opportunities. Interestingly, data in Mumbai revealed that four male vendors (three in Dadar and one in Vile Parle) had joined street vending after factory closures. A gender comparison in the context of previous occupations revealed that the number of female vendors who were employed as wage workers (in other vending stalls and as domestic workers) earlier was higher as compared to the male vendors.

Analysis of the data highlights a clear transition from regular wage employment to self-employment. In addition, there is also a tendency towards urban self-employment from rural agricultural wage work (4 per cent of the total vendors came directly from the agricultural wage work). According to the vendors, there is a strong preference to being self-employed than being wage workers. The most important reason is that self-employment gives greater autonomy. As wage workers, they are treated with disdain and are often underpaid. The rise in wages is not commensurate with the hard work they put in, in addition to the constant fear that they might lose their jobs. The transition from rural to urban self-employment also implies that the possibility of higher incomes and better lifestyles draws a large number of rural folk to this occupation. In almost all cities the percentage of regular wage workers among vendors far exceeds other trade or occupations. In Bengaluru it is 55 per cent, 57 per cent in Bhubaneswar, 47 per cent in Delhi, 66 per cent in Hyderabad, 47 per cent in Imphal, 75 per cent in Jaipur, 53 per cent in Mumbai and 52 per cent in Patna. Indore, Delhi and Lucknow had 61 per cent, 41 per cent and 40 per cent of vendors, respectively, who were unemployed before (see Table 1.8).

Table 1.8 Previous occupation of vendors

City	Occupation before street vending						Total
	Unemployed/ seeking employment	Agricultural labour	Home-based workers	Student	Casual wage worker	Regular wage worker	
Bengaluru	2 (1.0)	49 (24.5)	22 (11.0)	11 (5.5)	5 (2.5)	111 (55.5)	200 (100)
Bhubaneswar	52 (26.0)	3 (1.5)	1 (0.5)	2 (1.0)	27 (13.5)	115 (57.5)	200 (100)
Delhi	82 (41.0)	6 (3.0)	3 (1.5)	3 (1.5)	11 (5.5)	95 (47.5)	200 (100)
Hyderabad	39 (19.5)	4 (2.0)	24 (12.0)	0 (0)	1 (0.5)	132 (66.0)	200 (100)
Imphal	17 (8.5)	0 (0)	83 (41.5)	0 (0)	6 (3.0)	94 (47.0)	200 (100)
Indore	123 (61.5)	0 (0)	2 (1.0)	0 (0)	8 (4.0)	67 (33.5)	200 (100)
Jaipur	35 (17.5)	0 (0)	1 (0.5)	5 (2.5)	8 (4.0)	151 (75.5)	200 (100)
Lucknow	81 (40.5)	1 (0.5)	5 (2.5)	0 (0)	43 (21.5)	70 (35.0)	200 (100)
Mumbai	36 (18.0)	4 (2.0)	49 (24.5)	2 (1.0)	2 (1.0)	107 (53.5)	200 (100)
Patna	57 (28.5)	15 (7.5)	13 (6.5)	4 (2.0)	6 (3.0)	105 (52.5)	200 (100)
Total	524 (26.2)	82 (4.1)	203 (10.2)	27 (1.4)	117 (5.8)	1,047 (52.4)	2,000 (100)

Source: Computed by the author, based on field survey conducted in 2009–10.

Note: Figures within parenthesis indicate percentage in share.

Daily income

Looking at the data on daily income we see that in almost all cities majority of vendors had daily incomes in the range of Rs 100–200 (see Table 1.9). In Bengaluru the share is 55 per cent, 65 per cent in Bhubaneswar, 60 per cent in Delhi, 55 per cent in Hyderabad, 83 per cent in Jaipur, 88 per cent in Lucknow and 52 per cent in Mumbai. However, in some cities relatively larger share is found in lower-income group of Rs 50–100. Imphal has around 50 per cent

Table 1.9 Daily income distribution (in Rs)

City	Daily income (in Rs)						Total
	10–50	*50–100*	*100–200*	*200–300*	*300–500*	*500–2,000*	
Bengaluru	0 (0)	28 (14.0)	111 (55.5)	54 (27.0)	7 (3.5)	0 (0)	200 (100)
Bhubaneswar	10 (5.0)	47 (23.5)	131 (65.5)	10 (5.0)	1 (0.5)	1 (0.5)	200 (100)
Delhi	15 (7.5)	56 (28.0)	120 (60.0)	6 (3.0)	3 (1.5)	0 (0)	200 (100)
Hyderabad	7 (3.5)	39 (19.5)	111 (55.5)	34 (17.0)	7 (3.5)	2 (1.0)	200 (100)
Imphal	10 (5.0)	101 (50.5)	67 (33.5)	13 (6.5)	9 (4.5)	0 (0)	200 (100)
Indore	9 (4.5)	152 (76.0)	33 (16.5)	6 (3.0)	0 (0)	0 (0)	200 (100)
Jaipur	0 (0)	22 (11.0)	167 (83.5)	10 (5.0)	1 (0.5)	0 (0)	200 (100)
Lucknow	1 (0.5)	10 (5.0)	176 (88.0)	13 (6.5)	0 (0)	0 (0)	200 (100)
Mumbai	7 (3.5)	54 (27.0)	105 (52.5)	24 (12.0)	8 (4.0)	2 (1.0)	200 (100)
Patna	13 (6.5)	125 (62.5)	56 (28.0)	3 (1.5)	3 (1.5)	0 (0)	200 (100)
Total	72 (3.6)	634 (31.7)	1,077 (53.8)	173 (8.6)	39 (2.0)	5 (0.2)	2,000 (100)

Source: Computed by the author, based on field survey conducted in 2009–10.

Note: Figures within parenthesis indicate percentage in share.

while Indore and Patna have 76 per cent and 62 per cent of vendors in this income category, respectively.

Literacy

The low educational attainment often is one of the reasons for entry to this profession. The present study finds that most vendors have low levels of education (see Table 1.10). Interestingly 67 per cent of the vendors have had formal education, excluding those who could just sign their names. Relatively higher proportion is found

Table 1.10 Literacy rate

City	Educational attainment								Total
	Illiterate	Can sign only	Primary	Upper primary	Secondary	Higher secondary	Graduate	Postgraduate	
Bengaluru	27 (13.5)	45 (22.5)	18 (9.0)	52 (26.0)	44 (22.0)	9 (4.5)	4 (2.0)	1 (0.5)	200 (100)
Bhubaneswar	2 (1.0)	3 (1.5)	0 (0)	84 (42.0)	59 (29.5)	28 (14.0)	18 (9.0)	6 (3.0)	200 (100)
Delhi	40 (20.0)	24 (12.0)	2 (1.0)	89 (44.5)	24 (12.0)	17 (8.5)	4 (2.0)	0 (0)	200 (100)
Hyderabad	81 (40.5)	4 (2.0)	19 (9.5)	69 (34.5)	12 (6.0)	12 (6.0)	3 (1.5)	0 (0)	200 (100)
Imphal	93 (46.5)	26 (13.0)	1 (0.5)	47 (23.5)	16 (8.0)	10 (5.0)	7 (3.59	0 (0)	200 (100)
Indore	22 (11.0)	34 (17.0)	0 (0)	112 (56.0)	24 (12.0)	5 (2.5)	3 (1.5)	0 (0)	200 (100)
Jaipur	30 (15.0)	28 (14.0)	71 (35.5)	31 (15.5)	35 (17.5)	5 (2.5)	0 (0)	0 (0)	200 (100)
Lucknow	13 (6.5)	42 (21.0)	0 (0)	130 (65.0)	14 (7.0)	1 (0.5)	0 (0)	0 (0)	200 (100)
Mumbai	36 (18.0)	3 (1.5)	14 (7.0)	77 (38.5)	52 (26.0)	12 (6.0)	3 (1.5)	3 (1.5)	200 (100)
Patna	63 (31.5)	23 (11.5)	18 (9.0)	41 (20.5)	36 (18.0)	8 (4.0)	10 (5.0)	1 (0.5)	200 (100)
Total	407 (20.4)	232 (11.6)	143 (7.2)	732 (36.6)	313 (15.6)	107 (5.4)	52 (2.6)	11 (0.6)	2,000 (100)

Source: Computed by the author, based on field survey conducted in 2009–10.

Note: Figures within parenthesis indicate percentage in share.

in the upper primary and secondary education. Imphal (46.5 per cent), Hyderabad (40.5 per cent) and Patna (31.5 per cent) have the highest number of illiterate among vendors. What is interesting is that despite being illiterate they are conducting their business that includes maintaining accounts and having an inventory of goods bought and sold. The lowest number of illiterates can be found in Bhubaneswar, where only 1 per cent is totally illiterate and 1.5 per cent can only sign their names.

Notably eleven vendors in Bhubaneswar, Mumbai, Bengaluru and Patna are found to be postgraduates. The case of Mumbai can be highlighted here. Two male vendors in Kandivali and another vendor in Chembur were found to be postgraduates. Three of them had come from rural Uttar Pradesh in search of better-paid jobs in the formal sector in Mumbai. Since street vending is one of the easiest means of survival and requires only a small amount of financial capital, these graduates chose this profession. It is important to note that scarcity of employment opportunities in the formal sector is a primary cause for driving many educated individuals towards this occupation. It was observed that young male vendors joined this occupation initially either to earn some pocket money or to help their fathers and elder brothers. Over time they were forced to take up vending as their sole source of livelihood once they realised that little or no option was available to them and, as reiterated earlier, this occupation requires little capital investment, education and skill.

Household information

Besides socio-demographic and economic profile of the vendors, it is also important to analyse the information of households. This information includes the size of the household in terms of the number of dependents, parental occupation, types of household in terms of permanent or temporary structures throwing light on their living conditions and everyday struggles for existence.

Father's occupation

Not only vendor's previous occupation is important to explore; the occupational background of vendor's family, especially parents, is equally significant to analyse. While analysing father's occupation, it is found that most vendors' fathers were unemployed and the percentage is found to be relatively high in some cities including Imphal (63 per cent), Mumbai (87 per cent), Patna (85 per cent), Bhubaneswar (34 per cent), Delhi (30 per cent) and Jaipur (37 per cent) (see Table 1.11). Comparatively a large proportion of vendors' fathers were engaged in agricultural work including wage labour in others' land or small farmers. In Bengaluru, for example, 41 per cent of vendors and another 8 per cent stated that their fathers were engaged as agricultural labourers and small farmers, respectively. In Indore also almost 49 per cent stated agriculture to be livelihood of their fathers, while another 49 per cent stated self-employment to be the principal source of livelihood. In Lucknow 36 per cent stated agriculture to be the principal livelihood of their fathers while a substantial portion (64 per cent) stated self-employment as their livelihood. In Bengaluru (42 per cent), Hyderabad (86 per cent) and Jaipur (40 per cent), the self-employed section is relatively high compared to other occupations among fathers. It thus can be ascertained from the data that in majority of cases, vendors' fathers

Table 1.11 Fathers' occupation of vendors

City	Father's occupation					Total
	Unemployed	Agricultural wage labourer	Farmer	Self-employed	Driver	
Bengaluru	7 (3.5)	83 (41.5)	17 (8.5)	85 (42.5)	8 (4.0)	200 (100)
Bhubaneswar	68 (34.0)	26 (13.0)	50 (25.0)	56 (28.0)	0 (0)	200 (100)
Delhi	60 (30.0)	50 (25.0)	15 (7.5)	71 (35.5)	4 (2.0)	200 (100)
Hyderabad	2 (1.0)	12 (6.0)	14 (7.0)	172 (86.0)	0 (0)	200 (100)
Imphal	127 (63.5)	14 (7.0)	21 (10.5)	31 (15.5)	7 (3.59	200 (100)
Indore	2 (1.0)	56 (28.0)	42 (21.0)	99 (49.0)	1 (0.5)	200 (100)
Jaipur	75 (37.5)	2 (1.0)	35 (17.5)	80 (40.0)	8 (4.0)	200 (100)
Lucknow	0 (0)	7 (3.5)	65 (32.5)	128 (64.0)	0 (0)	200 (100)
Mumbai	174 (87.0)	1 (0.5)	14 (7.0)	10 (5.0)	1 (0.5)	200 (100)
Patna	170 (85.0)	10 (5.0)	4 (2.0)	14 (7.0)	2 (1.0)	200 (100)
Total	685 (34.2)	261 (13.0)	277 (13.8)	746 (37.3)	31 (1.6)	2,000 (100)

Source: Computed by the author, based on field survey conducted in 2009–10.

Note: Figures within parenthesis indicate percentage in share.

were engaged in self-employment such as street vending or petty shopkeepers or ran own-account enterprises which helped building up social contacts so that eventually their wards could take up self-employment. It is seen that some of the vendors serve as family helpers to their parents and later have taken over the activity.

Mother's occupation

In majority of cases mothers of vendors were housewives and not working. However, a few were also agricultural labourers mainly working as unpaid workers in family farms. In Bengaluru, 27 per cent of vendors have their mothers working as agricultural workers, while in Delhi it is 17 per cent, Lucknow 14 per cent and Indore 15 per cent (see Table 1.12). There were also self-employed among the mothers. In Bengaluru it is 14 per cent, Delhi 23 per cent and Hyderabad 21 per cent. It is interesting to find out that majority of street vendors in Imphal were women and they are first-generation earners as most of their mothers (nearly 89 per cent) were housewives themselves.

Table 1.12 Mothers' occupation of vendors

City	Mother's occupation				Total
	Agricultural labourer	Self-employed	Home-based	Housewife	
Bengaluru	55 (27.5)	29 (14.5)	3 (1.5)	113 (56.5)	200 (100)
Bhubaneswar	4 (2.0)	0 (0)	0 (0)	196 (98.0)	200 (100)
Delhi	35 (17.5)	47 (23.5)	0 (0)	118 (59.0)	200 (100)
Hyderabad	8 (4.0)	42 (21.0)	0 (0)	150 (75.0)	200 (100)
Imphal	12 (6.0)	9 (4.5)	0 (0)	179 (89.5)	200 (100)
Indore	30 (15.0)	9 (4.5)	0 (0)	161 (80.5)	200 (100)
Jaipur	1 (0.5)	8 (4.0)	0 (0)	191 (95.5)	200 (100)
Lucknow	28 (14.0)	10 (5.0)	0 (0)	162 (81.0)	200 (100)
Mumbai	5 (2.5)	3 (1.5)	0 (0)	192 (96.0)	200 (100)
Patna	7 (3.5)	1 (0.5)	0 (0)	192 (96.0)	200 (100)
Total	185 (9.2)	158 (7.9)	3 (0.2)	1,654 (82.7)	2,000 (100)

Source: Computed by the author, based on field survey conducted in 2009–10.

Note: Figures within parenthesis indicate percentage in share.

Dependency

The number of dependents in the vendors' households indicates the importance of the occupation as means of livelihood in terms of per capita income. In some instances, vendors were found to have up to fifteen to twenty family members to support. In the same thirteen vendors reportedly have a high dependence burdens. In majority of the cities the number of dependents varies from one to four. In Bengaluru the percentage of vendors having one to four family members to support is 78 per cent, in Delhi 54 per cent, in Imphal 58 per cent, in Jaipur 63 per cent, in Lucknow 63 per cent and in Mumbai 60 per cent. In Bhubaneswar, Patna and Indore the burden to dependents is slightly high with 66 per cent, 55 per cent and 53 per cent of vendors, respectively, having four to seven members to support. Hyderabad (28.5 per cent) and Patna (21.5 per cent) report cases of high burden of seven to ten family members (see Table 1.13).

Housing

The housing situation of vendors across cities is similar. Vendors in major cities live in one-room tenements. This indicates that space is a major problem for their living especially in cities like Bengaluru, Delhi, Kolkata and Mumbai. Most of them store their goods at home (will be discussed in Chapter 3) which means that living space gets further reduced. There are two types of houses that we have found – permanent and temporary structures. Permanent structures mean *pucca* housing which are made of cement and concrete and there is a permanent roof over the head. The temporary (*kuccha*) houses have tin walls or walls constructed with discarded cardboard pieces. The roofs could be of temporary material such as tarpaulin or of a more permanent nature. The temporary structures were seen mainly in urban slums. A majority (63 per cent) of street vendors lives in temporary structures (see Table 1.14). Other cities where temporary structures predominate are Delhi (56 per cent), Hyderabad (88 per cent), Jaipur (60 per cent), Lucknow (55.5 per cent) and Patna (74.5 per cent). This shows the pitiable plight of street vendors in these cities. Temporary structures have several implications. First of all, they are slums/shanties built mainly on public land. These are often demolished by the municipal authorities as they are considered illegal structures. The residents then are rendered homeless for a few days, till they recuperate their resources

Table 1.13 Total number of dependents on vendors

City	Number of dependents (in persons)						Total
	No dependency	1–4	4–7	7–10	10–15	15–20	
Bengaluru	1 (0.5)	156 (78.0)	39 (19.5)	4 (2.0)	0 (0)	0 (0)	200 (100.0)
Bhubaneswar	0 (0)	53 (26.5)	133 (66.5)	12 (6.0)	2 (1.0)	0 (0)	200 (100.0)
Delhi	6 (3.0)	108 (54.0)	62 (31.0)	22 (11.0)	2 (1.0)	0 (0)	200 (100.0)
Hyderabad	0 (0)	36 (18.0)	68 (34.0)	57 (28.5)	29 (14.5)	10 (5.0)	200 (100.0)
Imphal	1 (0.5)	116 (58.0)	67 (33.5)	12 (6.0)	4 (2.0)	0 (0)	200 (100.0)
Indore	0 (0)	48 (24.0)	107 (53.5)	31 (15.5)	13 (6.5)	1 (0.5)	200 (100.0)
Jaipur	1 (0.5)	127 (63.5)	45 (22.5)	26 (13.0)	1 (0.5)	0 (0)	200 (100.0)
Lucknow	1 (0.5)	126 (63.0)	46 (23.0)	26 (13.0)	1 (0.5)	0 (0)	200 (100.0)
Mumbai	0 (0)	120 (60.0)	67 (33.5)	10 (5.0)	2 (1.0)	1 (0.5)	200 (100.0)
Patna	0 (0)	36 (18.0)	110 (55.0)	43 (21.5)	10 (5.0)	1 (0.5)	200 (100.0)
Total	10 (0.5)	926 (46.3)	744 (37.2)	243 (12.2)	64 (3.2)	13 (6.0)	2,000 (100.0)

Source: Computed by the author, based on field survey conducted in 2009–10.

Note: Figures within parenthesis indicate percentage in share.

and set up another temporary shack in the same place. Besides this, they are also victims of the local mafia and municipal authorities that extort rents for allowing them to live undisturbed for a particular period of time. These shacks often do not have access to electricity or drinking water. This becomes an additional burden on the street vendor who has to get his/her supply of water from the nearest source. Safety also is another problem. Since these are temporary structures, thieves or burglars can easily enter inside with ease and carry away the goods stored. Dislocation in housing also means that the vendors' children that have been put in schools have to discontinue their schooling. Hence the future generation may be denied access to education. Sanitation facilities are almost always unavailable and open defecation is quite common. This leads to an unhealthy environment and spread of disease such as hookworms. Street vendors in Delhi were particularly affected by the Commonwealth Games, long before the games had started, under the garb of cleanliness. Moreover, their temporary structures were removed, then allowed to return and they had to find places far from their place of work. NASVI was able to intervene at a later stage in support of the displaced vendors. In fact NASVI's stand was that only those vendors operating in the areas near the venues of the Commonwealth Games could be relocated temporarily and that others should not be evicted at all. This did provide relief to a large section of the street vendors. This was one of the findings of our survey in Delhi. Street vendors living in permanent structures were found to be in Bhubaneswar (62.5 per cent), Imphal (98 per cent), Indore (76 per cent) and Mumbai (63.5 per cent). Table 1.14 indicates that the vendors in these cities are better off than other sections of the informal workforce. The popular myth spread by the middle class, media and also the authorities is that anybody and everybody

Table 1.14 Types of house

City	Types of house		Total
	Permanent	Temporary	
Bengaluru	74 (37.0)	126 (63.0)	200 (100.0)
Bhubaneswar	125 (62.5)	75 (37.5)	200 (100.0)
Delhi	88 (44.0)	112 (56.0)	200 (100.0)
Hyderabad	24 (12.0)	176 (88.0)	200 (100.0)
Imphal	196 (98.0)	4 (2.0)	200 (100.0)
Indore	152 (76.0)	48 (24.0)	200 (100.0)
Jaipur	80 (40.0)	120 (60.0)	200 (100.0)
Lucknow	89 (44.5)	111 (55.5)	200 (100.0)
Mumbai	127 (63.5)	73 (36.5)	200 (100.0)
Patna	51 (25.5)	149 (74.5)	200 (100.0)
Total	1,006 (50.3)	994 (49.7)	2,000 (100.0)

Source: Computed by the author, based on field survey conducted in 2009–10.

Note: Figures within parenthesis indicate percentage in share.

who migrates from the rural areas can set up a tarpaulin on pavements and start selling goods. This is obviously not true. The cities we mentioned with the exception of Delhi have a large number of vendors who live in permanent houses (Delhi has the largest number of street vendors at 3 lakhs), though a majority of them live in temporary structures. A large number of vendors were removed in an effort to sanitise the area. A large number of vendors have such precarious working conditions and are vulnerable to evictions. The Commonwealth Games took a heavy toll on the urban poor, including the street vendors.

Type of ownership of house

Patterns of ownership point out that most vendors across cities live in rented accommodations. In Bengaluru 69 per cent, Bhubaneswar 71 per cent, Hyderabad 81 per cent, Jaipur 65 per cent and Patna 65 per cent of vendors live in rented homes. The percentage of vendors living in own houses are particularly high in Mumbai (61 per cent), Lucknow (58 per cent), Indore (70 per cent), Delhi (61 per cent) and Imphal (87 per cent) (see Table 1.15).

Table 1.15 Ownership of house

City	Ownership of house		Total
	Rented	Owned	
Bengaluru	138 (69.0)	62 (31.0)	200 (100.0)
Bhubaneswar	143 (71.5)	57 (28.5)	200 (100.0)
Delhi	78 (39.0)	122 (61.0)	200 (100.0)
Hyderabad	162 (81.0)	38 (19.0)	200 (100.0)
Imphal	26 (13.0)	174 (87.0)	200 (100.0)
Indore	60 (30.0)	140 (70.0)	200 (100.0)
Jaipur	130 (65.0)	70 (35.0)	200 (100.0)
Lucknow	84 (42.0)	116 (58.0)	200 (100.0)
Mumbai	78 (39.0)	122 (61.0)	200 (100.0)
Patna	130 (65.0)	70 (35.0)	200 (100.0)
Total	1,029 (51.4)	971 (48.6)	2,000 (100.0)

Source: Computed by the author, based on field survey conducted in 2009–10.

Note: Figures within parenthesis indicate percentage in share.

Distance of workplace from residence

In majority of cases vendors reside close to their workplaces. In Bengaluru (64 per cent), Bhubaneswar (92 per cent), Delhi (61 per cent), Hyderabad (83 per cent), Indore (81 per cent), Jaipur (84 per cent), Lucknow (88 per cent), Mumbai (98 per cent) and Patna (86 per cent), vendors have residence within 1–5 km from their workplace, which helps to reduce the cost of transportation as also time in commuting (see Table 1.16). In Imphal 34 per cent live within 1–5 km from their workplace while another 22 per cent live 5–10 km away from the workplace. In Bengaluru and Delhi nearly 27 per cent and 31 per cent of vendors, respectively, have their residences 5–10 km away from the workplace. Often in a metro city or rapidly urbanising town, the cost of living in suburbs is relatively less compared to main city areas. In those cases, vendors prefer commuting to save the cost of rents.

Mode of transportation to the workplace

Vendors do not stay at the place where they conduct their business. At least some amount of travelling is involved for each vendor. According to Table 1.16, most of them, however, stay within a radius of

Table 1.16 Distance of workplace from residence

City	Distance between workplace and residence (in km)					Total
	0–5	5–10	10–20	20–30	30–60	
Bengaluru	128 (64.0)	55 (27.5)	15 (7.5)	2 (1.0)	0 (0)	200 (100)
Bhubaneswar	185 (92.5)	13 (6.5)	1 (0.5)	1 (0.5)	0 (0)	200 (100)
Delhi	123 (61.5)	62 (31.0)	14 (7.0)	0 (0)	1 (0.5)	200 (100)
Hyderabad	167 (83.5)	31 (15.5)	2 (1.0)	0 (0)	0 (0)	200 (100)
Imphal	69 (34.5)	44 (22.0)	50 (25.0)	32 (16.0)	5 (2.5)	200 (100)
Indore	162 (81.0)	37 (18.5)	1 (0.5)	0 (0)	0 (0)	200 (100)
Jaipur	169 (84.5)	26 (13.0)	4 (2.0)	0 (0)	1 (0.5)	200 (100)
Lucknow	177 (88.5)	9 (4.5)	14 (7.0)	0 (0)	0 (0)	200 (100)
Mumbai	196 (98.0)	4 (2.0)	0 (0)	0 (0)	0 (0)	200 (100)
Patna	173 (86.5)	27 (13.5)	0 (0)	0 (0)	0 (0)	200 (100)
Total	1,549 (77.4)	308 (15.4)	101 (5.0)	35 (1.8)	7 (0.4)	2,000 (100)

Source: Computed by the author, based on field survey conducted in 2009–10.

Note: Figures within parenthesis indicate percentage in share.

Table 1.17 Mode of transportation

City	Mode of transportation								Total
	Bus	Train	Auto	Cycle	Motorcycle	On foot	Cart	Tempo, truck, other	
Bengaluru	119 (59.5)	1 (0.5)	0 (0)	21 (10.5)	13 (6.5)	30 (15.0)	16 (8.0)	0 (0)	200 (100)
Bhubaneswar	0 (0)	1 (0.5)	3 (1.5)	96 (48.0)	92 (46.0)	8 (4.0)	0 (0)	0 (0)	200 (100)
Delhi	48 (24.0)	0 (0)	18 (9.0)	14 (7.0)	1 (0.5)	119 (59.5)	0 (0)	0 (0)	200 (100)
Hyderabad	47 (23.5)	1 (0.5)	6 (3.0)	33 (16.5)	1 (0.5)	111 (55.5)	1 (0.5)	0 (0)	200 (100)
Imphal	83 (41.5)	1 (0.5)	64 (32.0)	1 (0.5)	0 (0)	44 (22.0)	2 (1.0)	5 (2.5)	200 (100)
Indore	4 (2.0)	1 (0.5)	2 (1.0)	27 (13.5)	3 (1.5)	147 (73.5)	0 (0)	16 (8.0)	200 (100)
Jaipur	8 (4.0)	0 (0)	1 (0.5)	27 (13.5)	0 (0)	155 (77.5)	0 (0)	9 (4.5)	200 (100)
Lucknow	20 (10.0)	1 (0.5)	0 (0)	48 (24.0)	0 (0)	131 (65.5)	0 (0)	0 (0)	200 (100)
Mumbai	56 (28.0)	22 (11.0)	0 (0)	0 (0)	1 (0.5)	120 (60.0)	0 (0)	1 (0.5)	200 (100)
Patna	6 (3.0)	8 (4.0)	10 (5.0)	32 (16.0)	0 (0)	144 (72.0)	0 (0)	0 (0)	200 (100)
Total	391 (19.6)	36 (1.8)	104 (5.2)	299 (15.0)	111 (5.6)	1,009 (50.4)	19 (1.0)	31 (1.6)	2,000 (100)

Source: Computed by the author, based on field survey conducted in 2009–10.

Note: Figures within parenthesis indicate percentage in share.

5 km from their workplace. Over 77 per cent of the vendors in all ten cities stay within 5 km of their workplace. In Mumbai, 98 per cent of the vendors reside within this radius. In Bhubaneswar 92.5 per cent of the vendors residing within 5 km, whereas in Patna it is around 86.5 per cent and in Lucknow it is around 88.5 per cent. In Delhi, the vendors invariably live in shanties, which are located near their vending spots. Table 1.17 shows the mode of transportation that vendors use to arrive at the workplace. Most, 50.4 per cent, of vendors walk to their workplace. However, some of them may also use bicycle or bus. Very few vendors can afford motorcycles. Only 5.6 per cent of the vendors own motorcycles while 15 per cent own bicycles. About 19.6 per cent take buses. In Mumbai too, 60 per cent walk to the workplace, 28 per cent use the bus and 11 per cent use trains. In Patna too, most (72 per cent) vendors prefer to walk while some use bicycle (16 per cent). In Bhubaneswar, whereas most stay within 0–10 km from the workplace, 48 per cent of vendors have bicycle and another 46 per cent have motorcycles. As mentioned earlier, in Bhubaneswar, national policy was implemented and hawking zones were also identified first in India. This has obviously led to some degree of affluence among the vendors and as a result it is the only city where a sizeable section (94 per cent) can afford bicycles and motorcycles. In Imphal, motorcycles are not used much since most vendors are women. Buses are the preferred mode of travel of the largest group of vendors (41 per cent), followed by auto rickshaw (32 per cent). Around 22 per cent of the vendors travel on foot. In Hyderabad, about 56 per cent of the vendors walk to their place of work and back, whereas 23.5 per cent use the bus services and 16.5 per cent have bicycles.

Conclusion

The chapter highlights important socio-demographic features of street vendors across major cities in India, including not only tier 1 but also tier 2 and tier 3 cities. The idea is to assess the common attributes such as caste, religion, gender distribution, marital status, literacy, age, migration and household characteristics of a sufficiently large sample. Information on previous occupation, parental occupation and dependency help to understand the factors influencing entry to the occupation. These attributes differ across cities, also implying that the cultural connotations of the region also affect the characteristics. For example, Imphal presents a case where unlike all other cities, it has greater number of female vendors. However female vendors do not essentially earn higher income. Also, there are a number of older vendors in Imphal. While a large proportion in the total sample is from the Hindu community, Muslim vendors are found in places such as Hyderabad and Lucknow where the Muslim population is substantial. They may have joined the occupation due to social contacts or members from the same community may have helped in initiating and spreading the activity.

Low level of education is one factor behind entry to the occupation, parental occupation being another major factor. In most of the cases, parents are found unemployed or doing minor wage work. Some of the vendors had their parents in vending which have eventually helped those building social contacts. Again, in the case of migration we see, while migration from all parts of the country is high in tier 1 cities like Mumbai and Delhi due to their Hindi-speaking population, other cities like Bhubaneswar attract only the inter-district and migrants from neighbouring states. Apart from social contacts, language and cultural factors play a role in migrants' entry to street vending. Most vendors in cities like Bengaluru, Delhi and Mumbai manage to earn higher income due to large clientele base and this is also the reason behind greater migrants among vendors in these cities.

Although vending is opted for only by those who do not have an option to join the formal sector, data on previous occupation point out to a particular trend. Within the informal sector there is gradation and preference on types of job. In the sample comparatively greater portion report their previous occupation as 'wage work in casual jobs'. These wage workers have eventually taken up street vending as soon as they have accumulated some funds to start a stall. The reasons for preference for vending are independence, higher income and scope of adjusting work time.

Chapter 2

Informal markets

Structure, characteristics and sustenance

Street vendors operate in alternative shopping destinations which are not permanent and notified market places. They find natural markets for their products in places which generally witness large public gatherings, and allow convenient purchases for the customers. These areas are parks, sea beaches, bus terminus, railway stations, areas outside schools and colleges, hospitals and the like. However, locations of such markets vary across cities. These markets are either major transport nodes or public places such as hospitals, temples, gardens, schools and colleges that attract people from all nearby areas. According to the needs of the consumers, vendors supply goods and provide services to the customers at these places, termed as 'natural markets' (Bhowmik 2010). Products sold at the markets depend on the nature of the natural markets. If we take the example of hospitals, a substantial number of potential consumers such as relatives of patients admitted in hospitals and also the visitors make the surrounding of big hospitals a natural market for the vendors. Vendors outside a hospital would in most cases be found selling cooked food, tea and fruits. The demand for these items is higher in hospital areas. Vendors are smart entrepreneurs who understand the demand/supply theory and apply this in their business practices. Bicyclists need repair shops to have their tyres, chains and pedals fixed, just as much as car owners need tyre repair shops. Pedestrians need beverages, snacks and other articles on their way; thus these services have to exist, otherwise life would become impossible; vendors exists especially for those who cannot afford to buy expensive goods and services as they make the goods and services available at affordable prices.

The number of vendors and the frequency of pedestrians share a direct relationship as the more the frequency of pedestrians, the more vendors at a particular location. Also, if they are not required at those particular locations, then the vendors would not have any incentive to be at that place. People do not go to metro stations, bus stands, hospitals and offices because vendors sell there; however, they have particular requirements which are often sufficed by the services of the vendors, thus making them inevitable. It's difficult to comment whether the vendors are gaining more from such markets or the consumers, but it is clearly evident that more or less both consumers and vendors are dependent on each other, especially at the natural markets. These markets cannot be planned and of course the officials have to think of ways to incorporate these unplanned markets in their planned city while implementing the Act. These natural markets are public spaces and the characteristics of these markets are similar not only across India but also in all the cities of developed as well as developing nations around the world. The aim of this chapter is to discuss the structure and characteristics of street markets from the viewpoint of 'natural markets'. The chapter begins with an illustration of the nature of their market, the type of vendors operating, the various types of goods sold by them, age of their businesses, time of vending, the sources of their products (where they manage to get their wares), their access to wholesale markets and transportation of products. Let us discuss some of the natural markets that were formed historically which eventually have become part of cultural heritage of cities. Today, we cannot imagine these cities without these streets which have not only become a part of everyday lives of urban life but have also become shopping destinations for tourists.

Natural markets

Nehru Place (Delhi)

Nehru Place is a hub for IT (hardware), such as personal computers, servers, networking equipment and software products, documentation services and all allied services. There are also firms that deal exclusively with used and second-hand computer hardware, as well as small, one-room shops that sell software products. Other businesses that operate in the area are banks, multinational corporations, several restaurants and a theatre. Due to these facilities and inimitable identity of Nehru Place, thousands of buyers, users, shop owners and office executives visit this market on a daily basis.

As such, a visitor may find pavement vendors selling items such as printer toner cartridges, blank optical media, printer paper and even software from a small stall or cart. A large number of vendors could also be seen selling cooked food, tobacco and other goods which are required by the visitors. The concentration of a large number of vendors, who provide all sorts of services and sell all goods required by the market visitors, and executives working in surrounding offices shows that they are there because of prevailing demand for their products in this market.

Markets around metro stations and bus terminuses (Delhi)

Thousands of commuters use Delhi Metro and state transport services to reach their destination on a daily basis. Almost all the metro stations, bus stands and bus terminuses are surrounded by street vendors especially selling fruits, vegetables, tea and cooked food. Careful observations suggest that the metro stations and bus terminals are market place for rickshaw pullers as well, who stand near the stations and wait for the commuters. So these locations of vendors serve two sets of clientele: one the general travellers and also they cater to the needs of rickshaw pullers. A thoughtful analysis of items sold by vendors at these places substantiate the quest with regard to the concentration of a large number of vendors selling similar goods, as they cater to the demand of the commuters. If we take the example of Jhandewalan metro station, which is also surrounded by banks and MNCs, a large number of vendors can be found selling cooked food and tea. Vendors told us that they are selling there because this place has good business opportunities; one of them said that 'not everybody brings lunch from home, they need to eat something, not everybody can afford to eat at big outlets on a daily basis, and thus I am here to save them from starvation'.

At the Shadipur bus terminus, most of the vendors sell fruits and vegetables. The place is surrounded by residents of both middle- and lower-income groups, and the commuters find it convenient to buy necessary items such as fruits and vegetables from the vendors rather than going to the faraway markets. A vendor mentioned that 'large number of daily commuters give me good business opportunity; also I would only sell what people would buy. I am selling at the source and the destination of the people, it's convenient for them as well, as they don't have to change their way in order to buy the required things'.

Aminabad market (Lucknow)

There are mainly three types of street vending activities: daily, weekly and seasonal (especially during festive season). The weekly markets are very common across cities in India. This is primarily due to a large section of middle-class customers who prefer to buy weekly supply of fruits, vegetables and other groceries at relatively cheaper price. A large number of vendors in the city of Lucknow are involved in weekly markets in different localities on different days. The Aminabad market is one of the oldest markets of the city and it is one of the most famous markets of North India since the age of Nawabs. The market is situated in the heart of the old city and is surrounded by the localities of strategic importance towards all directions. The market constitutes a huge congregation of retailers and wholesalers, and a large part of business to the small towns of Uttar Pradesh is directed through this place. The market is an inevitable visiting place for almost all local tourists. Also, most of the bulk purchases in and around the city are done from Aminabad. Thus, over a period of time the market has developed into a mixed enterprise of wholesalers, retailers and street vendors. There are around 600–700 street vendors in the market, which is male dominated. Female street vendors are very rare and hardly 2–3 per cent of the total street vendor population is female. This could be attributed to probably the reluctance of Muslim men to allow women to participate in such activities as the area has a large number of Muslim traders and vendors. Women are generally employed in home-based activities like *Chikan work*. The product variety is something that cannot be specified for Aminabad as almost every product of every variety is available in the Aminabad market. Street vendors procure products from the wholesalers from Aminabad itself. Vegetable and fruit vendors bring their products from far-off *Mandis* like Sitapur Road Mandi. Most of the vendors live around Aminabad as the housing prices are not very high in the nearby *Mohallas* and also not far from affluent residential areas. This is also a criterion to select the place to vend. Commuting time is not much for the vendors of these areas. Vending starts around 10–11 a.m.

after one or two hours of cleaning and sorting. The street vendors in Aminabad are more united and informed than in other parts of the city. This market has seen the thick and thin in their struggle. Vendors faced many evictions driven by Lucknow Municipal Corporation. However, these evictions were followed by protests by the vendors against the authorities who later reoccupied the market places several times. The *Tehbazari* was abolished by the Lucknow Municipal Corporation in 2005. This had made the vendors know the relevance of the national policy on street vendors and their demand for implementing the Act. The reason behind selecting Aminabad is its historical relevance and multiplicity characteristic of its street vendors.

Chinhat (Lucknow)

The Chinhat market is situated on the outskirts of Lucknow city and the area is developing rapidly now due to the real estate boom in the adjoining areas of Lucknow. The market is located on the highway connecting Lucknow and Faizabad and a huge customer base is from the travellers who commute or come to Lucknow. Also the market serves as the supply district for pottery products and crockery to the nearby markets. The huge variety of vases, sculptures, lamps, chandeliers and wall hangings and a lot of decorative items made of fine-clay, plaster of Paris; ceramic-terracotta and so on are sold here. The market mostly consists of rural people who were inhabitants of the villages around Chinhat, now a part of the expanding city of Lucknow. Most of them are *Kumbhar* by community. The business for these people is high in summer because of the increased sale of pitchers but a large number of middlemen affect the profits in pot-making to a large extent. Most of the vendors in Chinhat market are also engaged in production with the help of their families and some of them are employed on wages. In the past few years some of the vendors have come to the scene for pure business purpose and are no longer involved in production. Products like clay utensils and pitchers are sourced and workers are 7–8 km from the Chinhat market. The designer crockery, statues and other products are obtained from Gorakhpur and Varanasi. During festivals their profit and sale are at maximum while it is worst during monsoon. The profit margin ranges from Rs 100 to 250 on sale of Rs 800–1000. Vendors are not associated with any kind of union whatsoever.

Markets on Fashion Street, Colaba and Bandra Linking Road (Mumbai)

Known to be the financial capital of India, Mumbai is also home to one of the largest number of street vendors in India. To name a few, *Chor* Bazaar (Mumbai Central); Crawford Market, Fashion Street and Colaba (South Mumbai), Linking Road (Bandra) and Dadar markets can be considered which are famous for street markets in Mumbai. The markets on Fashion Street, Colaba, and Bandra Linking Road are not only important shopping destinations but also located very close to the stations and sell a wide variety of items ranging from food products to fruits and vegetables, electronic items to clothes and accessories. One finds almost everything related to fashion such as clothes, accessories and electronic items. Often designer brand clothes – clothes having minor defects rejected by formal retailers which are procured by vendors from agents – are sold at one-fourth the original price. People from all economic classes of the society come here to shop. Youth frequently visit these places.

Dadar wholesale and retail markets (Mumbai)

Dadar market is featured in selling different products ranging from flowers, vegetables and fruits to garments and electronic items by both retailers and wholesalers. This is also considered as Mumbai's largest wholesale market for flower and vegetables. In case of flowers and vegetables, they arrive from different parts of Maharashtra, namely, Nasik, Satara and other nearby places, and trade to other parts of the city and suburbs. Located in Dadar west, the market has an interesting characteristic. The market starts at 4 o'clock in the morning as wholesale market for flowers and vegetables but at 8 o'clock in the morning onwards the same space is used by retailers selling a variety of products. Stepping out of Dadar station one will enter the market. The amount of bribes is not only vast but the system of the payment is also well coordinated between civic authorities, vendors and local goons. These informal arrangements have been in place since decades.

New Market (Kolkata)

This market has been in existence since colonial times, selling fashionable dress materials, food items, electronic items, shoes, utensils, craft items and daily necessities. Constructed in 1874 by the Calcutta Corporation for British residents, it is now a part of the city's cultural heritage.

College Street (Kolkata)

Similarly the College Street is the destination for book lovers in central Kolkata, a hub of publishing houses. This is also a large market for second-hand books. With historic significance of the location, the market is situated in the vicinity of so-called educational and intellectual hub of Kolkata, namely, Presidency College University, Calcutta University, Medical College and Coffee House. This market has intellectual and cultural significance.

Gariahat (Kolkata)

Another important market destination for street market lovers in Kolkata is *Gariahat* located in south Kolkata, which is well known for selling a variety of items but mainly famous for garments. Besides roadside stalls, there are also formal shopping outlets.

Women's markets (Imphal)

As mentioned earlier, street vending in Imphal is female dominated. Khwairamband market in West Imphal is the main market in the city selling a variety of items ranging from vegetables and fruits to craft items. This century-old street market is the largest women-dominated market in the entire Northeast India. The market is a mirror of women emancipation and matriarchal society of Manipur.

Markets for garments, perfume and street food (Hyderabad)

The street markets in Hyderabad are one of the oldest in India dating back to pre-colonial times. The markets have traditionally grown in and around the Charminar, the most famous historical monument. One of the most famous street markets, Laad Bazaar in the vicinity of Charminar, is famous for perfume, jewellery and garment shops. Between Laad bazar and Moti Chowk, there is this famous perfume market selling locally manufactured perfume 'ittar' since the times of Nawab of Hyderabad. Koti Sultan Bazaar is another street market near Charminar which is almost 200 years old. The market is famous for selling trendy women clothing and accessories. Pragati Gully, the street food hub in Sultan Bazaar, is a favourite breakfast destination for street food lovers. Likewise Pathar Gatti, Sindhi Colony and Sultan Bazaar are known for their famous *Hyderabadi biriyani, kebabs* and other *Mughlai* dishes.

Nature of business

Types of vending

By and large, there are two types of street vendors, namely, stationary and mobile vendors. Stationary vendors normally occupy a pitch on the pavement from where they sell their wares. In some cases, they may have makeshift stalls. The mobile vendors, on the other hand, can be of different types. There are those who sell their wares on pushcarts. These are the comparatively better-off sections because they are able to get a wider variety of the products they sell, such as vegetables and fruits. The stationary vendor, on the other hand, may have lower sales because s/he has constraints of space. At the same time, there are other sections of mobile vendors that are worse off than the other vendors. These are the women who carry their wares in baskets on their heads. Some of them may be fish sellers, but most of them sell vegetables. The limited size of the basket restricts the amount of goods that can be carried for sale (see Table 2.1). Jaipur has more mobile vendors, which constitute 66 per cent of the total vendors. Bengaluru and Lucknow also have a larger proportion of mobile vendors; the former has 48.5 per cent, whereas the latter has 45.5 per cent. Other cities have high proportion of stationary vendors. These include Bhubaneswar (92 per cent), Delhi (71.5 per cent), Hyderabad (80 per cent), Imphal (94.5 per cent), Indore (79 per cent), Mumbai (96 per cent) and Patna (72.5 per cent).

Type of products sold

Street vending was found to be the primary occupation for most male vendors, whereas it was a secondary occupation for most female vendors. Male vendors were engaged in selling all kinds of items, and majority were involved in selling products such as garments, household utensils, electronics and leather-made items. Interestingly, women were not engaged in selling electronic items

Table 2.1 Types of vending

City	Types of vending		Total
	Mobile	Stationary	
Bengaluru	97 (48.5)	103 (51.5)	200 (100)
Bhubaneswar	16 (8.0)	184 (92.0)	200 (100)
Delhi	58 (29.0)	142 (71.0)	200 (100)
Hyderabad	38 (19.0)	162 (81.0)	200 (100)
Imphal	11 (5.5)	189 (94.5)	200 (100)
Indore	42 (21.0)	158 (79.0)	200 (100)
Jaipur	133 (66.5)	67 (33.5)	200 (100)
Lucknow	91 (45.5)	109 (54.5)	200 (100)
Mumbai	8 (4.0)	192 (96.0)	200 (100)
Patna	56 (28.0)	144 (72.0)	200 (100)
Total	550 (27.5)	1,450 (72.5)	2,000 (100)

Source: Computed by the author, based on field survey conducted in 2009–10.

Note: Figures within parenthesis indicate percentage in share.

or leather-made goods. This is because the selling of these products requires substantial investment and involves considerable risk that only men opt for this. Women are more comfortable with those items which require small but day-to-day investment such as vegetables, cooked food and fruits.

The items sold by vendors consist of a variety of goods. Non-perishable items include clothes, metal utensils, plastic goods, leather-made goods and electronics. Perishable goods include vegetables, fruits, flowers, fish and cooked food. The preference of the vendors is for selling perishable food items. They do so because the prices of these items are less compared to non-perishable items such as household and electronic goods and they also constitute mass consumption goods. Data shows (see Table 2.2) that some cities have a greater proportion of vendors selling perishable goods, whereas in other cities, the proportion is slightly less. In Bengaluru 62.5 per cent of those covered were engaged in selling perishable food items. In Imphal, vegetable and fish sellers constitute about 74.5 per cent of the total vendors. Most of the vendors in Imphal are women who sell their goods in the local markets. As mentioned earlier, they come from poor backgrounds and hence, they sell these items as the

Table 2.2 Types of dominant products at the street markets

City	Types of products sold at the markets									Total
	Tea/ coffee	Vegetables, flowers, fish	Fruits	Electronics	Household utensils	Plastic, steel, cosmetics	Garments	Leather-made items	Cooked food	
Bengaluru	25 (12.5)	58 (29.0)	31 (15.5)	7 (3.5)	33 (16.5)	12 (6.0)	13 (6.5)	10 (5.0)	11 (5.5)	200 (100)
Bhubaneswar	4 (2.0)	27 (13.5)	32 (16.0)	5 (2.5)	82 (41.0)	9 (4.5)	2 (1.0)	39 (19.5)	0 (0)	200 (100)
Delhi	16 (8.0)	37 (18.5)	29 (14.5)	2 (1.0)	42 (21.0)	27 (13.5)	0 (0)	46 (23.0)	1 (0.5)	200 (100)
Hyderabad	1 (0.5)	23 (11.5)	46 (23.0)	0 (0)	68 (34.0)	27 (13.5)	6 (3.0)	29 (14.5)	0 (0)	200 (100)
Imphal	1 (0.5)	149 (74.5)	13 (6.5)	1 (0.5)	7 (3.5)	20 (10.0)	0 (0)	9 (4.5)	0 (0)	200 (100)
Indore	5 (2.5)	101 (50.5)	50 (25.0)	1 (0.5)	30 (15.0)	0 (0)	0 (0)	13 (6.5)	0 (0)	200 (100)
Jaipur	20 (10.0)	54 (27.0)	6 (3.0)	0 (0)	87 (43.5)	15 (7.5)	1 (0.5)	17 (8.5)	0 (0)	200 (100)
Lucknow	1 (0.5)	58 (29.0)	10 (5.0)	2 (1.0)	110 (55.0)	16 (8.0)	0 (0)	3 (1.5)	0 (0)	200 (100)
Mumbai	7 (3.5)	40 (20.0)	35 (17.5)	1 (0.5)	39 (19.5)	61 (30.5)	3 (1.5)	14 (7.0)	0 (100)	200 (100)
Patna	11 (5.5)	21 (10.5)	22 (11.0)	1 (0.5)	50 (25.0)	19 (9.5)	1 (0.5)	75 (37.5)	0 (0)	200 (100)
Total	91 (4.6)	568 (28.4)	274 (13.7)	20 (1.0)	548 (27.4)	206 (10.3)	26 (1.3)	255 (12.8)	12 (0.6)	200 (100)

Source: Computed by the author, based on field survey conducted in 2009–10.

Note: Figures within parenthesis indicate percentage in share.

capital required in this business is much less than that needed for non-perishable goods such as utensils and electronic goods.

Indore is another city where a majority sells perishable goods. Vegetables, fruits and fish are sold by 78 per cent of the vendors. A high percentage of vendors selling perishable food items also indicate that the vendors do not have much capital to invest in their trade. Thus, vegetables especially are largely sold by female vendors. The exceptions are the large vegetable vendors, who happen to be men. However, one can witness that in any market, women would invariably sell vegetables and these also happen to be in small quantities. This indicates that women vendors have low capital for investing in their trade. Fruit vendors are in a better position than vegetable vendors. The cost of fruits is higher than that of vegetables. The profit margin of fruit vendors is also quite high. In most cases, fruit vendors happen to be male. One can gauge the financial situation through the bribes given to the civic authorities. Normally fruit vendors pay higher bribes than vegetable vendors do. Since women vendors sell lower-priced perishable items such as vegetables, the bribes they give are smaller than those of men. The cities where non-food items dominate are Delhi (59 per cent), Bhubaneswar (68 per cent), Hyderabad (65 per cent), Jaipur (60 per cent), Lucknow (65.5 per cent), Mumbai (59 per cent) and Patna (73 per cent).

Presence of wage workers in street vending

Vending occupation is heterogeneous and peculiar in nature. By definition, it means self-employed and own account but many people are found to have worked as wage workers under other vendors while many others were employing wage workers. Besides keeping family members including children and spouse of vendors, the presence of wage workers is not an uncommon feature in the vending occupation in India. Nearly 12 per cent of the vendors are found who had started with wage work and then became self-employed street vendors. In general, vendors employ wage workers only when they accumulate sufficient amounts of capital for expanding their business and are in a position to afford wage workers. Vendors having high investment prefer women and children to be employed. Needless to mention, this is because they [women and children] can be paid very low. These wage workers are especially seen in cities like Bengaluru, Delhi, Hyderabad and Mumbai. The following two cases (see Boxes 2.1. and 2.2) from Mumbai do not only illustrate engagement of women and children as wage workers but also demonstrate the situation and conditions of the women wage workers in the activity.

Box 2.1 Children and women as wage workers and their conditions

The case of a vegetable vendor operating under the Chembur Flyover (Mumbai) is highlighted here. He has appointed eight people, five children and three women, the highest number of wage workers appointed in the activity in the area. Women and girls were appointed for cleaning the vegetables. Boys helped the vendor in weighing the vegetables. When the women and children were approached during field survey in order to understand the situation and the relation between employer and employees, they refused to disclose their ages at the first instance. Their employers also shied away from giving any details about them. However, a close discussion (on conditions of strict anonymity) with the vendor revealed that these children usually came from very poor backgrounds. Their parents had sent them for work. So the employers gave them work. The remuneration for the children was Rs 40 (for five hours) per day and Rs 50 for the women.

Source: Based on fieldwork conducted in 2010–11.

Box 2.2 Wage work to supplement vendor's daily income

Sudha (name changed), a vegetable vendor in Chembur (East) in Mumbai, earns Rs 3,000 which is very low because she has four dependents. Hence, she works as a wage worker in the morning with a vendor from about 8:00 a.m. till about 12 noon and earns an amount of Rs 50 for five hours as a wage worker. Thereafter, she starts her own business from 5:00 p.m. and continues through the night. She has no sufficient money to invest but wants to support her children's education.

Source: Based on fieldwork conducted in 2010–11.

Age of business

The number of years in business has an impact on their economic activities because it helps vendors to build social contacts at the market. The time determines relationship development with wholesalers, moneylenders and civic officials and police, and a longer time span also facilitates negotiation. Thirty per cent of vendors have been in the business over the past ten to twenty years while another 29 per cent have been in the business for five to ten years (see Table 2.3). Nearly 26 per cent of the vendors were relatively new in the market place as their years of business ranged between

Table 2.3 Age of business (in years)

City	Years of business						Total
	0–5	5–10	10–20	20–30	30–40	40–60	
Bengaluru	23 (11.5)	81 (40.5)	80 (40.0)	13 (6.5)	3 (1.5)	0 (0)	200 (100)
Bhubaneswar	51 (25.5)	68 (34.0)	67 (33.5)	12 (6.0)	2 (1.0)	0 (0)	200 (100)
Delhi	18 (9.0)	36 (18.0)	100 (50.0)	34 (17.0)	10 (5.0)	2 (1.0)	200 (100)
Hyderabad	54 (27.0)	67 (33.5)	50 (25.0)	22 (11.0)	5 (2.5)	2 (1.0)	200 (100)
Imphal	62 (31.0)	65 (32.5)	51 (25.5)	19 (9.5)	2 (1.0)	1 (0.5)	200 (100)
Indore	40 (20.0)	46 (23.0)	55 (27.0)	36 (18.0)	21 (10.5)	2 (1.0)	200 (100)
Jaipur	100 (50.0)	58 (29.0)	40 (20.0)	2 (1.0)	0 (0)	0 (0)	200 (100)
Lucknow	76 (38.0)	88 (44.0)	35 (17.5)	1 (0.5)	0 (0)	0 (0)	200 (100)
Mumbai	39 (19.5)	42 (21.0)	65 (32.5)	43 (21.5)	10 (5.0)	1 (0.5)	200 (100)
Patna	63 (31.5)	43 (21.5)	59 (29.5)	25 (12.5)	9 (4.5)	1 (0.5)	200 (100)
Total	526 (26.5)	594 (29.7)	602 (30.1)	207 (10.4)	62 (3.1)	9 (0.4)	2,000 (100)

Source: Computed by the author, based on field survey conducted in 2009–10.

Note: Figures within parenthesis indicate percentage in share.

one and five years, while about 3 per cent of the vendors said that they had been in the trade for more than thirty years. In Delhi, for instance, 50 per cent of vendors reported their age of business was between 10 and 20 years while in Mumbai this was reported by 32.5 per cent of vendors. On the other hand, in Jaipur, 50 per cent of vendors reported having business for less than five years. Similar are the cases of Bhubaneswar (25 per cent), Hyderabad (27 per cent), Imphal (31 per cent) and Patna (31 per cent). It can be explained by assuming that the newly urbanising cities are witnessing greater migration and street vending is considered as one of the easiest occupations to take up.

Time of vending

Time of vending varies from one location to another and it also depends on the presence of customers and demand from the customers. Time for vending is throughout the day but peak hour for the business varies according to the place. The peak hours of vending were observed to be from 07:00–10:00 a.m. and then again from 04:00–09:00 p.m. The busiest period was from 04:00–08:00 p.m. Customers invariably buy goods on their return from work. In case of Mumbai, the timing of vending is different. Vendors selling cooked food, such as *poha*, *sheera* and tea, are found at 04:00 a.m. near stations and near corporate offices. The customers for the cooked food are not working poor, but young individuals returning from night shifts in corporate offices, clubs and hostels. The slowest period of sale was during 11:00 a.m. to 03:00 p.m. In general, vending locations near the railway stations and bus stops enjoy business throughout the day and night and witness longer vending hours across the cities because these areas have the most footfall. As far as timing of vending and public space sharing are concerned, the case study of Mumbai can be referred. In Dadar (Mumbai), vegetable vendors come around 05:00 a.m. Apparently three vendors share the same place from 05.00–08:00 a.m. The incessant use of the same place will be explored in Chapter 3. Customers buy vegetables from vendors early in the morning at Dadar, often while returning home from morning walks. The analysis of the data showed that the location of the vendors and their services were completely dependent on the demand from the customers. This will be discussed later in this chapter.

Sources of products

Suppliers were found to be important players in the market because they not only supplied the products but also helped vendors in times of need. The main suppliers were the wholesalers, local vendors having large-scale business, retailers and shopkeepers at the respective market places. Mostly vendors do procure their goods from the wholesalers but vendors from same locality having large-scale investment also play an important role by not only providing products but also lending loans and others to them [vendors]. For instance, street vendors having a smaller investment, especially women, tend to buy products from those sources that are in the same location as their areas of business. In this way, street vendors that can afford only a small investment save on transport costs.

Access to wholesale markets

The places from where the vendors source their products and the suppliers are important elements. Access to wholesale markets is discussed here. Wholesale markets are located far away from the retail markets. Accessing wholesale markets is similar across cities in India – whether it is Agricultural Product Marketing Committee (APMC) markets in Vashi (New Mumbai) or *Muhana Mandi* in Jaipur. These wholesale markets not only support its local markets but also are linked to other wholesale markets across India. One such example is wholesale markets in Hyderabad (see Box 2.3). Let us discuss vendors' accessibility to Mumbai's APMC market. This case illustrates how vendors procure products from the wholesale markets. Vegetable and fruit vendors all over Mumbai get their goods from APMC Vashi wholesale market. Vegetable and fruit vendors from Chembur and Dadar do not face any difficulty to get their products from Vashi; they start at around 06:00 a.m. from Chembur and Dadar to source their products. The vendors from Kandivali and Vile Parle are not conveniently located from the Vashi wholesale market, so their commute starts at around 03:00–04:00 a.m. Vendors come by trucks, load their goods in the trucks or tempos and return by the same vehicles that they come in. Vendors mutually make weekly visits to wholesale markets. All vendors cannot afford to visit the wholesale markets every day. Vendors having high investment (Rs 25,000 and above) and affordability visit wholesale markets every alternate day but rest of the vendors manage to visit wholesale markets once or twice a week. Street vendors mutually decide the frequency of their visits to the wholesale markets. They jointly hire a truck or a tempo depending upon the number of vendors and quantity of the products they require, thereby enabling them to divide the cost of transportation equally among themselves. Socialisation among vendors and the process of accessing wholesale market are interesting but the conditions in which vendors access the wholesale market are precarious.

Box 2.3 Wholesale markets in Hyderabad

Begumpet, Laad Bazaar, Rythu Bazaar, Kothapet, Moosapet, Madina, Dilsukh Nagar, Sultan Bazaar, Mouzam Zai Bazaar and Shamshabad are main wholesale markets from where street vendors of Hyderabad make their products. Each of these markets specialises in specific items. These markets are also closely interconnected with other wholesale markets in other cities across country. For instance, for clothes, street vendors depend on agents based in Delhi and Mumbai who frequently visit Hyderabad. In case of vegetables and fruits, wholesale markets have developed in different parts of Hyderabad. Vendors go to the wholesale market closer to their workplace. In case of grapes, vendors travel to Solapur, which is famous for grape farming. As regards eatables, generally vendors make local purchases. The frequency of the purchase from the wholesale market depends on the items of vending. Those engaged in perishable items such as vegetables, fruits and flowers make their purchase on a daily basis. Other products transact on a weekly basis or fortnightly basis.

Source: Based on fieldwork conducted in 2011–12.

Investment and business expansion

The pattern and amount of investment in street vending show the size of the business and the entrepreneurship of the vendors. The investment pattern shows that females generally made lower investments than males. The female vendors (especially from Delhi, Mumbai and Kolkata) reported that if both the husband and wife were involved in vending, but had two different stalls, it was more likely to make larger investments in the husband's business. This is true not only of street vendors in India but also of vendors in other Asian nations. Murray in his study (1992) pointed out that female vendors in Asia save and hand over their savings to their husbands or use them for spending on a pilgrimage. However, the amount of work is the same even if the business or investment is small. The daily sale turnover also varied between Rs 500 and Rs 1,000.

Price setting

The price of one product at a particular location is mutually decided by all the vendors of the designated area or the street. However, setting the price of the product varies from product to product. For example, prices of perishable products depend on the quality and freshness of the products. It is also not possible to get returns from all perishable products. For instance, if one vendor buys one box containing 10 kg of tomatoes from the wholesale market, 2 kg will be damaged due to transportation and other factors. Therefore, the vendor will be able to sell only 8 kg. The vendor will aim to cover the cost of the damaged products through the sale of the remaining 8 kg, and this will affect the setting of the price.

Vendors admitted imposing an additional amount on the actual cost of any products. Therefore, the final price of the product becomes higher than the actual cost of the item. There are mainly two reasons behind this. First, vendors spend a significant portion of their income repaying the rates of interests on loans taken. This will be elaborated in the next section. Second, vendors pay bribes on a daily basis and the proportion of the bribes to their daily income is significantly high (5–20 per cent of total income). This will be described in detail in Chapter 3. However, imposing additional cost and raising the price of products are not always possible and sales get affected at times. This problem becomes even more acute when regular customers demand products at a lower price. Therefore, in order to cover the cost of procurement and bribes and all additional costs that go into making the final price of the product, vendors work for longer durations, increasing sales to generate larger incomes. This further leads to an increase in competition among the vendors.

Calculating profit

Profits of the vendors depend on the products they sell. There is a high profit margin on perishable items such as vegetables, fruits and cooked food as compared to other products. The profit margin of fruit and vegetable sellers was observed to be about 30–40 per cent. The profit margin was highest among vendors selling cooked food (at 40–60 per cent). Profit from other products, namely, garments, electronics, household utensils and leather-made goods, was observed to be up to 20 per cent. Vendors pointed out that profit on perishables such as vegetables and fruits depended on their freshness since consumers preferred buying fresh vegetables and fruits. The two odd seasons for vending are monsoon and summer. Their profit in the monsoon season is generally low as compared to rest of the year. In case of perishables, vendors try to sell fast in summer because perishables rot faster in humid weather. They also cannot stack enough stock in these two seasons due to lack of adequate storage facilities at the workplace. Therefore, vendors made less investment in these seasons, but recovered their losses during festive seasons such as *Ganesh Chaturthi* and *Diwali*. Need to mention, working conditions of vendors selling perishable products are precarious. The conditions will be described in Chapter 4.

Access to finance

Studies (Jhabvala 2000; Bhowmik 2001; Saha 2011a; Bhowmik & Saha 2013) show that street vendors have scarce financial resources for their business and need to obtain credit. Interestingly, the core issue is not that of access to credit for business purposes alone, but also for other important purposes that are in no way related directly or indirectly to income generation. Access to credit is one of the prime factors in the activity of these workers. The availability of low-cost easy credit of right amounts and at the required time can significantly enhance their earning capacity and employment status, and can thus improve the decency of work. Access to credit is therefore said to be the 'prime mover' of their business activity. Access to capital is an economic linkage that ties street trade to the economy, which in turn affects the vendors' economic activities, profits and potential business growth. Street vendors had access to capital from five different sources other than own savings such as capital from relatives/friends, local vendors or traders, moneylenders, wholesalers and banks or cooperatives. Own savings and friend/relatives are primarily used to get a business started, while all the rest are used to keep it running or for expanding the business activity.

Sources of credit

Street vendors primarily depend on the informal agents for their credit supply and end up paying large amounts of interest. In this study, five types of capital sources were observed – relatives, friends, local vendors or traders; moneylenders; wholesalers; informal saving groups created by a group of vendors; and banks or cooperatives through trade unions (see Table 2.4). Other than depending on these five courses to keep running or expanding the business on a daily basis, vendors depend on their own savings and friends and relatives to start the business.

As far as finance for their business was concerned, impressively about 51 per cent of the street vendors manage the business from their own savings. These include Delhi (75 per cent), Hyderabad (66.5 per cent), Imphal (91.5 per cent), Jaipur (62.0 per cent) and Patna (65 per cent). In Bhubaneswar, a relatively high percentage of street vendors (46.5 per cent) using their own savings seems to be possible because their incomes have increased rapidly since they got the security of vending zones. In the other cities, it is possible that their turnover was fairly high and therefore they could invest from their own savings. However, in all cases, including Bhubaneswar, the street vendors were not really large-scale business persons. So it was possible to refinance their micro-business through their own savings. One can understand why the street vendors in these cities preferred to use their own savings, no matter how meagre they were. The other sources of finance were prohibitively high. The other cities, not mentioned above, had less than 30 per cent of the vendors running their businesses through their own savings. Notably, in Bengaluru, none of the street vendors use their own savings for running their business. In Lucknow, it was lower at 25 per cent and in Mumbai 15 per cent depended on their own sources. The highest percentage in this regard was Imphal, where 91.5 per cent of the women ran their business through their own savings. As mentioned earlier, the alternative sources of funding carry high rates of interest, which often ruin the vendors or, as is the case of the female vendors in Imphal, they invest a small amount to run their business so that they are able to manage from their meagre savings. The most frequent source

Table 2.4 Credit providers

City	Sources (formal and informal) of credit						Total
	Own saving	Moneylender	Friends/ relatives/ local fellow vendors	Saving groups (informal)	Cooperatives	Wholesaler	
Bengaluru	0 (0)	200 (100)	0 (0)	0 (0)	0 (0)	0 (0)	200 (100)
Bhubaneswar	93 (46.5)	76 (38.0)	23 (11.5)	0 (0)	2 (1.0)	6 (3.0)	200 (100)
Delhi	150 (75.0)	42 (21.0)	1 (0.5)	0 (0)	6 (3.0)	1 (0.5)	200 (100)
Hyderabad	133 (66.5)	36 (18.0)	15 (7.5)	0 (0)	1 (0.5)	15 (7.5)	200 (100)
Imphal	183 (91.5)	17 (8.5)	0 (0)	0 (0)	0 (0)	0 (0)	200 (100)
Indore	34 (17.0)	130 (65.0)	0 (0)	1 (0.5)	2 (1.0)	33 (16.5)	200 (100)
Jaipur	124 (62.0)	15 (7.5)	0 (0)	1 (0.5)	0 (0)	60 (30.0)	200 (100)
Lucknow	50 (25.0)	150 (75.0)	0 (0)	0 (0)	0 (0)	0 (0)	200 (100)
Mumbai	30 (15.0)	130 (65.0)	15 (7.5)	3 (1.5)	12 (6.0)	10 (5.0)	200 (100)
Patna	130 (65.0)	50 (25.0)	9 (4.5)	4 (2.0)	1 (0.5)	6 (3.0)	200 (100)
Total	927 (50.7)	846 (36.9)	63 (3.15)	9 (1.0)	24 (1.2)	131 (6.7)	2,000 (100)

Source: Computed by the author, based on field survey conducted in 2009–10.

Note: Figures within parenthesis indicate percentage in share.

is from moneylenders. On the contrary, in Bengaluru, 100 per cent have taken loans from moneylenders, whereas in Jaipur, it is only 7.5 per cent who depend on the informal sources of capital. Lucknow with 75 per cent has the highest number of vendors relying on money-lenders for running their business, while 65 per cent of the vendors in each of the cities of Indore and Mumbai do so. The above were the cases where a majority of the vendors rely on outside sources for finance. In the case of those cities where a majority of the vendors relied on their own sources, we found the reliance on moneylenders much lower. In Bhubaneswar, 38 per cent took loans from money-lenders. In Delhi, it was 21 per cent, Hyderabad 18 per cent, Patna 25 per cent and only 8.5 per cent of vendors depend on moneylend-ers in Imphal. The other sources of funding were friends and rela-tives and wholesalers who gave them goods for sale in the morning and expected the cash return after adding the interest amount. Other sources which would involve very low interest rates are cooperatives and self-help groups (SHGs). These form less than 2 per cent of the total vendors in nine cities (excluding Mumbai).

The rates charged by moneylenders in all cities varied between 300 and 1,000 per cent per annum. However, in most cases, the moneylender expected to be repaid every month. Needless to say, the monthly interest was calculated by the moneylender. We asked vendors in these cities the amount they paid every month for the loan that they had taken. In analysing the difference between capi-tal and interest, we find that it was much more than the annual compounded rate. The street vendors were not capable of calculat-ing the interest amount on a monthly basis, so the moneylender always managed to skim off more than the stipulated rate. This was another way of keeping the vendors in perpetual poverty. To sum up, if we look at the sources of funding, whether from their own resources or from moneylenders, we find that in both cases the vendors cannot really break out of their poverty trap. In the case of the former, the source is limited and hence it could not lead to much profit. In the case of the latter, though funds may be more liberal, the interests charged offset any gains that the vendor can make. We also found that those who borrowed from friends and relatives paid high rates of interest (in some cases, as high as 100 per cent), though this was not as high as what the moneylenders charged.

It is important to mention that vendors cannot access credit directly from banks. Though vendors are able to open savings accounts, they face problems in availing loans from banks where they have their accounts as their occupation is not recognised. They cannot provide collaterals and their business cannot be termed as legal and 'permanent'. However, during this study, some cases came up wherein few vendors used bank loans indirectly for their business. These cases are highlighted below:

In Mumbai (two vendors) and Bengaluru (one vendor), three vendors applied for home loans to banks where they had their accounts. The banks granted them these loans in two instalments. They used a major part of the first instalment to create a foundation of the house. After verification by the banks, the second instalment was released. The vendors invested this entire amount in their business, not in completing the remaining construction of their homes. They built a temporary hut-like structure until their business prospered from the investment made after receiving the second instalment. When this investment started to bear fruit, they put the profits in building a concrete structure for their houses. This is not to say that the vendors have manipulated and used the loan amount for the purposes it did not intend to serve, but to impress upon the point that loans meant solely for business are extremely important for street vendors. In its absence, they have to sometimes resort to such solutions, if not for borrowing from informal sources at high rates of interest.

Introducer to the sources of capital

The linkages between the moneylenders and the vendors get established through a variety of channels. Sometimes, a fellow vendor initiates an introduction; at other times it could be friends or relatives (including parents and siblings). It is also not uncommon for moneylenders to introduce themselves to the vendors.

Across gender, fellow vendors serve as important links between moneylenders and the vendors themselves, especially for female vendors (Bhowmik & Saha 2013). For the males, fellow vendors and friends play an equally important role in connecting them to the moneylenders. As a matter of fact, it is very important to distinguish between fellow vendors and friends; fellow vendors in most cases become very close friends of the vendors on account of sharing of same business space for a considerable length of time.

Rates of interest

Calculation of rates of interest and the amount charged by moneylenders and wholesalers are forms of exploitation. The study showed that about 3 per cent of the total vendors did not pay any interest on their borrowing amount. This was because they borrowed from either very close friends or relatives. Most of the vendors pay more than 5 per cent rate of interest per month. However, around 10 per cent of vendors pay as high as 8 to 10 per cent monthly interest charges.

Amount, frequency and purposes of borrowing

Street vendors need to obtain credit primarily for their economic activities, but they also need money to take care of personal needs (about 20 per cent) such as sickness, marriage, house building and children's education. Since they are part of the informal sector, they do not have access to social security like formal sector workers. Thus, they manage money for their personal needs by borrowing from informal sources. Females borrow larger amounts for social security purposes than male vendors. Women mainly borrow money for their children's education and health care for their husbands and children. The high frequency of loans signifies that vendors fail to manage their needs, and their expenses far outweigh their earnings, which results in them falling into a debt trap. For instance, they borrow once, hoping to repay their debt. However, the interests get accumulated in such a manner that borrowing and repaying become a vicious cycle, resulting in continuous debt trap situation.

Street vendors' perspective on informal sources of credit

Despite the enormous debt situation of the vendors, it is interesting to observe how the vendors look up to the moneylenders. Vendors sometimes borrow money from relatives and friends who do not charge any interest whatsoever. Many vendors solely depend on moneylenders for their daily financial transaction. Hence, it is important to focus and highlight whether vendors look upon moneylenders or wholesalers as exploitative sources of credit or as survivors. Many vendors refer to the moneylenders as 'last resort' or even 'the sole money provider'. Some vendors like moneylenders' flexible attitudes. Three such cases have been illustrated below (see Boxes 2.4 to 2.6.) from different cities to show the positive aspects of moneylenders and wholesalers.

Box 2.4 Hassle-free short-term loans in Hyderabad

Vendors in Hyderabad city depend on moneylenders for hassle-free loans. The vendor in question operates in Koti area. He had taken a loan for his sister's marriage under the '100-day scheme'. An amount of Rs 10,000 was borrowed and a daily collection of Rs 120 was done by the moneylender from the next day itself. Therefore, the total amount of repayment summed up to Rs 12,000 after a period of 100 days. The rate of interest was to the tune of 73 per cent per annum. The loan taken by the vendor was for personal reasons and since he did not take loans often, he did not find the rate of interest to be very high. In fact, he found the loan very helpful because he could manage the loan without any collateral very easily. When he was asked, the vendor aptly pointed out that he required finance for various purposes, including social obligation purposes. Banks or any other formal financial sources will not easily supply these loans and even if they do, it will normally take time. However, one cannot wait until an emergency situation arises. In addition, vendors like him are assetless people and all they have to offer is a promise to pay back the moneylender his due on time. This type of social norm or trust works as the base of the entire activities of the vendors and moneylenders. Hence, in the absence of alternative credit sources, moneylenders are the only sources of finance. According to him, moneylenders' role cannot be misjudged only on the basis of rate of interest they charge for credit.

Source: Based on fieldwork conducted in 2011–12.

Box 2.5 Easy money by lenders in Kolkata

Most vendors in Kolkata consider the positive role played by moneylenders in their lives. This one was pointed out by a vendor who operates in Shyambazar area in north of Kolkata. He took a loan of Rs 15,000 for 90 days at a monthly rate of interest of 10 per cent, each month for three consecutive months from a moneylender. He realised that he had to pay back Rs 28,500 interest plus principal. Acknowledging that moneylenders charge high rates of interest, the vendor at the same time claimed that moneylenders are also the only easy source of credit. Some moneylenders have a very benevolent attitude towards vendors. They even described the money-lender as a father figure who seldom turns them down when approached. Banks, on the other hand, would confiscate a vendor's goods for defaulting on payments. According to them, besides the high interest, they have nothing to complain regarding the moneylenders.

Not all vendors like to buy goods on credit. A fruit juice seller in Shyambazar said that he takes goods on credit only during the mango and jackfruit season when the prices of these items soar and it is not possible to fetch all goods by cash.

Some other sources of finance were prevalent in the sample. One man in the New Market area said that he borrows money from the Krishi Gramin Bank in his village under the guise of investing the sum in agricultural works. He uses the money borrowed for business or even personal purposes. He said, 'If I say, I am a vendor in Kolkata . . . and I want money, will they give me money? They ask for papers. I don't have any'.

Source: Based on fieldwork conducted in 2011–12.

Box 2.6 Moneylenders as last resort in Patna

Most vendors take loans from informal sources such as mon-eylenders. However, this particular case in point is of a vendor in Patna claiming that the moneylender is his last resort. A street vendor in Patna had four daughters. According to him he took loans four times to marry off each of his daughters. He took loans at a monthly interest rate of 10 per cent, all of which he has successfully repaid. He said that he was able to marry off his daughters because there were moneylenders to help him with easy access to credit.

Source: Based on fieldwork conducted in 2011–12.

How do the informal street markets sustain?

Bribe payments

Bribe payment is a common feature in the business of vendors. Vendors pay bribes both in cash and in kind. The bribe in kind proves to be much higher than a cash payment as the local police and municipal officials pick up their products without paying for them. Different actors are involved in the whole bribe payments system. Street vendors manage to conduct business by negotiating with the police and the municipal authorities, in order to carry out their livelihood and avoid evictions. This understanding is solely based upon payment of bribes or a certain portion of their daily incomes as 'rents' to the authorities. Vendors who did not pay rents in the form of bribes admitted they are disturbed and harassed regularly. Therefore, paying bribes on a regular basis is considered to be one of the strategies for sustaining on the street. In spite of the Act coming into effect, vendors are still paying bribes but in different ways. These aspects will be discussed in detail in subsequent chapters of the book.

However, while one group of citizens are strictly against the vendors and their trade, another group of 'non-affluent' citizens, of which a major part belong to the lower middle class, depend on these vendors for their daily necessities. Street vendors thrive in the city and their numbers grow rapidly because their services are widely demanded by the general public. However, if these places are allotted to vendors along with proper regulations in the form of space demarcations, vending will not be a problem. It is also seen that shopkeepers use the adjacent space for advertisement and display purposes. Some small restaurants keep chairs on the pavements of busy streets for waiting customers, and they are not evicted.

Customers and their views on vending

Discussions with customers during this study brought out why vending activities were considered a menace. Interaction with fifty customers was conducted in Mumbai to understand their perspective on vendors. Some customers feel that road congestions and traffic problems were directly related to vending activities since they infringe upon parking areas. However, the ground realty is different and this aspect will be elaborated in Chapter 3. They also felt that vendors sold cheap quality products and other food items in unhealthy and unsanitary conditions, and charged high prices for products which resulted in extensive bargaining and so forth. On the other hand, a section of consumers felt that street vendors should get the licence to access public spaces and the authorities should provide them convenient places to conduct their business. Needless to say, the low-income group of citizens is more tolerant of vending activities than their elite counterparts.

Citizens benefit significantly from the products sold by the vendors, because they are cheap and diverse in range (as confirmed by almost 32 per cent of the customers). The second most important reason for preference is their easy accessibility and availability. About 26 per cent of customers confirmed this in the present study. Nearly 22 per cent of consumers said that the proximity of these stalls to their residences was also another important reason for their preference because it saved on commuting costs (see Table 2.5).

The study showed that the consumers bought a variety of items from the vendors. The highest percentage of consumers bought cooked food items because several college and office-goers relied on cooked food for their lunch since it is cheap and freshly prepared. Interestingly, most of the stalls located near hospitals, schools, colleges and office areas provided food to the consumers there. About 60 per cent said that they bought fruits from the vendors. Thirty-six per cent said they bought clothes, 34 per cent bought household utensils, while 24 per cent bought stationery and plastic items. Only 20 per cent of consumers preferred to buy vegetables from the vending stalls. All these products are daily necessities and they are bought at a much cheaper rate than those of formal retail outlets.

Table 2.5 Reasons for buying products from vendors

Reasons for buying products from vendors	Total sample (%)
Cheap rate of products and products of all ranges are available	16 (32)
Easily accessible and available at any time	13 (26)
Saves time to go to any other markets and saves money for local conveyance for them	10 (20)
Near home	11 (22)

N= 50.

Source: Primary data collected in 2010–11.

Thus, it can be concluded that the reasons for buying goods from street vendors are almost always related to their low price and easy accessibility. It is especially suited to the urban middle- and lower-income groups, who do not have the inclination to buy highly priced products from shopping malls. However, as the citizens report, there are both positive and negative sides of this activity (see Table 2.6). In many cases, the positive aspects far outweigh the negative ones, while in other cases the obverse is true.

A further analysis of the response of the customers revealed that 84 per cent of customers felt the goods were cheap, affordable and diverse. Forty-four per cent of customers felt the goods were accessible at all hours, and availability of door-to door service was a positive. A total of 38 per cent of customers said that the products bought from the vendors were at a proximal distance from their homes. Sixty-two per cent of consumers said that fresh products (raw fruits, vegetables and flowers or even cooked food) sold by vendors were one of the most attractive aspects of their business activities.

Customers also listed out the various negative aspects of vendors' activities, which is why the activity is considered a menace (see Table 2.6). Around 56 per cent of consumers reported that the roads get congested as the vendors carry out their activities in the parking areas. Nearly 60 per cent of consumers said that they sell cheap quality items, which are toxic and sold in unhealthy and unsanitary conditions. Some said that vendors charge very high prices for their products and excessive bargaining is required to buy them at modest prices. Four respondents mentioned that street vendors should get the licence to access public spaces and the authorities should provide them convenient places to conduct their business. Most of the consumers, belonging to the income group of Rs 5,000–10,000 were in favour of this occupation. This indicates the fact that the low-income group consumers are more satisfied with their activity.

Thus, it can be concluded that not all citizens oppose the vending occupation. However, citizens' group with high income residing in posh areas of the cities, due to their high economic and social position, often force the civic authorities to take action against the vendors and oppose any kind of move towards legalising them. Anjaria's (2006) observation of urban public space utilisation can be connected here. The responses of the citizens revealed that vendors do provide a valuable service to them by selling goods and services that fit their budget.

Table 2.6 Customers' perspectives on street vending

Positive aspects	Total (%)	Negative aspects	Total (%)
Cheap rate/reasonable price of the product and products of all ranges are available	42 (84)	Makes the road congested/crowded	28 (56)
Easily accessible and available at any time	22 (44)	Lack of quality	6 (12)
Saves time to go to any other markets and saves money for local conveyance for them	19 (38)	Needs excessive bargaining because street vendors initially charge a very high price	3 (9)
Fresh products	31 (62)	Service is not good	8 (16)
		Unhygienic	5 (10)
Total	50	Total	50

Source: Primary data collected in 2010–11.

Negotiating with customers

The number of street vendors has been growing over the last few years. This is due to a demand from urban citizens and working poor. With very limited business conditions, low capital and relatively high costs of operation, vendors rely on public relations tactics to keep their sales up. One of the strategies is to encourage customer loyalty, and vendors rely on their personal skills to keep their businesses afloat. Moreover, street vendors also exercise the trial and error method to look for better business opportunities that benefit both vendors and consumers. It was observed that the transaction between street vendors and their customers emerged out of a relationship of trust, one which assures quality of food and affordability, as vendors maintained quality products and variety. Vendors admitted they were sensitive to customer feedback, and implemented the learning in their business. This was highlighted as an important business strategy to retain customers, and extend the buyer–seller relationship for longer periods. Vendors shared that sometimes customers returned products that they bought if their quality is not up to the mark. This is particularly true in case of fruits. In such cases, vendors immediately change and replace the products with fresh ones to keep customers happy. Other tactics of attracting customers were observed, such as making catchy sounds, putting up colourful and bright lights and providing discounts during festivals.

Role of social network

Informal relationships among vendors were identified as the most basic component of vending in Mumbai. Trust among particular sub-groups, habitual exchanges of favours and mutual support among vendors and friends have been discussed in detail. The concept of 'structural economic sociology' developed by Granovetter and Swebderg in 2001 is based on three basic common principles, i.e. economic action is a form of social action, economic action is socially embedded and economic institutions are social constructions. Economic action is 'embedded' in ongoing networks of personal relationships rather than being carried out by atomised actors (Granovetter 1985). Granovetter described that network is a set of contacts or social connections among individuals or groups, since individuals are never isolated from the society (ibid.). Further, Granovetter (1985) explained that in 'a social embeddedness approach', economic transactions become embedded in social relations that affect the allocation and valuation of resources and financial markets differentially. Therefore, social embeddedness is defined as the degree to which commercial transactions take place through social relations and networks of relations that use exchange protocols associated with social, non-commercial attachments to manage business dealings (Granovetter 1985; Uzzi 1997). This study highlights the importance of social relations, social cohesion and social contacts in vending and shows how these factors help vendors to build trust, access finance, enter the activity and offer any help during emergency.

Kinship, ethnicity, religion and localism have an impact on the daily lives of street vendors at the marketplace, and these are the identifiable characteristics around which street vendors mobilise their resources. In the present study, it was observed that ethnicity played an important role in order to find employment in the market.

Localism is a more important identity in the market than ethnicity. This study showed that local origin played a decisive role in forming status groups. Local origin is with reference to provinces. Individuals identify themselves with the province in which they were born. Sharing the same local origin, language and same dialects with a person makes it a lot easier for one to receive hospitality or a warm welcome in the market and the rest follows, which the vendor might otherwise not be able to easily obtain. Another factor – good communication – is the key to building network and relationships with moneylenders, wholesalers and customers. A working knowledge of English helped them greatly in dealing with a particular class of customers. This is particularly seen in Mumbai and Bengaluru. In addition, sharing similar languages and dialects with fellow vendors, wholesalers and moneylenders helped in accessing loans.

Many of the market traders who were currently owners of stalls or employees and self-employed admitted they had entered the market with the help of their fellow locals. They also received help to search a house in the city. Localism gives people a sense of solidarity and security in the city. Cooperation and solidarity among vendors through the connection of a common local origin are obvious in the market as they do not have any other government assistance. It was also observed that people from the same local origin, community and religious group at the market go together to the wholesale market and procure their respective products. They also help each other to load and unload the products from trucks and tempos. Cooperation among market traders from the same locality even goes beyond their work environment. The significance of ethnicity and localism for market traders makes it easy for them to take action to monopolise resources in order to gain a competitive edge in the market.

Trust, too, plays a key role in the vendors' day-to-day business. Exchange of favours is a widespread mechanism among the vendors which assists their day-to-day life and helps them to flourish despite intense competition and lack of general trust over money. This mutual trust rests on an expectation of trustworthy behaviour and of reciprocal favours. Trust also helps to get money from the moneylenders as there is no liability of these vendors. Access to finance completely depends on the trust and relationship between vendors and lenders. However, it was observed that women formed better informal relationships at the marketplace than men. For instance, it is observed that lenders trust women as they are more reliable in terms of repayment of money on time. Women may be doing this even by going hungry for the day. Thus, it is understood that trust plays a key role in the activity of the vendors. The case below highlights the importance of 'trust' in the day-to-day lives of one of the vendors. Social network plays a decisive role in credit accessibility. Vendors can borrow easily from moneylenders, wholesalers and local traders for their capital requirements, provided they belong to the same community and place of origin as the vendors. On the other hand, for those vendors who belong to other communities and places of origin, it takes time to build trust and reputation to access capital. Once a good reputation and trust have been built with the lenders, vendors can even borrow money from the wholesalers for other purposes such as social security. It is perceived that factors such as number of years in business, language and origin of the vendors play a key role in building the two dimensions of trust and reputation even for those who are borrowing at a high rate of interest. Some vendors reported that it is important to build trust with lenders in order to get loans and credit for their business and other purposes. One such example of trust at the workplace can be highlighted through a case mentioned in Box 2.7. But at the same time, accessing credit from their own community and known persons does not give the liberty to bargain and finally they end up paying more than the actual sum.

Box 2.7 Prevalence of trust-based relationship at the workplace

Anil (name changed), 50, is a resident of Matunga (Mumbai) and sells fruits in Dadar. He is Hindu from a village in Maharashtra, who falls in the general category. He migrated to Mumbai in search of better income opportunities about thirty years ago. He started selling fruits at the age of 20 and has been in this business ever since. His income level is Rs 7,500 per month whereas his household expenditures exceed his income by Rs 1,500 every month. This results in a huge discrepancy which is covered mainly through borrowing at high rates of interest or lending from friends at the marketplace. While explaining the nature of borrowing-lending activities, Anil pointed out that personal bonding and mutual trust play an important role in determining loan transaction activities. Lenders are eager to lend money to people belonging to their own community and who speak the same language. Otherwise, it is a lot of trouble to borrow money even when vendors are willing to pay a high interest rate. Money is likewise borrowed for activities related to income generation and others. Anil pointed out, 'trust plays a key role in our day-to-day business. It is not easy to make a good rapport with the moneylenders. It takes time even when we borrow money at high rate of interest. Sometimes same language and same community promote the building up of good relationships with lenders. A highly informal relationship with the lenders makes the availability of loans much easier for purposes other than those which are directly or indirectly related to our business activities'.

Source: Based on fieldwork conducted in 2010–11.

Vending and its prospects

Scope of upward mobility

It was found that many vendors previously worked as wage workers under other vendors while many others employed wage workers. As explained, migrated vendors first began wage work to sustain their families in their respective villages. Subsequently, they accumulated sufficient capital, started street vending and expanded into large-scale vending businesses. Once vendors accumulate sufficient amounts of capital, they expand their business and are in a position to afford wage workers. Moving up in the occupation of street vending means increased income and expansion of the business. Most vendors saved some portion of their income to invest into their business, with an aim to increase income. As highlighted earlier in the chapter, highest amount of profit was seen in businesses with perishable goods; therefore, street vending for food showed sufficient opportunities for upward mobility.

The vending profession began with items such as vegetables, fruits and cooked food products, as they required low capital investment. Thereafter, the business was expanded to the next item, garments, which required mid-level investment. Eventually, after achieving a certain level of income, vendors progressed to electronic goods and leather-made goods that require substantial investments. Several vendors displayed signs of upward mobility in this manner. However, this mobility is restricted to vending and does not spill over to other traders. Most of the female vendors that were currently selling garments admitted to beginning with sale of vegetable and cooked food. They preferred to save money and invest in garment, though profit margin is marginal (about 15–20 per cent). On the other hand, male vendors preferred to continue with fruits and cooked food as the profit margins were higher. Thus, male vendors saved and then employed wage workers and expanded their businesses. Notwithstanding, it is important to mention here that vendors – who are selling perishable products and cooked food – face risk and obstacles such as the continued requirement of paying bribes (a detailed explanation and situation are described in Chapter 4). Working hours are prolonged and working conditions are precarious in these cases. While female vendors avoid such obstacles and risks, male vendors take up risk and continue with it.

Backward and forward linkages

Street vendors are 'micro-entrepreneurs' and their trade has important backward and forward sectoral and employment linkages. For instance, around 1,200 tons of vegetables are transacted daily in the APMC wholesale market in Vashi, Navi Mumbai, which is considered as the largest wholesale market in Mumbai. Interestingly, two-thirds of the total supply of vegetables is carried away by the street vendors and the rest one-third is bought by the formal stakeholders such as different hotels, restaurants and supermarkets. Therefore, in this way, street vendors directly help to clear the market of perishable agricultural products. They also provide market for the goods produced by micro- and small-scale enterprises. For example, locally made glassware, utensils and plastic moulded goods that are manufactured in household enterprises are marketed by the vendors. The section of workers that draws their livelihood from small enterprises thrives on the street vending activities.

This study has found that vendors help sustain another significant section of the informal workers, home-based workers. In Dharavi, the largest slum in Mumbai, many home-based workers, especially women, are actively involved in stitching garments and embroidery work. Many of them are wage workers, while others work on self-employed own-account basis. This wage work may come through the middlemen, employed by large garment manufacturers, who outsource to reduce manufacturing cost. The self-employed own-account workers are found to sell their products mainly through street vendors and, in some cases, local shopkeepers.

Additionally, vending also has important forward linkage effects. A significant section of the middle- and low-income groups depend on low-cost durables and food sold by vendors. Interviews with a section of middle- and upper-middle-class consumers revealed that factors such as low cost and easy availability draw them towards vendors. Consumers prefer to buy perishable items such as vegetables, fruits and flowers from vendors because they are fresh and prices are reasonable.

Women and children in vending

It was interesting to find somewhat a distinct pattern in terms of preference regarding types of vending and products that women sell. Female vendors do not prefer mobile vending. They would rather be found static at one place, in some cases near their home in peripheral areas. They mostly sell products such as flowers, fruits and vegetables. Most of the other items such as clothes (bed sheets, cushion covers, dress materials, T-shirts etc.), plastic items, locks and comb, cosmetics and fancy items are sold by male vendors. In some cases, husband and wife, along with children, work together on the street. While the male vendor deals with the customer, the wife helps the husband in unpacking/packing vending items. In case of food vending, the male prepares the food and the wife serves it and children wash the used plates. Sometime children look after the stall in the absence of their parents. Teenage sons of vendors help in bringing products from the wholesale market or help in exhibiting items on the cart or on the pavements. Streets are very unfriendly towards women vendors. They have to cope up at various fronts simultaneously. Besides civic authorities, female vendors face filthy remarks by male vendors and also by customers and passers-by. The police frequently harass them in many ways. They get more sense of security as being static and accompanied by other female vendors. The choice of product is also influenced by the need for security. They sell products which can be procured on the same day and which do not require any specific effort for overnight storage.

Conclusion

Despite the lack of proper legal framework and the informal nature of the activity, street vending is still operating successfully on the basis of mutual trust, social cohesion, social contacts and social networks. These factors are identified as important aspects to sustain and conduct their business at the market. Interestingly, prices of the products are decided and set mutually by the street vendors. Therefore, from the accessibility of wholesale markets to the mutual price setting, vending is based on mutual understanding. Indeed, it provides an 'alternative market' to the urban economy. In spite of the importance of their existence in urban economy, street vendors face many obstacles, constant threats and insecurity from the local leaders and civic authorities to access the market. As a result, vendors prefer paying bribes (73.25 per cent) to survive in the market, primarily because they occupy 'public space'. As a result, conflict arises, which is discussed in the following chapters. Street vending is an alternative market which is being perpetuated with different 'alternative' arrangements in the urban informal economy.

Needless to mention that street vending activity is associated with layers of vulnerability and insecurity. Notwithstanding, some vendors, especially women, stated that this occupation had transformed their lives because the potential to earn made them feel empowered. Not only had they become financially independent but also they had a say in making decisions in their household, particularly decisions relating to their children's future, education and so on. According to them, this was possible because they earned alongside their husbands and contributed to their household income. In addition, both male and female vendors were satisfied with this profession because it enabled them to support their families in cities as well as back home in their respective villages. Conversely, some vendors feel that there is an acute lack of dignity in their working lives and hence preferred to hide their 'occupational identity' from their friends and relatives. The questions of dignity, insecurity and uncertainty will be assessed in Chapter 4.

Chapter 3

Public space, politics and survival strategies

Work and employment of street vendors around the world are associated with the characteristics of precarity, uncertainty and vulnerability. These features prevail mainly because of the way in which they operate and establish their business in the public space. Some of the developing nations have recognised the activity and provided legal framework but most of them are hostile. In some important cities in developing nations like Bogota (Colombia), Mexico City (Mexico), Colombo (Sri Lanka) and Bangkok (Thailand), civic authorities have legally recognised these street vendors as workers and vending as an occupation. Despite having national policies (2006, 2009) on urban street vendors in India, they [vendors] have been ignored for decades until the recent past. In India, there happens to be no accurate data on the number of street vendors. Besides home-based workers, street vendors are one of the most unaccounted and undetermined groups in the informal sector (Chen 2007) in spite of being the most visible section in the urban economy. The Government of India (GOI) in 2006 estimated that 2 per cent of total population in metropolitan cities are street vendors. The problem with vending in India mainly arises from the fact that the activity has been considered illegal and a threat to modern urban living since decades. Vendors and their membership-based associations have struggled to change this attitude of urbanites, forcing the state to recognise their livelihood and existence as a vital part of urban life. However, only recently have their demands been fulfilled. The Street Vendors Act of 2014 has been passed to protect the livelihood of these vendors. Public space and rights over its utilisation is a necessary (although not a sufficient) precondition for a better life. Before exploring the politics over public space, however, it is important to understand the meaning of public space and how vendors use the space as source of livelihood, place of socialisation and extended household and so on. Vendors make contractual arrangements and paying costs for occupying space. This chapter shall help us understanding the way in which negotiation and politics take place while utilising public space. Urban public space has different meanings and connotations. While workers use it as a market place to generate income by buying and selling labour or labour products, civic authorities use it for rent extractions. Interestingly, Anjaria (2006) highlights the other side of urban space usage – the average-income city dwellers who regularly get benefits from the goods and services available at a low cost from the vendors.

There are many debates over public space and its utilisation. Lynch (1981) argues that urban public space is a common property resource to which everyone has equal and free rights of access. Conversely, Harvey (1973) states how important it is to understand that human practices create a distinctive conceptualisation of space before understanding the concept of space and cities themselves. He further argues that urbanisation can be achieved without exploiting the poor and highlights the concept of social justice and its relationship to urban spatial systems, the role of land as a commodity and the spatial implications of economic production in order to understand city space. While Lynch talks about assigning rights over the access and use of space; Harvey mentions the concept of social justice which entails that urbanisation is achievable without compromising the needs of urban working poor. As far as street vendors are concerned, the 'urban public space' for livelihood generation is a direct cause and consequence of vendors' status being a part of the informal economy and the extent of informality associated with their activities. Here, the argument of Hernando de Soto on informality is relevant. He delineates that absence of rights over ownership and use of public space perpetuates the informality. Though his argument is very simplistic, property rights over public space utilisation can be brought here where he (1989) talks about the existence of informality due to the absence of laws and regulations over the access and use of urban space. While David Harvey stresses on inclusive urban planning to ensure rights of equal access, Hernando de Soto has emphasised that the absence of laws and regulations among other factors is the most conspicuous. One can argue that this activity is characterised by sheer absence of any law or regulation (De Soto's emphasis on deregulation).

Alison Brown (2006: 10) uses the phrase 'urban public space' to refer to all physical space and social relations that determine the use of space within the non-private realm of cities. The 'urban public space' constitutes an essential element of the physical capital used by the urban poor to extract their livelihood (ibid.: 179). According to Brown, public space is not only 'physical space' but also a place for 'social relations'. In line of same thought put forwarded by Brown, urban space for street vendors is the only 'physical capital' available to them because in the absence of any other sources of capital, 'space' becomes an important 'capital' for them. In case of street vendors, let us understand social relation in the context of bargaining. Vendors use urban space not only for their livelihood but also for social relations that help strengthening their bargaining power with various actors at the market. They need bargaining power mainly for two purposes, namely, economic activity and building social relationship with others. Bargaining power is required to negotiate over rates of interests on borrowing with credit providers (moneylenders, wholesalers and others) and also over rates of bribes with civic authorities, local leaders and goons. This bargaining does impact directly their earnings and scale of operation. This can be called vendors' economic bargaining. On the other hand, vendors use bargaining power to build social relations with different actors such as customers, moneylenders and civic authorities. They develop good relationship and trust with customers. They bargain with fellow vendors who are relatively old at the market to sustain and to get help at the time of emergencies. Vendors also share their anger and emotions with other vendors and actors in the market. These social relationships, contacts and network help them sustain at the market. This helps vendors indirectly to enhance sustenance and scale of business. The reason behind developing social relationship is ultimately to strengthen their economic bargaining. This can be called vendors' social bargaining. Both economic and social bargaining are not mutually exclusive; rather, one is linked to another and also these take place in public space. Thus economic and social bargaining are exercised because of occupying the space. Therefore, the absence of (proper) legal frame and their strong social and economic bargaining with various actors become the reasons behind vendors' existence in the public space.

Public space has multidimensional aspects such as economic, sociological, political and legal. This study considers both the diverse aspects of street vendors' access and use of public space.

Space has an economic connotation. Considering De Soto's concept on market structure, the public space entails 'a form of capital' in the absence of any other source of capital which helps generate income. It also has a sociological interpretation, the existence of 'social relationships' that help to perpetuate this activity (Brown 2006). In other words, street vendors use social capital relations based on ethnicity, religion, localism and language as survival strategy in the urban economy (Brown et al. 2010). It carries a political meaning, because it is being used as a 'tool of exploitation' by a class of urbanites and local political agencies (both formal and informal). It has a legal aspect because of the absence of ownership rights, laws and regulations. As Harvey says, urbanisation is achievable without compromising the needs of working poor and urbanisation and modernisation should be 'inclusive'. However, in case of street vendors, who constitute a significant section of the urban working poor, they are considered a nuisance and an impediment to the modernisation process of cities, a by-product of migration and urbanisation. Nonetheless, they must not be 'left-out' but 'included' in the urban spatial planning process. Thus Harvey's (1978) concept of social justice is achievable but through 'redistribution' and 'inclusiveness'. One of the major hurdles in the path of ensuring 'redistributive justice' is the strong lobbies and nexus between builders, elite citizens' groups, the police and civic administration. The actors at the market consider it unprofitable to let vendors ply their trade in prime locations not even after the passing of the Act (notwithstanding that a section among them also takes bribes from vendors). Their powerful nexus, together with the state's lacklustre initiatives, stands in the way of achieving this.

Bribe payment becomes a system which is seen as an alternative strategy for survival and sustenance at the market. Street vendors prefer to pay fees legally to the government instead of paying bribes to the local police and the municipal corporation which can be a source of revenue collection. Some vendors stated that 'we would like to pay the amount as taxes instead of bribes for ours . . . space. We would even love to pay double the amount that we are paying now'. After the Act was passed, the situation has changed. While some civic authorities (like in Delhi and Mumbai) are now realising the importance of hawking zones for the vendors because this is the only way by which their 'rights to exist' can be realised, others are still reluctant to consider the Act (like in Kolkata). They (civic authorities) need to identify proper and feasible natural markets and provide hawking zones accordingly. It is difficult to build 'hawking zones' in areas where natural markets exist since these areas are otherwise occupied. On the other hand, the system of bribery being carried out (even after the passing of the Act) under the rule of the civic authorities is a testimony to the fact that the civic authorities are apathetic to this activity. Considering the argument built by Marjit and Kar (2009), the state is actually letting this informality and illegality to persist.

Denial of public space implies the perpetuation of informality. It implies a denial of dignity when street vendors' access and use of space in the cities are considered 'illegal' and 'encroachment' rather than a 'means of livelihood'. When vendors are denied a right to legitimately use the public space for carrying out business, they are also denied access to other forms of capital, namely, financial capital. But the question here is: why do vendors still exist on the urban space? When public space is denied to vendors, they find alternative arrangements to carry on with their activity – by paying bribes. Different informal market institutions are formed to facilitate. Issues related to bribe collection and the extensive process of bribe payment have been discussed later in this chapter. In the next chapter, working conditions with special emphasis on uncertainties and insecurities due to the illegal status of street vendors along with their living conditions and transition in their lives after coming to cities have been explored.

Rent seeking is a common feature in street vending activity. The rent-seeking behaviour of the civic authorities has been examined in this chapter. Vendors need to pay bribes primarily to the municipal corporation and the police. Bribes or rents are certain amounts that are paid by street vendors on a regular basis, sometimes even daily, for occupying public space. They pay these bribes from their daily income. According to the civic authorities, vendors illegally occupy urban space and paying bribes is a way of surviving in the market. However, bribe payment leads to another form of informality that has far-reaching implications on the vendors, the society and the economy at large. The amount of bribes is substantial and it imposes a financial burden on the payers which is completely unaccounted for and unrecorded. The process of bribe payment involves considerable harassment and exploitation.

This chapter unfolds various aspects of malpractices that are associated with the activity. It emphasises the nature of bribe payment and explores the actors involved in this whole process of payments and collections. Rent-seeking behaviour of the civic authorities is presented mainly based on the experiences while working with the Municipal Corporation of Greater Mumbai (MCGM) and the Guwahati Municipal Corporation (GMC). I had interacted with different stakeholders, mainly trade union leaders (from different trade unions) and street vendors across cities, to validate and cross-check the information. While conducting a study for the MCGM, informal and friendly discussions with officials from civic authorities also help to understand the current situation. The situation of the other cities is more or less similar. Numeric evidences show how much bribe vendors need to pay to sustain their businesses and to whom, what factors determine the amount to be paid as bribe, and what kind of bribes they pay. This chapter not only highlights the 'rent-seeking behaviour' of civic authorities but also shows how 'collection intermediaries' collect rent for the authorities and commission for themselves. The situation is same across the cities not only in India but also other cities in developing countries across the world. It is a part of regular activities of the vending profession. A study by Agnello and Moller (2004) on Cambodian vendors shows that vendors face harassment even after making bribe payments, and that their working conditions are affected by market insecurities and police intrusion. In Cambodia, in addition to the payment of taxes (vendors had to pay taxes after the formation of vendor unions), street vendors complained of paying 'other fees' collected as security and rentals and harassment against security and police personnel (ibid.). A study undertaken by R. N. Sharma (1998) revealed that around Rs 400 crore was collected as bribes annually from vendors in Mumbai in 1998. Undoubtedly, in a span of 18 years, the bribe collection has increased. The estimated amount of bribe is calculated on the basis of street vendors occupying BMC's land (ibid.). Therefore, if we consider all occupied space by street vendors and calculate the total amount of bribe, the total estimated amount of the bribe will be approximately triple the amount in the city of Mumbai. This raises the pertinent question as to whether states want to legalise this activity and control the rapid growth of vendors or want to continue the rent-seeking practices. This may be a partial explanation to the question raised by Marjit and Kar (2009) in their study arguing that the state wants natural growth of the informal sector.

A certain portion of vendors' daily income is termed 'rents' which is paid to the authorities and other civic bodies from the local market. Vendors who do not pay rents are harassed on a regular basis and are treated with disdain. It must be noted that bribes paid to the municipal authorities are greater than those paid to the police. In the process of making payments to the municipality and the police, the intermediaries are also involved to acquire their commissions (Saha 2014b). In most cases nearly 5–10 per cent of the vendors' daily income is appropriated by the police and the municipal officials (ibid.). The police are bribed on a daily basis, whereas the municipal officials extract bribes monthly. Non-payment of bribes results in either eviction or confiscation of goods. Bribes have been examined on the basis of demand and supply factors that are discussed at length later in the chapter.

Public space utilisation

Storage of unsold products

Storage facilities for unsold or new goods have always been a major problem for street vendors. Finding space at their place of work is very difficult. There are three ways of storing unsold goods. These are at home, at the workplace or at a shop/godown where they pay rent for the use of storage space. Many of the shops in the areas where street vendors operate are willing to store the goods of the vendors provided they pay a rent for their use. Some vendors find this convenient because it is close to the place of work as well as secure. However, many more, who may find the rents too high, have to use other premises for storage. Goods if kept in an insecure place are liable to be stolen or damaged. This problem is faced by most street vendors in all the cities (see Table 3.1). This is because the local authorities refuse to provide them with any storage facilities. As mentioned earlier, street vendors are regarded as illegal entities that encroach on public space and hence they should not be provided any facility to enhance their business. The exception is in Bhubaneswar, where storage facilities are available. In fact, among all the cities, Bhubaneswar is the only one that allows vendors to store their goods at the place of work. This is the only city, as mentioned earlier, which has evolved an effective street vending policy and later the Act. We found that only 1.5 per cent of the vendors store their goods at home, whereas 93.5 per cent keep them at the vending place in Bhubaneswar. Five per cent of the vendors rent out some space for storage. In the case of storage, we find that street vendors in a majority of the cities use their homes (57 per cent)

Table 3.1 Storage of unsold products

City	Places for securing unsold products					Total
	Home	Friends'/ relatives' place (free rent)	Vending place	Rented	Dealer	
Bengaluru	89 (44.5)	49 (24.5)	27 (13.5)	35 (17.5)	0 (0)	200 (100)
Bhubaneswar	3 (1.5)	0 (0)	187 (93.5)	10 (5.0)	0 (0)	200 (100)
Delhi	131 (65.5)	1 (0.5)	66 (33.0)	2 (1.0)	0 (0)	200 (100)
Hyderabad	133 (66.5)	4 (2.0)	9 (4.5)	54 (27.0)	0 (0)	200 (100)
Imphal	176 (88.0)	6 (3.0)	1 (0.5)	17 (8.5)	0 (0)	200 (100)
Indore	109 (54.5)	1 (0.5)	19 (9.5)	71 (35.5)	0 (0)	200 (100)
Jaipur	194 (97.0)	1 (0.5)	4 (2.0)	1 (0.5)	0 (0)	200 (100)
Lucknow	80 (40.0)	0 (0)	120 (60.0)	0 (0)	0 (0)	200 (100)
Mumbai	90 (45.0)	1 (0.5)	30 (15.0)	79 (39.5)	0 (0)	200 (100)
Patna	134 (67.0)	3 (1.5)	45 (22.5)	17 (8.5)	1 (0.5)	200 (100)
Total	1,139 (57.0)	66 (3.3)	508 (25.4)	286 (14.3)	1 (0)	2,000 (100)

Source: Computed by the author, based on field survey conducted in 2009–10.

Note: Figures within parenthesis indicate percentage in share.

as storage spaces. There are problems in this arrangement as well because most of the vendors live in hutments or slums which may not be very secure. Hence, family members take turns at keeping awake so that the goods are not stolen or tampered. In Bengaluru, 44.5 per cent of vendors store their goods at home and 24.5 per cent at friends'/relatives' place and 13.5 per cent store products at the vending place. In Delhi, 65.5 per cent store their goods at home, whereas only 33 per cent store them at their vending place and 1 per cent use rented space. In Indore, 54.5 per cent use their homes for storing, whereas 35.5 per cent store their goods at the workplace. Interestingly, Indore, Hyderabad and Mumbai have a large percentage of vendors that use rented space. In Hyderabad 27 per cent use rented space, whereas in Indore 35.5 per cent use it. Mumbai has the largest proportion with 39.9 per cent using rented space. In Delhi, Hyderabad, Imphal, Jaipur and Patna, more than 65 per cent of the vendors store their goods at home. For example, around 66.5 per cent of the vendors in Hyderabad and Patna store their goods at home, while these vendors form 97 per cent of the total in Jaipur. In Imphal, almost all vendors are women; 88 per cent of them store their unsold goods at home. One also may point out that these women vendors (in Imphal) face problems as they have to drag heavy loads on buses or in autos. In Jaipur, 97 per cent of the vendors store their goods at home, whereas only 2 per cent store them at the workplace. In Lucknow, 40 per cent of the vendors store at home and 60 per cent store at the vending place.

Multiple usages

Limited space for vending activity, together with rise in the number of vendors, has also led to multiple use of space. This is the direct result of intensification of competition. Many vendors decide among themselves to divide the use of the same working space over different hours of the day. In many places (especially in Mumbai and Delhi), we have seen that three different vendors occupied the same place during morning, afternoon and evening, respectively. These vendors paid bribes separately to the local agents and the local authorities, thereby giving triple the amount for the same space. This shows how intensively vendors are using public space currently, but in the absence of legal control these places are being utilised by agents and local authorities; and form a source of income. The civic authorities encompassing police and municipal authorities who are the 'regulators and controllers' of public space are in fact using the same to generate another form of income.

Place of socialisation

Street vendors use the space almost throughout the day. Vendors who sell perishable products assemble at their market place to go to the wholesale markets. The timing for assembling varies from place to place. In case of Mumbai, for instance, they gather at Kandivali and Vile Parle at around 2 o'clock in the morning and discuss payment and other matters with each other. Once the vehicle arrives, they leave the place to be able to reach the wholesale market (mostly in Vashi) before 5 o'clock in the morning and return to their market before 7:30 a.m. to start their business. Vendors selling garments, electronics and leather-made products prefer to go to the wholesale markets during lunch-time, preferably between 12 noon and 3 p.m. Therefore, the space is being used by the vendors throughout the day. Before leaving for the wholesale markets, vendors discuss not only business matters but also their personal lives with light conversations about movies and entertainment. They [vendors] use space as a place for 'socialisation'.

Ownership of public space among street vendors

The aspect of ownership of public space is interesting to discuss. It came out through interactions with many street vendors. Several street vendors across the cities are found to be paying rent towards the space that they are occupying. During the course of interviews with these vendors, the existence of a 'tenant–proprietor' relation-ship is found. While some vendors claimed to be tenants, others claimed to be the owners who leased out land to other 'tenant-vendors'. Their rights of ownership were based on the argument that they had paid enough bribes to the local civic authorities and leaders and therefore they held the right to the space. According to them, this sector would not be legalised and would not come under legal framework in the near future even after the passing of the Act. This current practice of renting out space began due to the expansion of social networks of the vendors as they brought their relatives or neighbours to the city and gave them work in their own stalls or appointed them as helpers (as wage workers). Later, some of these vendors left the vending job due to old age or other reasons and handed over the space of occupation, where his/her stall was set up, to these helpers. In the interviews, they revealed that although they had left vending, they did not leave their claims over the space they used years ago. The vendors who had been given these spaces to function needed to pay rent to these 'space-owners'. The 'owners' justified the rent-payment behaviour by say-ing that they (tenants) owe an obligation to them (owners). This is because they (tenants) were given the opportunity to work and earn in cities like Bengaluru, Delhi and Mumbai and were also provided with a source of livelihood, whereas in their towns and villages they were jobless and on the brink of starvation. However, interestingly, many current occupants said that they would stop paying rent if the owners refused the rent or if they died. However, it was observed that some vendors were still paying some nominal amount to the family of the owner even after the owner's death because they were obliged to the owner's family. It is interesting to look at how property rights are being created without any formal recognition of the property and it is being transferred to others.

Space is an extended home

The meaning of public space for women is more than just the workplace and therefore public space utilisation has even more implication for female vendors. Women treat their workplace as an extension of their homes and often bring their children to their vending stalls. Some female vendors interviewed across the cities reported that children do not study at home as they (female vendors) were not at home most of the day. They [female vendors] also feel that the workplace was a better place to study because it is airy and well lit, especially during the daytime, as compared to dimly lit homes. Women with infants carried them to the workplace as there was no one in the house to look after them. Leaving their children under the supervision of neighbours was also not an option since almost all of them were out to work.

Workplace becomes living space

Many cases were encountered in all the cities in which workplace was also the living space of vendors who lived there year after year. One such case of a male vendor from Chembur (Mumbai) can be mentioned. Despite his adverse circumstances, he did not fully participate in our study and therefore was not included in the total sample. Nonetheless this example has been used as an 'extreme deviant case'. He was an old man of about 65–70 years and his place of residence was his vending stall. He lived there and whatever he earned was sent to his family members back in his village in UP because he had no one in Mumbai. He chose to save on house rent and other costs, so he slept in his stall. However, during the monsoons because of torrential rain, he would take refuge with other people from his village in their rented rooms (his fellow vendors who are migrants like him often put up together in a small room to save upon rent). Surprisingly, he had no complaints about his life or the bare minimum arrangements he had for a safe existence.

Public space and its politics

Eviction, confiscation and rent extraction

Eviction drives reflect the attitude of civic authorities to the plight of vendors. Land is one of the most precious resources or physical capitals in urban economy. Politics and conflict arise on the way in which the space is utilised. In the present context of street vending, eviction, confiscation of goods and ever-increasing rent extraction are the outcomes of politics and conflicts that ascend surrounding utilisation of space. Nearly 66 per cent of vendors in the total sample reported evictions. Among the cities, Bhubaneswar, Lucknow and Imphal, 94 per cent, 92 per cent and 94 per cent of vendors, respectively, report having faced evictions while 68 per cent in Mumbai, 77 per cent in Patna, 66 per cent in Delhi, 56 per cent in Indore and 55 per cent in Bengaluru report evictions. Vendors in Hyderabad (63 per cent) and Jaipur (76 per cent) have reportedly not faced evictions (see Table 3.2).

Evictions and police harassments are regular features in the name of cleanliness and beautification, municipal norms, security concerns and so on. Most of the evictions are done by active consent

Table 3.2 Eviction

City	Eviction		Total
	Yes	No	
Bengaluru	110 (55.0)	90 (45.0)	200 (100)
Bhubaneswar	188 (94.0)	12 (6.0)	200 (100)
Delhi	133 (66.5)	67 (33.5)	200 (100)
Hyderabad	74 (37.0)	126 (63.5)	200 (100)
Imphal	188 (94.0)	12 (6.5)	200 (100)
Indore	112 (56.0)	88 (44.0)	200 (100)
Jaipur	47 (23.5)	153 (76.5)	200 (100)
Lucknow	185 (92.5)	15 (7.5)	200 (100)
Mumbai	136 (68.0)	64 (32.0)	200 (100)
Patna	155 (77.5)	45 (22.5)	200 (100)
Total	1,328 (66.4)	672 (33.6)	2,000 (100)

Source: Computed by the author, based on field survey conducted in 2009–10.

Note: Figures within parenthesis indicate percentage in share.

of the senior officials of the municipal authorities and other civic administration like all the cities. Most of the anti-encroachment drives are done without any prior information to the street vendors which in most of the cases, due to the presence of police, create panic among the street vendors and lead to huge physical and property losses for the street vendors. This sometimes seriously affects the livelihoods of small vendors like vegetable and flower sellers who usually work with very low capital. Often police resort to destroying the physical assets of some vendors in case they indulge in verbal protests on the venue. Eviction drives take place in all the cities but degree of the drives is more in other cities like Mumbai, Patna and Lucknow. Eviction and its associated harassments have been presented through the case of Imphal (see Box 3.1).

Box 3.1 Eviction and harassments – case of Imphal

Manipur has progressive laws for street vendors. Its Town Planning Act makes provisions for ten street vendors and three shops for every 1,000 population living in housing societies. However, we found that the municipal authorities have started to harass the vendors in the city. The municipality charges a small rent and takes Rs 10 per vendor every day as blockage tax for keeping the market clean. The vendors had complained that the municipal authorities did nothing to promote cleanliness. The area continues to remain dirty, posing a health hazard to the women vendors, and the municipal authorities keep collecting the blockage tax. The other major problem is eviction. Vendors not having licence (token from municipality) are frequently evicted and they have to run from pillar to post to get a place to sell. They are usually the main earning member in the family and decrease in income because of displacement has a negative effect on the food intake in the household. The vendors also complained of bribes that they have to pay to the authorities. Evictions and harassment take place only in the main market perhaps because it is a profitable area to work in. There are hardly any evictions or bribe taking in the areas outside the market. In other words, vendors work without harassment in areas outside the market.

Source: Based on fieldwork conducted in 2009–10.

Bribe payment: nature, types and process

Public space used by the vendors also feeds into the rent-seeking behaviour of a certain section. The procedure of bribe collection and the associated harassment are both the cause and effect of the informal status of vendors' business activities. This present study points to the fact that each vendor has to pay a significant portion of his/her income as bribes daily. The data collected through this study showed that in the case of most vendors, nearly 5–10 per cent of their daily income was usurped by the police and municipalities. Section 34 of the Police Act empowers the police to remove any obstruction on the streets, and the street vendors have to pay them bribes mainly to avoid eviction under this section. This is one of the reasons for further impoverishment of the street vendors. Vendors stated that if they pay higher bribes, they will face less harassment and intervention from the local police and the municipal officials. However, this did not mean that bribe payment would completely eradicate the harassment and confiscation of goods; it would simply reduce the degree to which harassment would take place on a particular day. Hence, it is an important alternative way to sustain in the market and it perpetuates the informality.

Around 14 per cent of the vendors across cities explicitly told us that they paid bribes to the authorities on a regular basis. However it does not mean that vendors in other cities do not pay bribes at all. In many instances it takes more hidden forms like goods in kind. Vendors in Bengaluru (44 per cent), Hyderabad (42.5 per cent) and Mumbai (30 per cent) told us if they stopped paying the bribes, the authorities would evict them and destroy their goods. The bribes ranged from Rs 2 to Rs 100 per day. We found that the highest bribe was paid by vendors who sell shoes or clothes in the Sunday market at the Red Fort. This market is illegal and it operates only one day of the week. But given the large number of people who flock to this place to buy durable goods, this one day saving is enough to last the vendors a week. However, the bribes too are very high. Most vendors pay between Rs 500 and 700 for the day. The highest are those that occupy the traffic islands. They pay Rs 1,000. In Mumbai too, the rates are fairly high, though not as high as the ones that are paid by the Red Fort vendors. As mentioned earlier, a census on street vendors conducted by TISS-YUVA in 1998 showed that the authorities collected Rs 400 crore annually and similarly in Delhi, it was found that around Rs 50 crore was collected from hawkers and cycle-rickshaw pullers. In fact the Chief Vigilance Officer had taken a strong view on this and asked the state government to take action against this malpractice. Extortion by the municipal authorities and the police (euphemistically called rent) is a bane for street vendors because it reduces their income considerably. Hence, one can see that besides the moneylenders, the municipal authorities too make it difficult for the hawkers to eke out a living. Rent seeking by the authorities somehow ensures the street vendor of 'trouble-free' vending. But this is not true. We found that paying rent did not necessarily protect them from evictions, though it may certainly reduce the number of evictions. A majority of the hawkers, with the exception of some cities, have been evicted from their workplaces and their goods have been confiscated. The exceptions where the majority has not been evicted are Hyderabad (63 per cent) and Jaipur (76.5 per cent). In Patna (77.5 per cent) have been evicted at some time (see Table 3.3). Confiscation of goods when vendors are evicted causes

Table 3.3 Bribe payment in cash

City	Bribe payment in cash		Total
	Yes	No	
Bengaluru	88 (44.0)	112 (56.0)	200 (100)
Bhubaneswar	3 (1.5)	197 (98.5)	200 (100)
Delhi	19 (9.5)	181 (90.5)	200 (100)
Hyderabad	85 (42.5)	115 (57.5)	200 (100)
Imphal	5 (2.5)	195 (97.5)	200 (100)
Indore	21 (10.5)	179 (89.5)	200 (100)
Jaipur	9 (4.5)	191 (95.5)	200 (100)
Lucknow	3 (1.5)	197 (98.5)	200 (100)
Mumbai	60 (30.0)	140 (70)	200 (100)
Patna	0 (0)	200 (100)	200 (100)
Total	293 (14.6)	1,707 (85.4)	2,000 (100)

Source: Computed by the author, based on field survey conducted in 2009–10.

Note: Figures within parenthesis indicate percentage in share.

major financial losses and leads them to indebtedness. In nearly all cases, with the exception of a very small percentage (less than 10 per cent), no receipt is given by the authorities when they confiscate goods. All too often, when the vendor goes to recover his/her goods after paying the fine, s/he finds that half the goods are missing. This happens in the case of clothes, which perhaps may land up in the houses of the authorities as gifts for their children and fruits. The confiscation of goods without receipt should be treated as a crime as it is nothing less than theft. In no civilised country is this confiscation done without giving a statement of what is confiscated. In fact the way the authorities treat the street vendors in this regard is totally appalling. For example, if a raid is conducted in the premises of a criminal, and a large quantity of fraudulent goods are found, the raiding authority will always take a panchnama containing the details of confiscated goods and signed by five witnesses. Unfortunately the street vendor does not get her/his legal relief. She/he is treated as a total outcaste, as someone who is even worse than a criminal, as no receipt is given for the confiscation of goods. Nature, types and process of bribe payment are discussed later in this chapter.

Bribes in 'kind'

The bribe in kind that vendors are required to pay is sometimes higher than the cash component and treated with less importance by the municipality and the police This was found to be true among some vendors. Bribes in kind are most apparent at food stalls. The police regularly eat snacks and vendors freely welcome them, especially the tea stall vendors who provide tea and snacks freely to the police. Interviews with vendors revealed that vendors believe in maintaining a 'good' relation by providing them 'food and other services' free of cost or at a subsidised rate. Thus they can later use this to bargain over bribe payments.

On the other hand, the municipality confiscates goods from the vendors and dumps them in the local municipal offices. Vendors (especially garment sellers, electronic goods sellers and household utensils sellers) reported some their goods got misplaced prior to them being released. Some local ward officials blatantly appropriate useful items from the pile of confiscated goods; others steal them. In both cases, we need to mention that municipal authorities do not provide any list of the confiscated goods.

Relationship between products sold and bribe

Bribe payments are contingent upon the volume of trade and the nature of products sold. If the volume of trade is considerably large or the per-day sale is high, the municipality and police demand steeper bribes. On the other hand, vendors selling perishable products have to pay more bribes; for example, tea vendors have huge sales and therefore have to pay more bribes. The same holds true for cooked food vendors. The highest bribe payers are those selling Chinese food, because these vendors sometimes sell liquor along with the food. Generally tea/coffee makers need to pay Rs 2,500 per month, a fruit and a vegetable vendor needs to pay monthly Rs 2,000 each, whereas a Chinese food seller needs to pay Rs 5,000 a month in bribes in Mumbai. It is seen that perishable product sellers pay high bribes as compared to others across the cities. The police and municipal officials use pressure tactics to extract higher bribes; for instance, they tell cooked food vendors that they run the risk of a fire breakout and so forth.

Multiple bribe payments to one particular place

As we mentioned earlier, one particular space is being used by at least three or four street vendors in certain places. Notably, all of them need to pay bribes separately to the civic authorities for securing their space for their particular shift to operate the business.

Commission to collection intermediaries

Collection intermediaries collect bribes from vendors and give them to the police and the municipal corporation. Though vendors were ambiguous about the identity of these collection intermediaries, they said that these persons were vendors in their localities who worked as intermediaries to facilitate the process of rent seeking or bribe collection between the vendors, the municipal officials and the police. The amount of bribe collected by them is divided into two groups – one amount, the exact percentage of which is unknown, is kept as commission and the other is distributed between the civic authorities and the police. The echo behaviour of the police and municipal bodies is therefore another 'instrument' of harassment for the vendors. The amount of bribe is both fixed and regularly demanded by the civic authorities.

Process of bribe payment: demand-driven situation

It is important to know how these bribes are collected. The entire bribe payment system is demand driven. Though the process itself is completely illegal and different layers of illegalities are intertwined, the system operates perfectly in a well-coordinated manner. This process has been elaborated based in the case of Mumbai. It was difficult to get such detailed information at each city level but the similar process of bribe collection is practised in almost all the cities in India. The number of actors involved in the process may vary from city to city and location to location. There are mainly two groups involved in the collection process. First group is the civic authorities, namely, municipal officials and police (as mentioned earlier). Second ones are those street vendors who double up as collection intermediaries. Interestingly, street vendors reported that the number of these intermediaries has been increasing over the period, thereby raising the question, what is the role of these intermediaries in the process of bribe payment and collection?

This begs the question, how do street vendors pay the bribes? There are two broad ways by which street vendors make bribe payments. First, street vendors pay directly to municipal officials and police while negotiating the retrieval of their products and settle it with the civic authorities themselves. Second, these intermediaries collect bribes from vendors and pay the authorities. These vendors who act as intermediaries also know when the civic authorities visit the marketplace. In the entire process, 'collection intermediaries' facilitate the bribe collection process. It is estimated that one street vendor needs to pay bribes to around 43 different actors in the civic administration and police combined, including payments to 'collection intermediaries' and 'zero numbers'. The 'zero numbers' are professional informers from the markets, who are also street vendors by profession. The above example is from Mumbai. The following case (see Box 3.2) of bribe payment and its process in Mumbai has been explained. Mumbai can be considered a typical case characterised by existence of different layers and involvement of various actors in the bribe extraction process.

Box 3.2 Bribe extraction process in Mumbai

There are around thirty-four direct actors from the BMC involved in the process of bribe collection, including the gate-keeper of the local ward office. Although the amount and percentage paid to each of the actor could not be ascertained, the process can be understood from the description below. There are mainly two levels of BMC from which evictions are authorised – local ward office and the main BMC office.

Local ward level

It is relevant to the context to explain the current structure of the BMC that looks after public space and street vendors first before exploring the function of the bribe payment system. Apparently, the process is very complicated but on close observation, its structure and, in fact, the entire process appear very structured. The twenty-four wards under the BMC are alphabetically named as A, B, C, D, E, F (South, North), G (South, North), H (West, East), K (East, West), L, M (West, East), N, P (South, North), R (South, Central, North), S and T. There is a 'Licence Superintendent' (LS) who looks after the aforementioned twenty-four wards. There are twenty-four 'Assistant Licence Superintendents' (ALSs) under the LS and each of twenty-four ALSs is in charge of one ward. These twenty-four ALSs report directly to the LS.

One Senior Licence Inspector (SLI) and one Senior Inspector (encroachment) [SI I] are appointed under an ALS in each ward. Under one Senior Inspector (encroachment), there are four lorry inspectors (sometimes the number of lorry inspectors varies), one godown clerk and twelve labourers who are appointed to ensure that the city's urban spaces are kept free from encroachment and other issues pertaining to public space utilisation. These seventeen officials from the local ward take action and conduct eviction drives whenever they receive complaints from residents' associations or 'zero numbers' (or professional informers) regarding encroachments and their spillover. Therefore, these officials from the BMC have the autonomy and the power to confiscate the goods of these vendors and even evict them. Thus vendors and their leaders have to negotiate directly with this group of officials from local ward office and bribe the seventeen officials to prevent their goods from being confiscated or them from being evicted. Vendors reported that bribes are distributed among these officials and that they never reach the LS and ALSs. But nobody really knows what happens because this action is very difficult to explore.

Bombay special squad

The Bombay special squad and ward officers (removal of encroachment) are appointed to look after public space. The first one, comprising some officials from the department of vigilance of municipal office, is involved in the bribe collection process. They are appointed and controlled by the main BMC office. One squad is in charge of vigilance and is popularly known among street vendors as 'special' with respect to the area. For instance, they are known as the *Andheri Special* in Andheri, *Kandivali Special* in Kandivali, *Bandra Special* in Bandra and so on. Their inspections are unannounced.

One vigilance team comprises one Senior Inspector, one godown clerk and around twelve labourers. Their team gets spread over in two lorries. Vendors need to pay them as well. Sometimes it is direct payment and sometimes it is through 'collection intermediaries'. Thus fourteen officials are involved in collecting bribes directly under Bombay special squad and vendors need to pay bribes to each of them too.

Ward officers – removal of encroachment

Another group of officers is appointed by the *ward office* (removal of encroachment). The BMC appoints a team of two labourers and one lorry inspector to look after unauthorised demolition sites. Therefore vendors need to negotiate with them as well. This is because the ward officers in charge of removal of encroachment (is often known as WRE) and its team often visit different vending sites to threaten vendors. A three-member team is also part of bribe collection. Therefore thirty-four BMC officials – who are working at the ground level – are involved directly in the payment and collection of bribe. Most importantly, lorry inspectors and lorry drivers seem to possess a lot of information on each vending location, time of vending and even name of each street vendor.

Police and their operation

Only a few police officers are involved in the collection of bribes. Each area has a beat marshal appointed by the local police station and a mobile 'wireless' team responsible for monitoring city and overseeing space utilisation. The shifts of these beat marshals are on a 24-hour rotation, with two shifts of 12 hours each. Those on the night shift frequently harass the vendors but are unable to do much beyond that because they have no authority to confiscate the vendors' products. The manner in which the police harass the vendors is as follows: they file a charge which has a monetary component. A receipt of the charge with the amount of Rs 1,250 is handed over to the vendor. While on paper this appears to be the practice, the situation on the ground is somewhat different, because negotiations between the vendors and the police are never on record. If the police arrest ten vendors, ten individual receipts of Rs 1,250 need to be prepared. Therefore the total amounts to Rs 12,500 against the ten receipts. The police–vendor conflict and its resolution being an everyday affair, the vendors bargain and negotiate with the police to reconsider the penal charge. Invariably, the police provide a solution based on a cost-benefit analysis and charge a lump sum amount of Rs 5,000 from the ten vendors. They make two copies of the charge, one for Rs 1,250, which goes into the local corpus of the police, and the other amount is unaccounted which they pocket. This results in a win-win situation wherein the vendors have to shell out only Rs 5,000, with each vendor contributing Rs 500, instead of Rs 1,250.

Source: Based on fieldwork conducted in 2013–14.

When do municipal officials conduct raids?

The municipal corporation raids the street vending sites whenever the general public files a complaint against congestion. As mentioned earlier, 'agents' are fixed by civic authorities (they are known as zero numbers in case of Mumbai). These intermediaries also file *false* complaints for congestion. The municipality and police conduct raids on receipt of the complaint. Not surprisingly, these intermediaries complain whenever they are in a mood to raise their 'commissions'. Sometimes these informers go to the extent of bargaining and blackmailing the officials from municipality and police if civic authorities do not increase their commission. They threaten these civic authority officials that they might go up the chain of command and complain about malpractices of these petty officers. To abet the raid, they also inform the civic authorities about the places where raids should to be organised and the municipal officials act upon the information they receive from them. The police are not authorised to confiscate goods or evict the vendors; they approach the municipal officials to do so.

Citizens' perspectives on the use of public space

As reiterated earlier, understanding the concept and therefore the pertinence of public space is critical to this study. One of the main reasons for the growth of this sector is because of demand from the general public. As mentioned earlier, we interviewed fifty consumers from different sections across four places, the main intention of which was to garner positive and negative responses, including viewing the issue from the consumers' viewpoint in this context.

The late 1990s saw non-governmental organisations (NGOs) and citizens' associations blaming the hawkers as the reason behind growing urban congestion and its associated problems (Anjaria 2006). They maintained that vendors illegally occupied the pavements and footpaths, causing congestion and unhygienic conditions, which in turn led to overcrowding and occasionally road accidents. According to these elite groups, hawkers represent a part of the metropolitan space which has gone out of control (ibid.). Hawkers and their illegal occupancy depress the real estate value of an aspiring world-class city (ibid.). These citizens' associations are often successful in convincing the authorities that evicting the vendors will ease many problems.

Builders' lobby

The growth of real estate is taking place at a very fast pace in all the selected cities in this study. As a result, multi-storeyed buildings are being constructed on a large scale and builders' lobby is gaining prominence in the cities, along with power and money. The growth in urbanisation is also accompanied by a greater rise in the number of working poor who migrate to the cities in search for a livelihood. Records of various trade unions confirm that the number of street vendors is growing steadily in all the cities, especially fast-growing cities. The needs of the working poor are not recognised or taken into account when land is acquired for real estate development, such as the construction of malls, shopping plazas, multiplexes and housing complexes, by different builders, who often use modern spatial urban planning techniques for the development of such area. Builders prefer locations which have proximity to the major transport nodes or important places of interest (the sea line or parks). These areas are also where street vendors find a ready 'natural market' for their wares. This clash in interest for the same area makes it difficult for vendors to continue business as they face threat from the builders. According to many street vendors and some union members interviewed in this study, builders are also connected with local politicians and civic authorities. They often exercise influence coercing the vendors to evacuate these prime locations, not realising that the vendors draw their sole means of livelihood from these places. This study highlights one such case where builder lobbies and other important aspects of vending, including issues over illegality, led to gross injustice for a street vendor.

The reason behind the murder of Kapoorchand Gupta, former general secretary of Shahid Bhagat Singh Hawkers' Union (SBSHU) in Mumbai's suburb Kandivali (West), on 20 November 2012 at 10:10 p.m. on M G Road, opposite the swimming pool in Kandivali (West), can be discussed briefly in the context of builders' lobby. Two hawkers, named Shiv Prasad Kesari and Shiv Bharadwaj, were arrested from Nashik the next day in connection with this murder. According to the investigating team of police, the prime reason for the murder was that Mr Gupta had allegedly caused a loss of Rs 4,000,000 to these two moneylenders and had jeopardised their moneylending business (*The Indian Express*, 23 November 2012). However, a meeting with SBSHU's leaders and other street vendors from the vegetable market in Kandivali (West) revealed that the amount of loss was not less than Rs 6,000,000. His murder case unfolded many things. Among several glaring aspects that have come to the fore is the fact that the builders' lobby might be linked to Mr Gupta's murder.

Mr Gupta was also not liked by the builders' lobby. The builders of market complexes and housing societies were trying to evict the vendors and make their spaces of business hawker-free zones before laying foundation of their building projects. The builders claimed that hawkers led to the diminution of market valuations in their locations because people in principle preferred 'hawker- and clutter-free' locations. Therefore hawkers and their businesses caused losses to builders' lobby and sometimes these losses amounted to several crores of rupees. An incident that took place on Mathuradas Road in Kandivali (West) can be linked in this context. One builders' group had called on Mr Gupta to convince him to evacuate the spaces because the builders knew that Mr Gupta had considerable influence on the hawkers and that he alone could convince the vendors to relocate. Mr Gupta rejected the builders' proposal and a clash ensued between the builders' lobby and Mr Gupta in which even money changed hands. This sort of case might have a link with the murder of Mr Gupta. We have not come across such cases in other cities but both street vendors and trade union leaders, especially in Bengaluru and Delhi, shared same concerns.

Survival strategies in the public space

Negotiation with different actors

In spite of their wide visibility, vendors across cities face harassment at the workplace. They survive by paying different forms of bribes, which have existed for a long time now. In Mumbai, between 1988 and 1997, there was a *pavti* (unauthorised occupation cum refuse removal charges) system for street vending in Mumbai in which vendors used to pay Rs 5–10 per day to the BMC which entitled them to vend (Anjaria 2006). According to a survey conducted in 1997 by Tata Institute of Social Sciences (TISS)-Youth for Unity and Voluntary Action (YUVA), 22,000 vendors were issued such pavtis on a daily basis. As Anjaria pointed out, this pavti was a formal recognition of an informal, officially unrecognised, yet widespread, activity. Similarly, in Guwahati, every vendor pays Rs 20 per day to the Guwahati Municipal Corporation (GMC) against receipt towards maintaining cleanliness at public place. This practice continues even after the passing of the Act. Therefore, this makes a contradictory situation. On one hand, vending activity is considered legal and on the other hand, civic authority is making revenue from them on a regular basis. Thus, in the form of a *pavti/receipt*, there was an official recognition of an unofficial practice. It is evident that the state used to collect revenue from an officially illegal population. Vendors mentioned that although pavti system in Mumbai was there only for eighteen months, many among them still have the pavtis and hope that the system would one day be reactivated in the form of tax.

Ironically, street vendors across cities manage to conduct their 'unofficial' business by negotiating with the police and the municipal officials. This understanding is solely based upon payment of bribes as 'unofficial rent' to the authorities. It means that to earn a livelihood and to avoid large number of evictions, they need to pay a certain amount as bribes. This study revealed that vendors who did not pay rent in the form of bribes were disturbed and harassed regularly. They were required to pay bribes primarily to three main groups—the municipal officials, the police and local agents fixed by the local authorities. Bribes were paid both in cash and in kind, although the bribes paid in kind were much larger than those paid in cash. While the bribes to the police were paid on a daily basis, bribes to the municipal officials were paid when the vendors faced the threat of eviction and confiscation of their goods. It was also noticed that local policemen often take away their products without paying for them, in case the vendor is unable to pay bribes in cash. The amount of bribe depends on the vending activity and volume of business. In case of the municipal corporation, after confiscating goods from the vendors, the officials normally issue a 'bill' or 'receipt' indicating the amount that vendors need to pay to release goods from the municipal office. This amount often exceeds the investment in business. Vendors have to negotiate with officials to have the goods released at an amount lesser than that mentioned on the 'receipt' and the payment system is totally 'informal'. The entire process of negotiation and informal exchange between the vendors and the officials takes place after official hours, which is usually after 5 p.m. After negotiation and release of the goods, vendors need to return the 'receipt' to the municipal officials which go unregistered.

Besides local authorities, another peculiar category of bribe seeker was also noticed in the market, evident in every city considered in the study. Vendors talked of a certain 'agent' of the police and the municipal corporation that collect bribes from vendors in the locality. Though vendors did not provide details on his/her personal identification, they said that s/he is a vendor in their locality who works as an intermediary to facilitate the process of rent seeking or bribe collection between the vendors and the municipal officials and the police. The amount of bribe collected by the agent is given to the two groups, after keeping aside a certain percentage as his/her 'commission'. The exact percentage of this commission is not clear and it is very difficult to calculate it too and it varies from case to case. The 'agent' therefore is another 'instrument' of harassment. S/he normally collects the bribe amount by force by promising that the police and municipality would not approach them anymore.

Negotiation at individual level

The municipal officials raid the places subsequent to being informed. They start eviction drives and confiscate goods from vendors. Once they confiscate the goods, vendors need to go to the local office in order to release the products. They need to bargain over the amount to be paid to release them. While leaving the municipal local office premises, officials even suggest to the vendors to give a token amount to the gatekeeper, so that the gatekeeper does not squeal on them to the higher-ups.

The municipal officials generally go for inspections during the day, avoiding the peak hour of business. While the reason for doing so is not altogether apparent, the officials assume that their bribes will get compromised if the vendors are not let free to pursue their business. The decision to visit a particular location is made 'strategically' and in an organised manner. It is interesting to note that if one of the vendors learns of such a visit, news about a possible raid spreads instantaneously throughout the marketplace. The smaller, more vulnerable vendors pack their items and retreat to the small lanes and hide their wares. When the municipal officials leave, they resume their business. It is astonishing to see how resiliently they pursue their trade despite the insecurity. When they were asked about their experiences, one of them (in Mumbai) replied, 'This is not uncommon, we have been witness to this ever since we started business. This is an everyday affair with them (civic authorities). Our day starts with this mental preparation.'

Negotiation through collection intermediaries

In general, 'collection intermediaries' negotiate with the civic authorities on the amount of bribe to be paid and how to make that payment. One or two vendors from each street or same locality are engaged as collection intermediaries. They have to ensure a good rapport with the local authorities so that their fellow vendors can trust them. They negotiate with civic authorities on behalf of the street vendors by virtue of them being 'leaders' and collect money from them on an everyday basis to pay the municipality and the police. The collection intermediaries for municipal officials and police are different sets of persons. These intermediaries also keep some portion of the collection as commission, although they do not admit this. Their fellow vendors are however convinced that a substantial portion of the bribes is pocketed by these agents, because despite paying bribes to these intermediaries, the civic authorities make frequent visits, almost daily, to harass them. Hence the vendors feel that a significant amount of bribe meant for the civic authorities is being kept as commission by these intermediaries. In this context, one important aspect needs to be mentioned, which is the way payment is made. A case from Mumbai can be referred. The intermediaries provide the collected bribe amount in 'closed envelopes' which is popularly known among vendors as 'pudi'. The concept of *pudi* is famous in the markets and ironic. The intermediaries negotiate with the authorities every day by giving pudi. The pudi implies 'envelope'. Receivers do understand the 'extralegal' arrangements that are made by them to let the 'illegal' vendors thrive in the market. This malpractice even happened several times while we were conducting survey for the MCGM in Mumbai. During this survey, we observed that MCGM officials (lower level) received this *pudi* from one of the intermediaries.

Congestion over public space: the reality

Civic authorities and residents' associations always blame street vendors for being the main cause for traffic congestion. Vending stalls sometimes spill over to the streets and crowds of customers gather around the stalls obstructing free flow of traffic. However, the ground reality is quite different which was noticed during field work. The main reason for the bottleneck and congestion situation across cities is because of personal car parking and auto/taxi parking. We can retrieve an example from Mumbai. In Chembur, for instance, the two roads perpendicular to the Chembur Railway Station Road which are connected to the Ambedkar Garden are the main areas for traffic congestion. Most of the hotels, restaurants and bars are located on these two roads. As a result, private cars, auto-rickshaws and taxis park there. Notably, vendors occupy the footpath, not the road. In Dadar, the main reason for congestion is the parking of private cars and taxis. In Kandivali and Vile Parle, private car parking and restaurants are the main reasons for congestion.

Another important aspect of road congestion that needs to be highlighted is the extension of private space of shopkeepers in areas in Mumbai such as N.G. Acharya Marg (Chembur), DeSilva Road and Ranade Road (Dadar), Akruli Road and M.G. Road (Kandivali) and Hanuman Mandir Road (Ville Parle). The shopkeepers deliberately blame street vendors for occupying footpaths; however, they treat footpaths as extended business areas. The shopkeepers put up placards, display boards or even hang out their wares in cots and thus add to road congestion. Street vendors have reported that some of the shopkeepers act as 'informers' to municipality and police for conducting sudden eviction drives. It is noticed that vendors do not come to the main road and customers also do not create any congestion, even though the bargaining process between customers and vendors takes a little long time.

Awareness of hawking zones

Vendors' awareness about the hawking zones was collected which also helped to understand how far unions are active in disseminating vital information (see Table 3.4). In Bhubaneswar, Hyderabad and Imphal the situation is slightly better as 89 per cent, 68 per cent, and 70 per cent of vendors in the respective cities are aware of the hawking zones. Slightly better situation on awareness prevails in Delhi (46 per cent), Mumbai (33 per cent), Patna (34 per cent), Jaipur (28 per cent) and Bengaluru (22 per cent). The worst conditions prevail in Indore (5.5 per cent) and Lucknow (2 per cent). The information dissemination on the hawking zones helps to understand the spread of information on the Act (2014). The following case (see Box 3.3) shows the positive aspects of civic authorities of Jaipur on how they [authorities] tried to frame and designate vending zones for the vendors.

Table 3.4 Awareness of hawking zone

City	Awareness of vending zone		Total
	Yes	No	
Bengaluru	44 (22.0)	156 (78.0)	200 (100)
Bhubaneswar	178 (89.0)	22 (11.0)	200 (100)
Delhi	93 (46.5)	107 (53.5)	200 (100)
Hyderabad	137 (68.5)	63 (31.5)	200 (100)
Imphal	140 (70.0)	60 (30.0)	200 (100)
Indore	11 (5.5)	189 (94.5)	200 (100)
Jaipur	57 (28.5)	143 (71.5)	200 (100)
Lucknow	4 (2.0)	196 (98.0)	200 (100)
Mumbai	67 (33.5)	133 (66.5)	200 (100)
Patna	68 (34.0)	132 (66.0)	200 (100)
Total	799 (40.0)	1,201 (60.0)	2,000 (100)

Source: Computed by the author, based on field survey conducted in 2009–10.

Note: Figures within parenthesis indicate percentage in share.

Box 3.3 Construction of hawking zones in Jaipur

Jaipur Development Corporation (JDC) and Jaipur Municipal Corporation (JMC) tried to make provisions for settling
street vendors in the city. The first step was to provide spaces
for 180 street vendors in two markets, namely, Vidhyadhar
Nagar and Murlipura. These spaces, comprising permanent
stalls, were provided by the municipal corporation. There
are 100 such stalls in Vidhyadhar Nagar market. These were
set up in 2002 and the vendors were allotted these stalls at
Rs 9,000 per stall. The amount could be paid in four annual
instalments of Rs 2,250. Eighty street vendors were allotted
places in Murlipura market. These stalls were given to them
in 2005 and each had to pay Rs 26,000, a fairly high cost.
The amount was collected at one time. It is not surprising that
shopkeepers and private owners bought these places. Besides
these ventures, the JDC plans to select fifty new places to
accommodate 3,000 vendors. The prices of the stalls will be
on the basis of the local price of land. It is expected to be high

as land prices are appreciating rapidly. Moreover accommodating 3,000 vendors is just too small a number considering that there are at least 40,000 vendors in the city. Both the JDC and the JMC have promised to provide sanitation facilities, drinking water and electricity in the new markets. This would be of great help to the vendors, especially the women. Drinking water would provide more hygienic conditions for food vendors. The JMC has also agreed to provide licences to the existing vendors. It will build hawking zones near places of tourist interest and other spots. After these zones are finalised the corporation will provide dustbins and other facilities for the vendors. Vendors will be provided spaces of 6 × 6 sq. ft. for each pitch.

Source: Based on fieldwork conducted in 2009–10.

Conclusion

Vending activity is considered as a threat to development, urbanisation and modernisation. It shows that another section deliberately utilises their informal existence as an instrument of rent extraction. They are kept under the cover of informality since they help a section of urbanites to extract supernormal profits. The vendors are actually victims of the influential nexus of bribe collectors that include civic officials, police and also some 'influential vendors' who have acquired the trust and confidence of the cohesive group of vendors. Staying afloat in the vending profession is a tedious and long process which involves transferring money at various levels. In the event of a complaint made by a citizens' group, the actors involved quietly organise themselves and start the process of rent extraction. Ironically, the 'congested spaces' are never actually 'evacuated' because vendors return and occupy the places after a few days. The entire process to redress the complaints and grievances of urbanites seem to be an eyewash; their complaints just facilitate yet higher rent extraction. On the other hand, vendors who are already financially overburdened from regular bribe payments are further tortured and harassed in the name of 'encroachment removal and keeping city urban space clean'.

Bribe collection procedure, the rates and timings of raid are well organised and 'sharply' undertaken whereas the police intrusions seem to be more dependent upon the 'mutual bargaining process'. This also forms a well-coordinated informal market institution which is directly and indirectly helping vendors to sustain in the market. This makes the municipality acutely exploitative compared to the police, apart from the fact that the municipality's rent-seeking process is more organised, making it possible to extract a larger amount as bribes.

Street vendors prefer to pay fees legally to the government instead of bribing the local police and the municipal corporation. One of the vendors stated that 'we would like to pay the amount as taxes instead of bribes for our . . . space. We would even love to pay double the amount that we are paying now'. A trade union activist (name withheld) made an important point. He said that the bribes that most vendors pay are completely unaccounted for money. The municipality and the police who collect this money do not turn it over to the government. It goes in the pockets of the officials involved. Legalising the vendors would mean the loss of this sum to the corrupt officials. But bribes can be avoided, and both parties involved, that is, the government and the vendors, can benefit. If the government issues business licences to the vendors and legalises their trade, they will be ready to pay some amount directly to the government in tax, instead of paying bribes. This will enable the government to increase its revenue, and the street vendors will also get legitimised, which will solve many of their problems, including access to formal credit. Street vendors prefer the security that comes with legalisation and are even willing to pay taxes or registration fees (as *pavti*) to benefit from legality. In the current scenario, in the absence of social security and formal credit arrangements they face a competitive disadvantage and have to take care of themselves and their business on their own.

Almost 70 per cent of the vendors said that they suffer from threats of evictions, and actual evictions have occurred up to three times per year. During the raids, vendors' goods are confiscated and almost 70 per cent of vendors reported that at times the goods are returned damaged or are not in entirety. Vendors have tried to reconcile themselves to this situation given the irregular nature of their trade. Their lack of effective unionisation makes them even more vulnerable to exploitation, since it becomes easier for the authorities to evict them if they are dispersed. The aspect of unionisation and its role in vending will be highlighted in detail in Chapter 5. Unionisation provides vendors with a platform by which they can unite to express their demands and press for their rights. Despite having a weak representation of street vendors in unions, some success stories are discussed in the succeeding chapter, including the reasons for poor representation and challenges faced by vendors. Denial of accessing public space leads to denial of other resources such as formal financial credit. On the other hand, vendors need to pay bribes to different actors in order to survive in this market.

It is clear that there is an unaccountable capital involved in street vending. From the view of capital, around 5–20 per cent of the total daily income of the street vendors goes towards bribes which are completely unaccounted for and unregistered. Hernando de Soto (2000) describes this as 'dead capital'. According to him, illegal payment is loss of capital which is unregistered and unaccounted, especially in the informal sector in the developing countries. He terms this loss as 'dead capital' for the government. By legalising this activity, the state could make this 'dead capital' into 'active capital' which could become a source of revenue collection. One can argue here that property rights can be assigned for occupying public space. Nonetheless assigning property rights will still not solve the problem. This aspect will be critically analysed in the last chapter. Once their right to use public space for an income-generating activity is secured, they can be adequately brought under the sphere of taxation. Taxed money can be a source of revenue for the state as De Soto argued. However, the bribe payment has its impact on vendors' lives, which are discussed in Chapter 4. The questions on how does the bribe payment impact vendors' lives and what kind of exploitation and harassment do civic authorities and local actors involved in it are addressed in the next chapter.

Chapter 4

Livelihood insecurity, uncertainty and vulnerability

Denial of dignity towards street vendors and street vending as a profession begins with the denial of access to public space. In the absence of legal permission from the civic authorities for occupying space, street vendors face constant threats of harassments and eviction. As a result, their work becomes highly insecure and uncertain. Standing (1999) refers to seven different forms of work-related insecurities, namely, labour market insecurity, employment insecurity, job insecurity, work insecurity, skill reproduction insecurity, income insecurity and representation insecurity. I believe that all these work-related insecurities can lead to livelihood insecurity. This is the larger issue encompassing all other insecurities and uncertainty which are resulting from the way vendors operate their business. In this context, different forms of harassments, eviction, insecurity and uncertainty and how street vendors become vulnerable at the workplace have been focused in this chapter. Additionally, competition at the marketplace and prolonged working hours are presented. Thus long working hours, insecurity and uncertainty and their impacts on their lives have been illustrated in this chapter. There is an acute lack of dignity in their working lives and hence they preferred to hide their 'occupational identity' before their friends and relatives. There were a few cases in which acute lack of dignity was noticeable. One vendor (from Mumbai) who had a vending stall in Vile Parle but resided and stored products in Jogeshwari talked about difficulties of being a female vendor during her daughter's marriage. Her relatives also stopped contacting when they came to know about her profession. Let us begin discussing the working conditions of street vendors.

Conditions at work

Daily working hours

One of the important factors to consider for understanding the working conditions is working hours in a day. On an average, vendors' work hours range from eight to twelve hours per day (see Table 4.1). We can now turn to discussing the number of hours that the vendors spent on vending. Most of the vendors in these cities said that the longer number of hours they worked would in turn mean more income. Hence we find that in most cases, vendors work more from eight to twelve hours a day. This does not include another important aspect, namely, cleaning of goods before displaying them up for sale. In the case of vegetables, this exercise is extremely important as very few clients would prefer to buy unwashed vegetables. Hence, the number of working hours increases because the cleaning time ranges from one to four hours a day. Those who vend for five to ten hours constitute 82 per cent in Bengaluru. Of

Table 4.1 Daily working hours

City	Working hours per day					Total
	2–5	*5–10*	*10–12*	*12–15*	*15–18*	
Bengaluru	8 (4.0)	165 (82.5)	24 (12.0)	3 (1.5)	0 (0)	200 (100)
Bhubaneswar	10 (5.0)	15 (7.5)	50 (25.0)	109 (54.5)	16 (8.0)	200 (100)
Delhi	8 (4.0)	172 (86.0)	17 (8.5)	3 (1.5)	0 (0)	200 (100)
Hyderabad	2 (1.0)	172 (86.0)	24 (12.0)	1 (0.5)	1 (0.5)	200 (100)
Imphal	6 (3.0)	99 (49.5)	62 (31.0)	33 (16.5)	0 (0)	200 (100)
Indore	3 (1.5)	39 (19.5)	99 (49.5)	55 (27.5)	4 (2.0)	200 (100)
Jaipur	2 (1.0)	146 (73.0)	33 (16.5)	19 (9.5)	0 (0)	200 (100)
Lucknow	2 (1.0)	195 (97.5)	3 (1.5)	0 (0)	0 (0)	200 (100)
Mumbai	15 (7.5)	92 (46.0)	75 (37.5)	13 (6.5)	5 (2.5)	200 (100)
Patna	168 (84.0)	20 (10.0)	3 (1.5)	8 (4.0)	1 (0.5)	200 (100)
Total	224 (11.2)	1,115 (55.8)	390 (19.5)	244 (12.2)	27 (1.4)	2,000 (100)

Source: Computed by the author, based on field survey conducted in 2009–10.

Note: Figures within parenthesis indicate percentage in share.

these, 85 per cent spend around two hours in cleaning their goods. Hence even those working four to eight hours a day have to spend at least two hours in cleaning their wares. In Bhubaneswar, we find that 54.5 per cent of vendors work for more than twelve hours a day plus two hours in cleaning. So each vendor spends approximately between twelve and fifteen hours a day. In Delhi too, 86 per cent of the vendors spend between five and ten hours plus two hours for cleaning and display. In Hyderabad, 86 per cent of the vendors spend five to ten hours and in Imphal, 49 per cent of the vendors spend five to ten hours while another 31 per cent spend ten to twelve hours. The case of Imphal is especially striking, because almost all vendors are women. In other cities, we found that women workers work less than the males because they are engaged in other activities at home which include cleaning, cooking and childcare. Hence their income too is lower than that of men. The case of Imphal is particularly pathetic because these women spend between ten and fourteen hours a day for their work (including two hours for cleaning their goods). We have also mentioned earlier that most of the women prefer to store their goods at home. This constitutes additional time spent on transport. Women could take up such strenuous and time-consuming activities only if they are extremely hard-pressed for gainful employment. In Indore and Mumbai, 73 per cent and 46 per cent of street vendors, respectively, work five to ten hours a day and another two hours may be added for cleaning. In other cities such as Lucknow, 97 per cent of the vendors work shorter hours, between five and ten hours along with two hours for cleaning the products. In Patna, 86 per cent of vendors spend less than five hours for vending but the time taken for preparation may be longer.

Street vendors are found to work long hours and the average working hours for most vendors varies from eight to twelve hours per day. Compared to the long working hours, the amount earned is a lot less and most importantly, even by extending their hours of work, vendors are not able to raise their income sufficiently. Vendors work from early mornings to late evening, sometimes even late at night. Vendors who sell perishable items such as vegetables, fruits and cooked food have high profit margins. At the same time, however, the working conditions of these vendors, especially vegetable vendors, are miserable. Most of the vegetable vendors are women, because this kind of vending requires very low level of investment in comparison to the other types. The activity begins as early as 4:30 a.m. and ends as late as midnight. Vegetable vendors work from 5:00 a.m. till 12 midnight, and they work every single day of the year.

Working hours and uncertainty due to competition

The number of street vendors has been increasing continuously across cities. This is mainly because vending does not require any skill, formal education or high capital investment. The rise in number of vendors has led to the spilling over of vending activities in certain areas which were earlier unoccupied. Limited space and rising numbers of vendors have resulted in competition over the limited area, and concurrently the work. This competition has affected vendors' survival strategies as well.

Despite the long hours that street vendors have to work to stay afloat, they are unable to raise their income to sufficient levels. Personal spaces have also reduced. Long hours of work affect their health and well-being. The total vending space has been impinged further due to builders' lobbies and the evictions undertaken by civic authorities coupled with the restriction over their movement in certain areas. Some vendors resort to competitive price cutting to attract customers and use other advertising strategies to sell their wares and increase their sales volume. At times, they sell their products at the cost price.

The competition among street vendors has been steadily rising with their growing numbers. Vendors have been forced to evolve better and newer methods to face competitiveness in the market, which forces them to seek the economies of scale. Market traders have realised that scaling up their business helps them to stay competitive and to maximise profits. Increased competition takes its toll on the vendors' health and well-being because they increase their working hours to increase income. The following case (see Box 4.1) depicts the reason behind such competition and condition due to this competition.

Box 4.1 Competition among vendors at the workplace

Ramesh Gupta who is in his early seventies is illiterate. He lives and works in Dadar (Mumbai) and has to support a family of five. He is a vegetable seller. He migrated from Uttar Pradesh sixty years ago. He started street vending when he was 12 and has continued it ever since then. His income level is low.

He reminisces about the days of his early entry to this profession, when the situation was completely different. There were few persons who were in this business. There was no competition and overcrowding in this activity. The income that he earned sufficed for him and his family. As days passed, tougher times crept in. Since there was a serious shortfall in the demand for and supply of formal sector jobs, a considerable number of people resorted to this activity for earning money. This profession too has seen massive expansion in terms of numbers and types of activities.

Due to massive overcrowding, his personal space at work has reduced and increasing number of entrants in the trade means that the profit margin also has reduced considerably. Initially it was not difficult to eke out a living from this profession. Now the situation is completely different. This old and feeble man has to work almost ten hours a day to earn that depleted amount in income. He explained the situation in his own word: 'I have been in this activity since I was 12 years old. I have spent 60 years in this area. We were only 10 on this road and now we are more than 1,000. Our total space is the same. Only our personal space has been reduced. I have noticed that the profit margin has decreased compared to what it used to be. Competition has increased. I used to spend 5 hours a day but now I spend 9–10 hours to survive'.

Source: Based on fieldwork conducted in 2010–11.

Conditions before visiting wholesale markets

The severe work schedules have a direct effect on the lives of vendors who have to visit the wholesale market at midnight to procure their goods on time. Most of them have to leave very early and reach home only at night and again leave the next day for the same work. These vendors hardly have time for sleep or family life. The lack of a proper time to sleep and constant struggle to earn affect their health severely but vendors in most cases are left with little choices but to stick to their tedious routine.

Safety and insecurity of work

The existence of street vendors is not only about a section of poor people trying to earn a livelihood in the informal sector, but also about the provision of valuable services to the urban population. According to Article 39 (a) of the Indian Constitution, 'any citizens, men and women, have equal right to an adequate means of livelihood' (NCEUS 2006: 10). However, the ground reality is that street vendors are by and large considered unlawful entities and eyesores, and are consequently subject to constant harassment by the local police as well as the municipal authorities. This is usually seen to result in a concomitant financial burden of bribes to smoothen the path of their daily vending beat. Non-legalisation is the main problem of this occupation and all vendors were found to be operating without licences which leave their job uncertain and insecure. The lack of legal recognition for the activity and constant fear of eviction and including threats of impending evictions impose constant psychological pressures on the vendors.

As far as workplace is concerned, vendors suffer from their personal insecurity and fear of theft of goods since it is still dark when they come to the marketplace. The prolonged duration of work severely affects them. In case of female vendors, in addition to vending activities, they perform all their household chores, including cooking for the family members, washing, cleaning and so forth, before going to their vending stall or even after coming back home. Long working hours also imply that they have very little time to attend to the needs of their children and very little time to rest or to relax. Street vending is often carried out in busy market places under direct sunshine and amidst lot of sound and air pollution. As a result they often suffer from illnesses like hyperacidity, high blood pressure or migraines that many vendors have stated. In spite of working for so long, they do not earn sufficiently to meet all of their families' requirements and have to resort to frequent borrowing. The increase in earnings is not commensurate with the long working hours. Besides, vendors have to be mindful of competition. Competition for limited space has led the vendors to work harder and longer to eke out a living. The following case (see Box 4.2) explains the general life of a woman vendor from dawn to dusk who is still unable to earn sufficiently as to free herself and her family from the clutches of poverty.

Box 4.2 Insecurity and uncertainty of income faced by female vendors

Uma, 52, sells fruits at Dadar (Mumbai). She began vending fruits when she was 22 years old. Born and brought up in Dadar, Mumbai, she has been in this business for over thirty years now. Her husband is sick. She earns Rs 15,000 per month and her household expenditure is Rs 9,010 per month. The expenditure includes items such as food, house rent and medicines for her husband and her mother-in law, education expenses for her children, provisioning for children's entertainment and the rest of the amount goes into savings. When somebody in her family falls ill it puts considerable pressure on her and she is forced to approach the moneylender who charges exorbitant rates of interest. She has to support six people and meet all of their requirements. Women like her constitute the most vulnerable section of this class since they are subject to various kinds of harassment both in their personal and professional lives. Excerpts from her interview: 'My husband is ill and cannot work. As the sole earning member of my family, I need to work hard for long hours to sustain myself and my family. The recent hike in the process of essential items including food and medicines has led to an increase in my household expenditure, whereas my income has not risen proportionately. I suffer a lot due to the uncertainties of the profession and obligations of the family.'

Source: Based on fieldwork conducted in 2010–11.

Gender differences in work

The quantity of goods sold by female vendors is less compared to the males. They feel insecure about going to the marketplace at early hours of the dawn or even at dusk. It was seen that the investment of female vendors was typically less than that of males and therefore the daily income pattern showed that the female vendors typically earned less than their male counterparts. This is because of the types of products that they sold. Female vendors typically sell those items which require low capital investment, only a working capital, whereas male vendors sell items requiring relatively larger capital and investment. This gender bias is reflected in the sale of goods such as leather-made products and electronic goods. The goods which are expensive have been treated as sophisticated products. When male vendors were asked as to why female vendors generally avoided selling these items, the male vendors reported that 'they (the women) lack technical knowledge and experience of selling these sophisticated items'. On the other hand, when female vendors were asked the same question, they (females) stated that it was due to the lack of savings to invest in these types of products. Thus the lack of funds is the main factor that restricts investment in these types of products. When husbands of the female vendors are involved in the vending business too, other problems developed. The total amount of money being limited, the amount got divided between two separate businesses. It is obvious that the female vendors invested a lesser amount while the husbands' business got priority. Another reason why the women are found to earn less is because they divide their work time between vending, childcare and household chores. When taken into account the time spent for cooking and attending to children, the females are found to work nearly eighteen to twenty hours per day. It is noticed that women usually bring their children to the vending place. This created diversion of attention and less sale, thereby resulting in less income. However, their male counterparts devoted comparatively more time and attention to income-earning opportunities. Let us explain the following case (see Box 4.3) which illustrates the working conditions of a woman vendor in Mumbai.

Box 4.3 Working conditions of a woman vendor

Chandra Bala, 51, is a female vendor selling vegetables on a small vending stall in Kandivali (Mumbai). She migrated from a village in UP thirty years ago. She is a Hindu and belongs to the general category. Illiterate, she joined this activity when she was 21 years old. She earns Rs 9,000 per month, close to her place of residence in Borivali with eight family members. Her household expenditure always exceeds her income and she bridges the gap by borrowing some amount to cover her expenses. The reason for her high expenditure is her large family. She is a widow and needs to work hard to support the family.

She faces a tough time since the costs of procurement and transportation have gone up severely while her income has remained stagnant. She is required to look after her children and perform all the household chores without any help. She is uncertain about the future since this job does not fetch her enough money to meet all her family's requirements. She described her day thus: 'I wake up around 4 o'clock in the morning, then go to the wholesale market to collect the vegetables. I clean the vegetables for two to three hours and I keep the vegetables in the market where I sit. I come back home and cook for my children and then again go to the market and start the activity. When I come back home, it is already midnight. I work for the whole year. If I don't work for one day, my children will sleep without meals, since I am the only breadwinner in my family.'

Source: Based on fieldwork conducted in 2010–11.

Financial debt and its impact

Vending is based on daily transaction and it requires capital to start the activity. They start their business either from their own savings or depending on other informal sources such as moneylenders, friends, relatives and wholesalers. Interestingly about 50 per cent of vendors manage by their own savings. As mentioned earlier, some vendors access credit at exorbitant rates of interest from mainly moneylenders and wholesalers. As a result, vendors fall into debt trap which is perpetual and chronic in nature.

Dependency on informal sources

Moneylenders and wholesalers are the predominant actors in providing credit to street vendors. They set up their own rules and regulations for lending money. They also maintain their records and provide an individual copy of loan transaction to each vendor. They have their own ways of running the business and often provide loans through various schemes. Mode of interest payment leads to exploitation and vulnerability. Therefore, it is interesting to look into their modes of operations and how the informal loan market operates. It is evident that personal trust and norms govern the lending and borrowing activities (instead of collaterals and security) but high rates of interest payment lead to debt traps.

Mode of operation of moneylenders

Moneylenders formulate their own schemes, rules and regulations of lending money and collection process. There are mainly four different types of loan schemes prevalent. These schemes are based on the daily repayment method and loans are provided for 33 days, 66 days, 100 days and 200 days. From the data collected during this study, one common thing noticed among moneylenders is that they prefer to lend money on a day-to-day basis. Additionally, they prefer to provide short-term loans of small amounts because it has a 100 per cent recovery rate and the rate of return is higher if they lend on a day-to-day basis. Moreover, the vendors are under constant supervision and pressure to repay the money on time. Moneylenders ply their business and interestingly similar schemes of informal credit provided by them [moneylenders] are found not only in one city but across cities. Two different cases of day loan systems are discussed below (Boxes 4.4 and 4.5):

Box 4.4 33-day loan scheme provided by moneylenders

Laxmi is a 55-year-old woman selling vegetables in Chembur (Mumbai). She is Hindu, belongs to the general caste and is illiterate. She is married with eight dependent members in the family. She had migrated from Chennai in Tamil Nadu almost fifty years ago and has been in this business for forty-five years. Her daily earnings are around Rs 300. Her household income together with that of her husband is around Rs 12,000 a month and her monthly household expenditure is Rs 11,500.

She wanted to borrow a sum of Rs 6,000 for 33 days under the Rs 200-per-day scheme. At the time of borrowing, she was informed that the rate of interest is 10 per cent for 33 days. This was even recorded. Moneylenders maintain their records and copies of the record of such calculations were seen during the field work of this study.

Analysing the situation, it was found that Laxmi actually got a loan of Rs 5,500 only, as opposed to Rs 6,000. She had to pay a processing fee of Rs 500. She also had to pay Rs 100 while closing the amount which was mandatory. Therefore, she had to pay Rs 6,700 (33 x 200 + 100) to the moneylender against an actual amount of Rs 5,500. The moneylender extorted Rs 1,200 from her as interest. Thus, if we calculate the actual rate of interest, it was 22 per cent per month, as opposed to 10 per cent previously stated by the moneylenders.

Source: Based on fieldwork conducted in 2011–12.

Box 4.5 100-day repayment scheme offered by moneylenders in Hyderabad

Apart from moneylenders, informal financial groups which are not registered as credit agencies also operate in Hyderabad. A major part of credit borrowed by vendors is through moneylenders. There are two different patterns of moneylending. Among these, one is the 100-day scheme. In this case, if the moneylender lends a vendor Rs 10,000 for 100 days at the rate of 10 per cent per month, here the vendor has to return Rs 12,000 at the end of the 100-day period.

Likewise in Mumbai, the vendor gets Rs 9,500 in hand because Rs 500 goes towards processing fees and other formalities in Hyderabad. One may be surprised to notice how these informal mechanisms are similar across cities. This is an important part of transaction where the vendors are required to pay a significant amount of money as hidden transaction cost for the sum borrowed. In other words, the vendor has to pay Rs 2,500 for the sum borrowed.

Source: Based on fieldwork conducted in 2011–12.

Mode of operation of wholesalers

About 7 per cent of the total vendors take credit from wholesalers or suppliers of their products. They provide two different types of loans, one on a monthly 10–15 per cent rate of interest if vendors require loans for social security or any other emergency purposes. Another loan is provided for their business purpose, wherein wholesalers do not charge any rate of interest in cash. This is more complex, and, in such cases, vendors often end up paying more than the actual amount. An example will elaborate on the second type of loan. Vendors get products from the wholesalers on day-to-day transaction basis. Sometimes, wholesalers provide a short-term loan for vendors' business and do not charge any rate of interest. In this way, trust-based relationship is created between suppliers and vendors. Vendors are always in need of credit for their business or other purposes. When vendors require a large amount of products for investing in their business, wholesalers often provide such loans but they impose an extra 15–20 per cent on the products. This happens during festival seasons. Therefore, vendors also do not think of the amount that they are getting from wholesalers. Importantly, vendors prefer to get credit or loan from wholesalers than moneylenders. They believe that their relationship with wholesalers is on a day-to-day basis and if they get loans from wholesalers, this relationship will get stronger and wholesalers will even stand by whenever they require loans. Some of the vendors think the same way for moneylenders.

Borrowing for non-income-generating purposes

Vendors are not recognised as legal entities in the market and their businesses are deemed 'illegal'; the state does not have any direct social security programmes for them and they often borrow to meet their social security requirements. There are broadly two purposes – economic and non-economic – on which vendors borrow money. Street vendors mainly borrow money for their business activity across cities in India (Bhowmik & Saha 2013) but except Mumbai. In Mumbai, vendors frequently borrow for social security. Mumbai also presents an example where moneylenders are engaged in usurious practices unlike other cities in India. This is due to high demand for loans and absence of any other parallel sources of finance (ibid.). However, borrowing money at usurious rates of interest for non-income-generating purposes from informal sources such as moneylenders and wholesalers eventually leads vendors into a debt trap. The amount and purpose of borrowing have an implication in the perpetual debt trap situation for street vendors. The informal credit has important effects upon the lives of street vendors.

Vendors stated that they often fell into a debt trap. This may be because of their borrowing for non-income-generating activities such as social security and high amount of deposit for house rent (especially in Delhi, Mumbai and Bengaluru). However, the amount and frequency of borrowing for social security were observed to be more for other purposes such as deposit for house rent and economic activities. As mentioned earlier, the study revealed that about 82 per cent of vendors borrowed for their business activities in fifteen major cities of India (ibid.). On the contrary, the present study revealed that vendors borrowed mainly for social security in Mumbai. Vendors that do not avail any institutional or non-institutional benefits manage it through their savings or borrow from their close relatives, who are considered internal sources, who do not charge interest. The rest avail social security either from the micro-insurance schemes through the trade unions or by borrowing at high rates of interest from informal lenders such as wholesalers, moneylenders or even relatives. These constitute the external sources for social security. In Mumbai, it is seen that a majority of the street vendors (56 per cent) kept their savings in banks and cooperatives or borrowed from relatives to support themselves in situations of crises, while 11.75 per cent used their membership in trade unions for credit (Saha 2011a). A substantial number of vendors (32 per cent) resorted to borrowing at high interest rates in times of crises (ibid.). Interestingly, this assessment reveals that there is a growing concern among many vendors that they need to find their own ways to finance themselves in their times of need.

Social security providers

There are two principal external sources of social security: trade unions and informal sources. Unions mainly provide micro-insurance services, a part of Janshree Bima Yojana (JBY) scheme. Informal sources consist of wholesalers, moneylenders and relatives who provide financial support for social security. Among these three sources, moneylenders are the most important and this study showed that 39 per cent of vendors took loans from them for social security as well as business. Wholesalers and relatives play an important role in this regard. The trend for males and females was observed to be similar. Around 42 per cent of males and 37 per cent of females depended on moneylenders for social security (Saha 2011a).

Nature of debt trap

Loans taken for social security purposes include financial exigencies arising out of ill health, accidents, marriages, death of the income-earner and so on. The amounts vary depending on the purpose they serve. A few different cases have been highlighted to show the severity associated with indebtedness of the vendors owing to informal borrowings. The case depicted in Box 4.6 brings out a daily credit scheme and the exorbitant interest charged by the lenders. This case also highlights a situation of debt trap due to borrowing for social security. A case illustrated in Box 4.7 discusses how generations are trapped in the chain of loans and its consequences. The case discussed in Box 4.9 brings out how 'multiple loans' result in debt traps. Moneylenders also prefer to provide short-term loans of small amounts because it has a 100 per cent recovery rate and the rate of return is higher if they lend on a day-to-day basis.

Box 4.6 Debt trap due to borrowing for social security

A female vendor (Mumbai) borrowed Rs 200,000 for her husband's operation in 2001 in Chennai. She was forced to borrow from three different sources: moneylenders, fellow vendors and a bank at an interest rate of 5 per cent per month. So far, she has managed to repay half the amount, i.e. Rs 100,000, and now she has to repay the other half at 3 per cent per month. She has been allowed this reduction in interest rate since she has already repaid half the amount. Now she is paying almost Rs 3,000 per month.

In addition to this, she had borrowed an amount of Rs 100,000 at 5 per cent per month for her father's poor health. She sold their land and paid Rs 50,000. Now she is paying an interest rate of 2 per cent per month as interest on the remaining Rs 50,000. In addition to these two loans, she had borrowed Rs 150,000 at an interest rate of 1 per cent per month from the bank for her children's education three years ago. Now she is paying Rs 1,500 per month as interest towards this loan. Therefore, altogether she is paying Rs 5,500 per month as interest for her various loans. Evidently, all the loans were for purposes of social security.

She pays interest to all the lenders on time. Sometimes she is able to do so only after borrowing from others. The interest on short-term private loan is higher than long-term loans. Thus, she is a victim of the chain of debts. During this study, she revealed that local moneylenders readily give loans to women vendors since they always pay back along with the interest amount on time. When asked about her survival strategy, she smiled innocently and said: 'It is a part of my business and my life, there is no choice but to continue with the struggle'.

Source: Based on fieldwork conducted in 2011–12.

Multiple debt traps

It is seen that when a loan is taken from a moneylender at an exorbitant rate of interest, not only the individual but also his/her next generation gets trapped in the chain of debts. The following case (see Box 4.7) highlights such a situation.

Box 4.7 Perpetual debt trap situation

Kamlesh is a 24-year-old who sells electronics goods, residing in Mahim (Mumbai). He runs his stall in Dadar and has been in this business for ten years. Hindu by religion and belonging to the general category, he had just been able to complete his primary education when he was forced to join the business. Married with a family of six, this vendor originally hails from Uttar Pradesh and had migrated to Mumbai fifteen years ago along with his family. His monthly income is about

Rs 12,000, while his expenditures total Rs 9,000 per month. His savings are paltry. He is a member of a union.

This young man's father had taken a loan from a money-lender at a high interest rate which he was unable to pay back during his lifetime. As a consequence, the son is now obligated to repay the loan along with the interest amount to the mon-eylender. Hence, Kamlesh is financially overburdened with the repayment of the loan and meeting his family's requirements. As he narrates, 'My father had taken money for this (vending) activity. After his death, I am still paying the rate of interest. I am in a debt-trap situation'.

Source: Based on fieldwork conducted in 2010–11.

Women and loan

Women vendors are engaged in this occupation either to support their husbands and family or due to widowhood. However, they have less capital to start as well as continue the operation of their businesses. Although female vendors are engaged in vending activity which requires less capital, they are still pushed to borrow money. Neither they get money from their husband nor do they have savings to start the business. On the other hand, moneylenders and wholesalers prefer to lend to female vendors rather than their male counterparts. The reason is that the women vendors are very good at repaying loans. They never fail to pay back the dues in time. Many female vendors said they would prefer to go hungry than be a defaulter. This characteristic of female street vendors makes them prone to exploitation by moneylenders. The rate of recovery of the loan is higher in the case of female vendors than male vendors. However, lenders charge same amount of interest rates from female vendors. Notwithstanding, moneylenders provide loans to female vendors at low rates of interest for the first loan or the first instal-ment of the loan to attract them. Thereafter, moneylenders charge higher amounts with each subsequent loan or instalment of the loan. As a result, female vendors fall into a 'multi-debt-trap'. The following two cases (see Boxes 4.8 and 4.9) highlight how these vendors are vulnerable to exploitation when emergency strikes and they are forced to borrow. These cases also show the sincerity and commitment of female vendors towards the repayment of loan.

Box 4.8 Emergency requirement of credit

Poonam sells vegetables in Chembur (Mumbai). Once her son was critically ill and required hospitalisation; therefore, she borrowed Rs 5,000 from a wholesaler at a monthly interest rate of 2 per cent. She was given three months to pay back her loan. She paid interest for three months. One day the wholesaler demanded the money back immediately, before the completion of three months, because he needed it for some emergency. Therefore, she had to repay the amount that she had borrowed, which forced her to borrow Rs 3,000 overnight from another moneylender at a monthly interest rate of 3 per cent.

Source: Based on fieldwork conducted in 2010–11.

Box 4.9 Multiple debt trap for a woman

Shova is a vegetable and fruit seller in Chembur (Mumbai). She took a loan of Rs 100,000 for the purpose of building a house. She borrowed money from a moneylender at a monthly interest rate of 2 per cent. No conditions for repayment were set. She paid Rs 2,000 monthly for one year and then stopped for three months because she had to pay her son's school fees. When the moneylender started pressurising her to pay, she got scared and paid Rs 6,000 immediately. Since she had no savings, she had to take loan from another moneylender at a monthly interest rate of 5 per cent to repay the first moneylender. She repaid Rs 6,000 to the second moneylender, but is still paying her debt to the first moneylender.

Source: Based on fieldwork conducted in 2010–11.

Moneylenders and tactics of their business

It is seen in all the cities that moneylenders play an important role and create another level of informality. The case of Kapoorchand Gupta's murder case has already been introduced. In the context of moneylending business, this case can be reiterated which shows that moneylenders can become the rulers of the loan market in the absence of alternative sources of credit. The market is monopolised by moneylenders and hence they exercise an extremely strong influence and can go to any length to extract their interests/profits. The murder of Kapoorchand Gupta at the hands of two moneylenders highlights how moneylenders can act if anyone interferes in their businesses.

The accused made a statement which showed that he was both personally (because Gupta had caused him a loss of over 40 lakhs) and professionally (Gupta was a constant threat to his moneylending business and had to be eliminated) unhappy with Mr Gupta. The accused hawkers who are also moneylenders have stalls near Kandivali station in Mumbai. One is a native of Maharashtra (Nalasopara); the other vendor is a person from Uttar Pradesh (Ghaziabad) and has been staying in Mumbai for seven years.

Mr Gupta, as the union secretary, was deeply involved in the fights of hawkers especially against high-interest-charging moneylenders. This was what apparently led to his murder. The death also brings out the harsh realities in the moneylending business. These cases have emerged from the discussions with the union members and other street vendors from Kandivali vegetable markets. The following are some of the tactics of the moneylenders that they adopt while plying their lending business:

1   The case of Mr Raghukar Sudama Gaud (Kandivali, Mumbai) can be illustrated here to show how moneylenders cheat vendors. Mr Raghukar Sudama Gaud, a resident of Mathuradas Road, borrowed an amount of Rs 200,000 from Shiv Prasad Kesari (one of the accused) in early 2011 at 10 per cent monthly rate of interest. However, he could not continue paying the monthly rate of interest. Due to this, Mr Kesari demanded a total amount of Rs 400,000 (including principal and total rate of interest) from Mr Raghukar Sudama Gaud which he had to pay back by end of September 2012. Needless to say, Mr Gaud could not pay. In order to retrieve the amount, Mr Kesari demanded Mr Gaud's house in his name which was denied by Mr Gaud. One evening, Mr Kesari invited Mr Gaud for drinks and dinner, and allegedly took Mr Gaud's thumb impression (as Gaud was illiterate) on a paper which stated that Mr Gaud had sold out his house to Mr Kesari against Rs 1,000,000.

Next morning, when Mr Gaud realised what had happened, he approached Mr Kapoorchand Gupta. Mr Gupta took him to the police and filed a case against Mr Kesari and he was arrested. This is just one example. According to street vendors and union leaders, such incidents happen almost every day in Mumbai and perhaps in all the cities across India.

2   In many instances, when vendors are unable to pay back the loan amount, the money is retrieved by acquiring the spaces where stalls exist (although there are no papers or legal documents stating the owner's name). If hawkers are unable to pay the rate of interest and the principal amount to the moneylenders, they have to hand over their place to the moneylenders, and the moneylenders sell out that place to other vendors. Therefore, although no ownership rights exist over the space, moneylenders make business from it and generate profits. This shows that while one section (poor and marginal street vendors) is grossly exploited due to the informality, another section (moneylenders) significantly benefits from it. In the past, Mr Gupta had intervened several times in situations like these. In addition, Mr Gupta interfered with moneylenders many times in their calculation of rate of interest and identified the loophole in calculation and intentional errors made by the moneylenders in it.

3   Moneylenders generally tend to target small and marginal vendors with low capital bases and whose businesses are small and tend to rely more on borrowing. Moneylenders know that these street vendors will not be able to pay back the loan easily within the stipulated time. Therefore, these vendors can be exploited and be perpetually debt-trapped. Due to the absence of other credit sources, vendors borrow credit from moneylenders which is easy to access. Vendors do not realise this trap situation and even call lenders their 'saviours' and 'godfathers' or as a 'last resort'. A case narration has been highlighted to depict this situation.

A fruit vendor (name withheld) in Kandivali approached a local moneylender for a loan of Rs 10,000 for business. The moneylender readily gave him a loan of Rs 10,000 at 10 per cent monthly rate of interest. But he actually gave the vendor an amount of Rs 9,000 after deducting Rs 1,000 as 'transaction cost'. According to the vendor, the moneylender emotionally supported him. The vendor also revealed that the moneylender asked him to approach him without any hesitations in future whenever he needed money. The lender further said that since he had loaned money to the vendor, the lender should now be treated as a 'friend' and that the vendor should invite him for dinner and drinks. Subsequently they went to a local bar and had drinks together. The vendor had to pay the bill of Rs 1,200. Finally the amount that was available to the vendor for investing was Rs 7,800 or less. However, the interest that he has to pay is on the loan amount of Rs 10,000. Also, the payment will be made on a daily basis at a flat rate of interest. This means the total payment of rate of interest will be much higher than actual calculated amount.

Bribe payment and its impact

Nearly 39 per cent of the vendors pay 5–10 per cent of their monthly income as bribes. Around 21 per cent of the total vendors pay 10–25 per cent of their income as bribes. Vendors understand the need to 'replace' bribes with 'taxes' and recognise the state's role in doing so, which could save them the daily harassments they face at the marketplace. The issue of harassment faced by vendors at the workplace is an important one. The following two cases illustrate impoverishment due to bribe payment (see Box 4.10) and the extent and impact of harassment faced by vendors (see Box 4.11). However, the degree of associated harassments varies from area to area and vendor to vendor.

Box 4.10 Impoverishment due to bribe payment

Mangesh Karande (name changed), 37, is an unmarried vendor residing in Mahim (Mumbai). He sells garments in Dadar. Hindu by religion, he belongs to the Scheduled Caste (SC) category. He is illiterate and has been a vendor for over twenty years. He earns Rs 4,500 per month, while his household income is Rs 7,500. His household expenditure is Rs 7,000 per month.

He attributes his impoverishment to the bribes he is forced to pay. A large portion (Rs 50 per day as he sits near the main road) of his income goes towards the payment of bribes to the local authorities. Vendors like him are desperate for government regulation. On the one hand, they suffer from the lack of a proper space for business and on the other, they have to pay a sizeable portion of their income as bribes to the authorities. He states that people like him are willing to pay double the amount of bribes as taxes to the government. He explains his situation thus: 'We would like to pay the amount as taxes instead of bribes for ours . . . space. We would even love to pay double the amount that we are paying now.'

Source: Based on fieldwork conducted in 2010–11.

Box 4.11 Harassment through bribes

Surendra Patil (name changed) is a 55-year-old garment seller in Dadar. He is Hindu by religion and belongs to 'general' caste category. He is illiterate. He is from Mumbai and has been in this business for over twenty-five years. He is married and there are five members in his family who are entirely dependent on him.

Surendra states that apart from regular problems of credit and unsuitable job environment, there have been growing incidences of harassment at the workplace. They are unduly affected because of the casual nature of their job, in addition to the constant threats of eviction and bribe payments. Surendra says that bribe-seeking instances have gone up in the last three to four years which are seriously hampering his productivity, efficiency, income and consequently their standard of living. The government is apathetic to their situation.

Source: Based on fieldwork conducted in 2010–11.

Gender and bribe payment

Although vendors, irrespective of whether they are male or female, face threats of eviction and are harassed regularly, the behaviour meted out to female vendors can best be termed 'abusive'. However, there are also a few among them who also exchange lewd comments and remarks with the municipality and the police whenever any argument breaks out among them; however, the majority suffer

meekly. Female vendors selling vegetables, fruits, flowers and gar-
lands have small stalls and they easily manage to run away whenever they spot municipality officials in the market. Compared to
female vendors, male vendors are found to have a slightly better
relationship with the police because they are better at negotiating to
reach a workable solution with regard to bribe payments.

Female vendors also face specific challenges such as the difficulty
of dealing with male dominance at the workplace. The attitude
of the police officials is softer towards female vendors, especially
towards those who sell less and are in the most miserable conditions. Same officials do not even take bribe from such female vendors sometimes. This situation, however, varies from place to place.
The attitude of the municipality is completely different. If male vendors go to the municipality office after their goods are confiscated,
they are always treated better than female vendors. Besides, female
vendors seldom enjoy dignity at their workplace.

Attitude of the municipal officials

Attitude of the municipal officials towards street vendors needs to
be discussed. An interesting case was encountered on the revisiting field during October–November 2013 which was part of the
MCGM project. I along with other researchers went to a field trip
in Dadar (one of the study locations considered under MCGM project). The main purpose of the project was to identify and demar-
cate the principal vending locations and best ways in which vendors
could be regulated. We were accompanied by some MCGM officials in their vehicles. The senior inspector (encroachment) and the
lorry inspector kept calling somebody (perhaps the 'zero number')
saying that vendors need not worry as they would not conduct any
eviction. Nevertheless, as soon as we reached the spot, there would
a commotion among the vendors. The lorry inspector raised his
(only male lorry inspectors get appointed by the MCGM) hand to
pacify vendors, which indicated that vendors need not worry as
there would be no eviction. Soon after getting that indication, vendors would settle down as usual. The lorry inspector turned to us
expressing his gratification over the amount of control and muscu-
lar strength he exercised. The street vendors were constantly in fear
seeing this man approaching and a simple waving of the hand had
the power to subdue their fears. A definite power relationship exists
between civic authorities and vendors.

Conclusion

It has been mentioned in the beginning of this chapter that vending as a profession has had different impacts on the lives of vendors. Some view the effects as 'positive and affirmative' and despite the odds (discussed in Chapters 2 and 3), it does seem to offer the only opportunity to earn a decent livelihood. Despite the vulnerabilities and insecurities associated with this activity, many vendors (more than 65 per cent) opt for vending as an occupation. Distinguished from wage work, street vending provides scope for independency and autonomy at work. Moderate investments can be made and hours of work are flexible. Even the income can be varied. Interestingly, vendors mention that they can make their own decisions. Thus even with a small amount of investment, income can be earned. This income plays a transformational role especially for the female vendors. About 80 per cent of total male vendors stated that vending had transformed their lives, particularly when it came to livelihood. Many female vendors (mainly those who migrated) shared their opinions and experiences. When they (female vendors) used to live in their villages or at homes, they had little idea of the world and how to earn a living. But now, self-dependency has changed their lives and it has also helped to change their perception of the world around them. They realise the value of good health and nutrition and education and they know how to make their children's lives better. They are able to make rational decisions at home and they know how a part of income should be saved up for future contingencies and a part should be reinvested. Even with low levels of education, they know how to deal with customers, bribe collectors and moneylenders. The capability to share the expenditure of the household and increase the cash flow in the household along with husband has instilled in them confidence and a sense of self-worth. They are no longer able to withstand abuse from husbands or in-laws. Vendors rightfully agreed that they can no longer stand the thought of being confined within the home. Their workplace has given them the much needed space to claim and establish their independence. One female vendor stated, 'when we were in village, we could have not imagined coming out from house to work; and now we cannot imagine staying at home'.

Insecurity and uncertainty of working hours, income, harassments and evictions are all pervasive in the lives of vendors. In spite of these, vendors do not fail to recognise the fact that vending as a livelihood has liberating effects upon their lives. Notwithstanding the positive impacts, it stands undenied that vendors face a lot of challenges in plying their trade. Vendors stated that uncertainty and continuous harassments are most important challenges. At every stage of business, they have to negotiate with the state and other stakeholders. It is at this juncture that organising for a common struggle assumes such great importance for these informal workers.

Chapter 5

Negotiations, organisations and collective bargaining

Introduction

The right to collective bargaining is central to the ILO's concept of 'decent work' and is an indispensable part of democratic procedures. The aspect of decent work will be elaborated in Chapter 6. Realising the impact of freedom of association and the right to collective bargaining upon improving the plight of both formal and informal workers, the ILO has made the right to freedom of association an important part of its decent work agenda. The declaration concerning the aims and principles of the ILO, called the 'Declaration of Philadelphia', which has been appended to the Constitution of ILO, reaffirms that freedom of association is essential for sustained progress (Gopalakrishnan 2008). The fundamental right to livelihood is actually promoted by this right. It promotes the right to work with the right to bargain against exploitation. The Preamble to the Constitution of the ILO states that recognising freedom of association among workers would not only lead to their overall welfare but also promote lasting peace among nations all over the world.

ILO clearly stresses its objective to achieve an environment in which adequate opportunities of income and employment are secured and social protection for workers is achieved. The concept has become even more important in the present world of globalisation, and in order to achieve welfare maximisation for all, every member should have the right to participate in the decision-making process so that it is made legitimate and sustainable. Interestingly the right to form associations and organise a joint struggle is so important that it is both covered under their rights at work and is an indispensable component of their social dialogue. Several ILO conventions such as the Freedom of Association and Protection of the Right to Organise Convention, 1948 (No. 87) and the Right to Organise and Collective Bargaining Convention, 1949 (No. 98) are essential components of the social dialogue process (Anker et al. 2003). It means that it is workers' right to form associations to realise other decent working standards. This becomes even more significant for vulnerable and marginalised workers engaged in the informal sector as it ensures their basic rights at work. The bargaining power becomes simpler in the existence of employer–employee relationship. Bargaining remains indeterminate in case of self-employment where this relationship is imperceptible. This holds true in case of street vendors too. Membership-based organisations (MBOs) play an instrumental role in organising workers in both formal and informal sectors. MBOs can be defined as 'those in which the members elect their leaders and which operate on democratic principles that hold the elected officers accountable to the general membership' (Chen et al. 2007: 4). Trade unions, cooperatives, workers committees, savings and credit groups such as self-help groups (SHGs), producer groups and so on are categorised as MBOs (Chen et al. 2007). The democratic governance structures of MBOs are intended to provide both internal accountability (since leaders are elected through democratic process and are accountable) and external legitimacy (ibid.).

As far as trade unions/associations working for street vendors are concerned, Self-Employed Women's Association[1] (SEWA), National Association of Street Vendors of India (NASVI), National Hawkers Federation in India (NHFI) and Nidan are a few among others. They have been working effectively for initiating policy dialogues at the local, regional, state and national levels. The main role of these organisations is to negotiate with local authorities when the vendors are threatened by them.

Self-Employed Women's Association

Self-Employed Women's Association (SEWA), formed in 1972, is a trade union of women who earn their livelihoods by running small businesses. It is the first and the largest trade union in India's informal sector with a strong membership base of 966,139 workers (as of 2008). Addressing the need for capital as the major constraint of its members' business, SEWA Bank was set up in 1974. SEWA helps promote SHGs to access microcredit. SEWA has also promoted NGOs and cooperatives run exclusively by women and catering only to women through which street vendors can access institutional credit (Chen et al. 2007: 14). Their microcredit programmes have been highly successful. Street vendors have used the standard loan from SEWA Bank as investment capital to upgrade their mode of selling but recently, SEWA Bank introduced a special working capital loan exclusively for street vendors, which is called a 'daily loan', where vendors can borrow in the morning at the start of business and repay the loan at the end of the day after close of business.

SEWA has played a significant role in formulating policies and laws. But it also has important role in organising and mobilising vendors at the city level. A case of SEWA Delhi can be highlighted. SEWA Delhi submitted a proposal in the year 2005 to the Municipal Corporation of Delhi (MCD) City zone office to get a market exclusively for women vendors where they can work without harassment. After consistent struggle, SEWA Delhi established a women's market (Mahila Bazaar) at Tagore Road in 2009. Over 200 women vendors from different parts of Delhi vend without facing any harassment. In order to develop it into a model market, SEWA members undertook the task of cleaning, construction and development of the site. A security guard and a cleaner were also appointed, dustbins installed and shades put up to protect the vendors from heat and rain. In addition, the basic facilities of toilet and drinking water were also secured for the women vending in the market. This happened after consultation with the MCD. Women vendors were mobilised for coming to the market through regular meetings and home visits which also worked as a platform to unionise them and address their concerns.

National Association of Street Vendors of India (NASVI)

NASVI,[2] an independent vendor federation and a founding member of the international alliance of street vendor organisations called StreetNet, was set up in India in 1998. The federation's main aim has been to bring together trade unions and cooperatives that represent street vendors so that they [vendors] can carry out their trade smoothly. NASVI has gone a step further and devised social security schemes for its members. It has pressurised the state to implement the national policy for urban street vendors. In 2005,

NASVI adopted a scheme that would provide multiple benefits to its members which included insurance coverage for health, house and property, accidental and natural death, and permanent and partial disability. Members are required to pay an annual premium in the range of Rs 70–100 towards this scheme. NASVI also attempts to provide credit accessibility to street vendors through the promotion of SHGs, cooperatives, trusts, federations and different micro-finance institutions. NASVI has started building direct links between street vendors and those organisations providing financial assistance. NASVI is not only working in one particular city but its members are actively raising their voice for their rights across the cities in India.

Nidan

Another large membership-based organisation is Nidan in Patna. It is a highly successful hawkers' organisation operational in several towns of Bihar. Its group insurance scheme is the hallmark of its many achievements, designed to cover health-care services for street vendors such as hospitalisation costs and life insurance. Initially, Nidan organised several programmes for street vendors to familiarise them with different insurance schemes of the Life Insurance Corporation of India (LIC) and the General Insurance Corporation of India (GIC). Thereafter, it helped its members get enrolled in several insurance groups in Patna and other towns (Bhowmik 2006).

This chapter focuses on the challenges faced and strategies adopted in organising street vendors in India. Against this backdrop, this chapter is based on the discussion and reflections which have been drawn from different organisations' perspectives on how they [organisations] address the issues of vendors on the period between 2008 and 2015 considering both pre- and post-Act situations in Delhi, Kolkata, Mumbai and Guwahati to analyse the role of MBOs in different types of cities in India. We have considered NASVI and NHFI because these two have the largest affiliation with trade unions. Other trade unions and associations who are actively working for street vendors have been considered. Azad Hawkers' Union (affiliated to NASVI), Shahid Bhagat Singh Hawkers' Union and Bombay Hawkers' Union (both are affiliated to NHFI) have been considered in Mumbai. NASVI-affiliated NGOs/unions – Society for Social Transformation and Environment Protection (sSTEP) (an NGO working actively in Guwahati and has a representative in the

TVC) and All Assam Street Vendors' Association (AASVA) – have been considered in Guwahati. Jai Hind Calcutta Hawkers' Union (affiliated to NASVI), Hawker Sangram Committee (affiliated to NHFI) and Kolkata Street Hawkers' Union (KSHU) (affiliated to CITU) have been taken into account in Kolkata.

The union/association activities in mobilising street vendors across cities in India are same. Union activities depend on the nature and types of the problems that the vendors face from the civic authorities (both police and municipal officials). The representation of street vendors at unions is thin across India, primarily because of peculiar and heterogeneous nature of work (Saha 2011b). Working hours for street vendors are long. Most vendors cannot find time to attend meetings or activities organised by the unions (ibid.). While unionisation is not necessarily a solution to their problems, some vendors opined that unionisation has an empowering effect (ibid.). This chapter will elaborate on these issues, though its main intention is not only to explore the reasons behind low unionisation among street vendors but also to highlight the struggles and challenges of unions while organising street vendors. Discussions here are based on interactions with street vendors and key resource persons, the latter of whom are from MBOs, union leaders and current union members. They played an instrumental role in providing vital information on the strategies of organising vendors in every city.

The analysis is based on in-depth interviews with key respondents who are actively involved in MBOs/unions and street vendors from these aforesaid unions. These interviews with key respondents help understand the organisation from the inside because these interviewees are in a position to make decisions for the vendors. As the key respondents were reluctant to disclose their names and information about their organisations, their identities have not been disclosed. Their positions in their organisations and other important aspects from an organisational perspective have nonetheless been mentioned in order to gauge the work they do to promote collective bargaining. These cases helped develop the role of unions, reasons for the success and failure of unionisation and the dynamics of these unions. Notwithstanding, these members are vendors themselves and are presently working towards mobilising the street vendors. They were working as small vendors initially, but over a period of time have become owners of small enterprises, and have even employed a number of wage workers who also carry out the administrative work and other responsibilities in their respective unions. The main aim of these union leaders is to empower street vendors in the process of mobilising them in an organised manner for a common cause. All the members and leaders of the unions stated that it is very easy to work for the vendors as insiders, because as insiders they were able to achieve many objectives. According to them, only insiders can understand the problems associated with street vending and work towards eradicating them while associating with the insiders.

Despite low unionisation among street vendors, MBOs, especially trade unions, have a big role to play in organising vendors against various forms of harassment. Unions mainly play a role in securing the trade of the vendors by ensuring their right to public space utilisation. Some unions follow a participatory mechanism through which vendors try to find solutions to their problems. Unions mainly focus on negotiating with the civic authorities, forming cooperatives for accessing working capital and providing social security and awareness training programmes. The most common form of harassment faced by vendors arises from the rent-seeking activities of the authorities, some intermediate bribe collectors and local leaders.

Statistics on street vendors in Ahmedabad, Bengaluru, Delhi, Imphal, Kolkata, Mumbai and Patna showed that less than 20 per cent of the street vendors are unionised in major cities, whereas in Ahmedabad, 40 per cent of street vendors are unionised under SEWA (Bhowmik 2001). However, it varies from city to city. The ground reality of union membership is different. For instance, about 50 per cent are members of different trade unions in Mumbai. In particular, 53 per cent of male and about 48 per cent of female street vendors are members of different trade unions (Saha 2011a: 450). This is indeed an impressive statistic. In-depth discussions with the street vendors, however, revealed that only 47 street vendors out of 400 are actively involved with union (around 12 per cent of the total sample population) (ibid.). These 47 vendors are actually regular in attending meetings and organising themselves, and are even trying to mobilise other street vendors. Therefore, the question of active participation remains same in other cities across. The rate of unionisation among females is lower than among males; activeness among females is prodigious compared to their counterpart. Trade unions or other MBOs stage protests against civic authorities whenever the authorities do something that goes against the interests of the street vendors. They do not refrain from going to jail, and in any case, they obtain stay orders from the court to temporarily stop the civic authorities.

Union activity

Awareness programmes and union membership

Not all organisations were found to be well organised in terms of their functions and activities. Effective leadership and mobilisation of vendors are easiest and most efficient ways to increase membership. Very few unions were found to be well organised in terms of their functions and activities. This scenario is same across all cities in India. There is a lack of awareness among street vendors about the roles and functions of union, their basic rights and even about the Act. There are a few organisations which are particularly focusing on the awareness. In this regard, among all, Shahid Bhagat Singh Hawkers' Union, based in Kandivali area in western suburban Mumbai, can be noted. This union not only conducts several awareness programmes to educate its members about their duties and rights but also makes the vendors aware about the circumstances under which the municipality and police confiscate goods and enforce evictions, including the amount of fines to pay the municipality and police once vendors are caught. While interacting with its members (vendors) it is found that they know both (original as well as revised) national policies on urban street vendors and the Act that was passed in 2014. Vendors are taught about different social security provisions that they can avail. Union members also facilitate meetings on a regular basis in which different training programmes take place. Interestingly this union also campaigns for universal social security schemes in order to mobilise as many vendors as possible under social protection. On the contrary, Hawkers' Sangram Committee (affiliated to NHFI) in Kolkata is more into increasing memberships. This union is visible and has also strong hold of its members but the ground reality is somewhat different. When members of this union were asked about the union activities, vendors expressed their unhappiness, and reported that the union concentrates only on its membership and its rallies. Vendors are often threatened by the union leaders if they express unwillingness to join rallies or meetings.

NASVI-affiliated unions, on the other hand, are more into the advocacy level along with conducting awareness programmes. In addition, these unions focus too on union membership, but the leaders from these unions believe that movement will come from mass representation. The main agenda is 'mass mobilisation and confrontation'. Needless to say, these unions are most visible in the all the cities. For instance, memberships of Azad Hawkers' Union (Mumbai), Jai Hind Calcutta Hawkers' Union (Kolkata), sSTEP and AASVA (Guwahati) are spread over the city. They have their membership covering all major nodes of the vending locations.

Facilitating to access finance

An overwhelming majority of vendors across India obtain credit from informal sources and pay out a large part of their incomes in interest payments (Bhowmik & Saha 2013). As discussed earlier, vendors are found to access credit from informal sources and end up paying high rates of interest (amounting to roughly 5–10 per cent of their earnings per month) on the borrowed sums. Since most vendors have limited knowledge of arithmetic, they are defrauded by moneylenders and end up paying interest continuously. However, some unions are organising SHGs to provide low-cost credit to vendors. The lack of general awareness about its benefits and the aversion of some vendors to joining such organisations lead them to further being exploited by these moneylenders. Besides awareness programmes, Shahid Bhagat Singh Hawkers' Union (Mumbai) facilitates credit facility to vendors since 2006. Post Act, Azad Hawkers' Union in Mumbai (July 2014) has also started providing credit facility. Interestingly unions which are helping provide credit also support in organising social security for the vendors, including the provision of micro-insurance services. A fraction of the vendors avail of formal credit organised by the trade unions through a registered cooperative credit society operating in some areas. They also give group loans at very low rates of interest to members (vendors) who approach the society through the unions. Union membership in this case is vital, because the union stands as guarantor for the vendors. The following case of Shahid Bhagat Singh Hawkers' Union (see Box 5.1) can be discussed as the union has been providing credit for the past one decade. They provide credit on a regular basis.

Box 5.1 Role of unions in facilitating credit to vendors

A cooperative credit society has been registered under the state government to provide loans such as personal loans, educational loans and loans for economic activity, and the cooperative receives money for these from the state government. The cooperative gives loans to MBOs. Shahid Bhagat Singh Hawkers' Union acts as a mediator for vendors which helps them (vendors) avail credits facility from the cooperative. According to the rules and norms, a vendor can acquire a maximum of Rs 30,000 as a loan from the cooperative. Each vendor in the organisation gives money to the organisation according to the vendor's volume of trade (at a minimum of Rs 10 per day) and the organisation thus accumulates money that is used as 'working capital'. The vendor can then take a loan from the accumulated funds at a nominal rate of interest.

According to the ten key respondents from the selected three MBOs, this type of cooperative is very successful in giving low-cost credit to the vendors, and the repayment rate is also high. Despite the work done by the cooperative, the take-up rate is small. This is due to the low rate of active unionisation. According to one of the active union members, around 2,500 vendors are involved in such cooperative and social security schemes in Mumbai, while Mumbai has 250,000 street vendors according to the records of most unions. Failure to register themselves with the unions debars vendors from obtaining the benefits of formal credit availability.

Source: Based on fieldwork conducted in 2010–11.

In the sample, as mentioned, a relatively high number of the vendors (46.7 per cent) obtained credit from informal sources, namely; moneylenders, friends and relatives, fellow vendors, and wholesalers; and paid out a large part of their incomes towards interest payments. Interestingly, a fraction of the vendors avail of formal credit organised by the trade unions through a registered cooperative credit society (1.2 per cent) operating in some of the cities (especially Bhubaneswar, Delhi, Hyderabad, Mumbai and Patna). The following case narrative from Delhi (see Box 5.2) shows how vendors are benefitted from the union and also how the union facilitates to provide low-cost credit to its members.

Box 5.2 Credit accessibility and role of trade union

Sukhbir (name changed), a 42-year-old vendor (Delhi), had taken a loan to buy a cart for vending. He used to work for another vendor as a wage worker, prior to becoming a vendor himself. Unable to find sources of finance, he approached the society through the union. In his own words: 'I used to work as a wage worker and my employer used to torture me day in and day out. Finally, I decided to become a street food vendor and for which I need to buy a cart. I approached several organisations in vain for money. I soon got in touch with the union (name withheld on request) and they said they initiate the loan by standing guarantor if I joined their union. I readily became their member and got the loan of Rs 10,000. Their working capital requirement was nominal. The benefits that I have accrued from my business far exceed the loan and the interest charges. The membership norms are very suitable for people like me who do not have any other collateral to offer. They are able to understand my dilemma because they are part of the trade. I feel more vendors like me should join unions if they want formal low-cost loans'.

Source: Based on fieldwork conducted in 2010–11.

Organising social security

The need for social security cannot be ignored. Vendors need credit for various purposes, among which social security requirements are one of the most important. Studies show that street vendors in Mumbai, Patna, Delhi and Hyderabad borrow money for non-economic activity, especially for social security purpose, which lands them in a debt trap (Bhowmik & Saha 2013: 170). It was found that unions provide social security to their vendors through the JBY under the group insurance scheme of the Life Insurance Corporation of India (LIC). The following (Box 5.3) is a case of Shahid Bhagat Singh Hawkers' Union that convinces its mobile vendors to avail social security benefit.

Box 5.3 Role of union in facilitating social security benefits

Shahid Bhagat Singh Hawkers' Union urges its mobile vendors to avail group insurance scheme. The scheme includes insurance coverage for health issues, house and property, accidental and natural death, and permanent and partial disability. It is a group insurance scheme, which needs a minimum of twenty-five members. Members pay an annual premium. The annual premium for an individual vendor is Rs 169, which is very affordable, even for the poorest. Under this scheme, each vendor could receive Rs 15,000 to 75,000 in the case of an accident, and the vendor's family would receive Rs 75,000 after his/her death. Further, this scheme also covers scholarships for the education of the vendor's children. A maximum of two children of the vendor could benefit, and each child could receive Rs 1,200 per year as a scholarship. One organisation has even helped to arrange money for a vendor's son to pursue higher studies.

Source: Based on fieldwork conducted in 2010.

Managing competition

Unions help to reduce cut-throat competition among street vendors, which arose in India due to the inadequate number of unions/ associations for street vendors and the inactivity of unions and associations. Trade unions can also help to regulate the number of vendors by restricting their entry to the profession. One of the cases has been noticed in Kandivali (Mumbai), where the union tried to regulate vending in a constructive way. First, the union, through its credit and social security programmes encourages the children of the member-vendors to study and find formal sector jobs or secure positions in licenced trades so that they do not have to depend on street vending (especially for the next generation). They even provide loans to their members to get licence for shops. They [union leaders] encourage upward mobility and also restrict the number of vendors. Interestingly, all key respondents noted that limiting the number of street vendors would also solve many problems. It would be easier for the government to issue licences if there are fewer vendors and they would get more easily regularised. The relationship among vendors too could be regulated. Key respondents across cities reported that the rise in the occurrence of internal troubles among vendors due to ever-increasing competition and limited public space in which they operate to be cause for conflict. The relationship of competition must be replaced with one of cooperation, in which vendors fight for their common demands in unison, in order for the authorities to listen to them. Unions could be instrumental in uniting the vendors. Along with this, there is also the need to encourage self-regulation and self-compliance among vendors. They must realise that it is their duty to keep the city clean and also to see that the products they sell are in no way harmful or toxic and conform to minimum standards of hygiene. Unions often conduct different environment- and hygiene-related awareness programmes for their members.

Vendors' perception about unions

On one hand some street vendors reported that membership of trade unions makes them feel 'empowered'; on the other hand some of them expressed the opinion that it is a waste of time to attend regular weekly and monthly meetings. The union members' activities often interfere with their work, and many street vendors think that if this time were devoted to vending activities, at least it would provide them with some more income. As a result they cannot take time off from work to attend union meetings. This is not only true in case of India but the attitude of vendors across Asia is similar. Studies show that street vendors are loosely organised (Kusabake 2006; Nirathron 2006). Hence union participation is mostly a pen and paper affair. Vendors prefer paying bribes to joining a union.

Many vendors are critical about unionisation and some of them expressed their dissatisfaction and frustration about the union and its activities.

Only 12 per cent of the total number of street vendors are actively involved with unions. Most vendors feel that actively working with unions is a waste of time. They think that unions sometimes give them false hope in the name of providing licences and so forth. For instance, unions in Mumbai promise to get licences from the MCGM, for which they charge Rs 500 a year (figure as of 2009) as a processing fee from each vendor. This was the case before the Act was passed. Needless to say, this has been interpreted as another form of exploitation. Many vendors do not like this attitude of unions and many of them therefore refrain from any affiliation to unions and question unions' commitments. Some of the vendors prefer paying bribes to being charged for riding on false hope. Another fact – though less evident – is rampant corruption within vendors' organisations where leaders forge close alliances with stakeholders (police, municipality, builders' lobby) and work on their behalf in order to appropriate a suitable 'commission'. The absence of effective and honest leadership is one of the greatest impediments in this sector. Vendors therefore prefer to maintain a cordial relationship with the civic authorities and the police. This may be one of the reasons why vendors avoid participating in any union activities whatsoever, which results in their [vendors] representation being thin at the union.

Role of organisations in legalising street vending

The Street Vendors (Regulation of Vending and Protection of Livelihood) Act, passed in March 2014, is indeed a victory and a result of a long struggle from below. Unions have a role to play in spreading awareness regarding rights and duties of each vendor, organising them in their collective struggle and persuading the state administration to implement the provisions of the Act in shortest possible time. Representatives from organisations such as NASVI, NHFI, SEWA, Nidan, Manushi and other trade unions had been called upon to participate at each level of consultation and in drafting of the central law on vending. Their valuable comments and inputs had been given due priority while framing the Act. Nevertheless, the organisations still continue to play an important role in implementing the provisions of the Act.

The United Progressive Alliance (UPA) government through its National Common Minimum Programme, set up NCEUS in 2004 to protect unorganised/informal sector workers. The NCEUS was engaged in identifying the problems faced by small and micro-enterprises. The Prime Minister's Office (PMO) recognised the importance of urban street vendors for their significant contribution to the urban economy. The task force was formed through which the draft of the national policy on urban street vendors in India was submitted. The National Policy on Urban Street Vendors was framed in 2006 and subsequently the policy was revised in 2009, when the street vendors were recognised as urban service providers. As mentioned earlier, the policy recommended the issues related to registration; issuance of identity cards; monitoring the facilities; identifying areas for vending with no restriction; setting the terms and conditions for hawking; taking corrective action against defaulters; and collecting revenue. The policy of 2006 and the revised one in 2009 stated that TVCs were to be formed on a ward-wise basis and changes were introduced in its composition as well. The importance and roles of TVC are also outlined in the Act.

Even after the Act, the conditions of street vendors across the country have hardly improved. Membership-based organisations played a crucial role in legislating street vendors. For instance, NASVI and SEWA protested to consider the policy in 2009. On the contrary, there have been regular reports of harassments, evictions and tortures inflicted on vendors. Finally, the Hon'ble Supreme Court of India issued an order on 9th of September 2013 to protect the rights of vendors, mentioning how the problem of street vendors have aggravated because of 'lackadaisical attitude of the administration' and failing legislative mechanisms, clearly specifying that within a month of receipt of the order, chief secretaries of state governments and administrators of Union Territories are required to direct their respective district administrators to form TVCs and implement all other policy provisions contained in the National Policy of Street Vendors 2009. Important to mention, some civic authorities like Kolkata (Kolkata Municipal Corporation [KMC] and Bidhan Nagar Municipal Corporation [BNMC]) had not started doing anything about the Act as of June 2014. The officials from the civic body stated that it was too early to expect any changes at the ground level. It is in this context that unions like HSC and KSHU have referred to the Supreme Court order and pressurised the civic authorities to form TVCs and conduct the survey

as per the order until the Act is implemented. At the TVC, participation of all stakeholders are ensured: municipal authorities, trade
unions, NGOs and hawkers, including women and those from SC,
ST and OBC categories. The TVC is entrusted to decide upon issues
such as determination of natural market, vending and no-vending
zones, preparation of street vending plan and undertaking a survey
of street vendors. In the Act it is mentioned that no eviction shall
take place till a survey on existing street vendors has been completed and certificate of vending has been issued to vendors.

Town vending committee (TVC) and the role of unions in it

Civic authority, namely, municipal authority, is supposed to form
the TVC. Officials are supposed to be aware of the Hon'ble
Supreme Court's Order on street vendors issued in September 2013,
the National Policy on Urban Street Vending 2009 and the recent
Act (2014). But not all civic authorities across cities in India know
this development of legalising street vending. For instance, KMC
and BNMC and their departments concerned were not aware of
the Act as of December 2014. Nevertheless the unions are now constantly putting pressure on municipal authorities (mainly all the cities) towards implementing the Act.

Formation of TVC: case of Mumbai

MCGM, deceptively, has positive intention to implement the provisions mentioned in the Act. Accordingly, a number of meetings
were held with different NGOs and other stakeholders towards formation of TVC, and it was formed in the month of January 2014
on the lines of Supreme Court order. The TVC consists of thirty-five
members including five special invitees. The chairperson of the committee is the commissioner; 40 per cent representation will be from
vendor associations; 20 per cent representation will be from civic
authorities consisting of one designated urban local body (ULB),
one planning authority (MMRDA), one Traffic Police and Superintendent of Police; 10 per cent representation is from elected members of ULB (nominated councillors); 10 per cent representation is
from resident welfare associations and community-based organisations (CBOs); 10 per cent representation is from banks (SBI) and
insurance company (LIC); and 10 per cent representation will be
from NGOs, doctors, lawyers and town planners. There shall be

different rules, regulations and mission for each stakeholder. However MMRDA, banks (SBI) and LIC shall have inclusive policies and mission that can be captured once the TVC gets formed formally. Within a year of TVC formation, two meetings were held. According to the Supreme Court order, it was mandatory to form TVC and conduct a survey among vendors. Therefore, the MCGM conducted a survey in the month of August in 2014. Lorry inspectors were appointed by the Department of Licence and Invigilation of the MCGM. It took about four to six days, depending on the size of ward, to survey. Lorry inspectors were in charge of taking photographs and verification of vendors at the place of vending location and then distribution of forms. Vendors were given fifteen days to fill the form. Later, around ten or eleven ward officials at each ward office were to collect filled-in forms. In the process of survey, union members ensured that each vendor received form and lorry inspectors did not take any bribe while inspecting the vendors and distributing the forms. Union members monitored the entire process.

Formation of vending committee (town and zones):
case of Guwahati

The municipal authorities recognise the contribution of vendors towards the urban economy in Guwahati. Officials from the Guwahati Municipal Corporation are aware of the Hon'ble Supreme Court's Order on street vendors issued in September 2013, the National Policy on Urban Street Vending 2009 and the recent Act (2014). They have positive intention to implement the provisions mentioned in the Act. Accordingly, meetings are being held with partner NGOs and other stakeholders towards formation of a twenty-member town vending committee (TVC) apart from the chairperson and the convener of the committee. The GMC has decided to form a TVC as an apex body. The chairperson of the committee will be the commissioner, and convener of the committee shall be appointed. The twenty-member TVC comprises the following: 40 per cent (8 members out of 20) representation is from associations of street vendors; 20 per cent (4 members out of 20) representation is from civic authorities consisting of one designated ULB, one planning authority (GMDA), one Traffic Police and Superintendent of Police (SPO); 10 per cent (2 members out of 20) representation is from elected members of ULB (nominated councillors); 10 per cent (2 members out of 20) representation is from resident welfare associations and CBOs; 10 per cent (2 members out of 20) representation is from banks (SBI) and insurance company (LIC); and 10 per cent (2 members out of 20) representation is from NGOs, doctors, lawyers and town planners. There are different rules, regulations and mission for each stakeholder. However GMDA, banks (SBI) and LIC are the primary stakeholders in implementing inclusive policies and missions.

Interestingly, the GMC has decided to form one TVC and zone vending committees (ZVC) to be formed under TVC. This is to function smoothly. There are six zones demarcated by the GMC such as South, East, West, Central, Lokhra and Dispur. Thus the GMC has been divided into six ZVCs. The composition of members of ZVCs will be same as TVC. The TVC will be the decision-making body and ZVCs will execute and implement the policy which will be set by the TVC. The GMC appointed a city-based NGO to conduct a survey on street vendors as part of implementation of the Act. However, after conducting survey, not much work towards issuing licenses has been done so far.

While the higher officials are seen to be proactive in implementing the Act, the lower-level officers who are entrusted with the actual implementation have shown reluctance to accept the provisions of the Act. According to them, despite their unwillingness, they are bound to follow rules and regulations. They said that it would be difficult to implement the Act point to point at ground level.

The GMC shows its clear disapproval of keeping vendors on the road. However, adding that existing hawkers will not be removed from their current position (especially in areas like Fancy Bazaar and Pan Bazaar), if needed they shall be rehabilitated or relocated within a 200-metre radius from their current location. However, some officials expressed that since roads are narrow, vendors on the road also imply crowding and congestion. Hence vendors need to ply in proper market-like structures in each location designed especially for the purpose.

The GMC also expressed concern that Guwahati has a significant number of mobile vendors unlike other cities in India and therefore measures must be taken to regulate them as well as static vendors. Concerned about the safety and welfare of general citizens as well as vendors, the GMC feels that mobile vendors need photo identity cards duly signed by the civic body concerned. This is nevertheless a point ahead in including even mobile vendors and their concerns in the present agenda.

Nevertheless, union members expressed that hardly any discussion takes place in the TVC meetings. This is true not only of a particular city but also in other cities. Each meeting is held for 30 minutes and issues and agenda points are pre-decided by the commissioner, which are supported mainly by the residents' associations. Even if union members try to put their opinions or views, mostly those are overlooked in the TVC meetings.

Challenges faced by the unions

There are a few challenges that union face while organising street vendors. First, heterogeneous characteristics of the occupation make it difficult for unions to organise. As mentioned earlier, nine leading types of vending are prevalent across cities in India. Each category has its own mode of operation. In addition, wage workers are found to be working under self-employed own-account street vendors. This complex nature of the activity makes it even more difficult for the union to organise the vendors. All union members reported that across all categories of vending, organising vendors who sell *Chinese* food is most difficult, especially in Bengaluru, Delhi and Mumbai. Let us discuss this. These vendors serve *country liquor* along with *Chinese* food items. This food is served mainly in the evening. This type of vending exposes vendors to severe forms of harassments as authorities take advantage of this. On this ground authorities, mainly police, threaten vendors with confiscation and damage of the stalls. This is because they [vendors] work with 'fire', and accidents might occur at any time. Therefore, these vendors do not want to enter into any confrontation with the authorities. They like to solve it by negotiating at individual levels with the authorities by paying bribes to avoid all strife. Unions too fail to convince them. Notably, both police and municipal officials charge more bribe from them as compared to other types of vendors.

Second, there are many layers of informality, illegality and personal vested interests involved in this activity. As a result it is difficult for committed and loyal leaders to continue with it. In this context, an interesting comment made by the acting general secretary of Shahid Bhagat Singh Hawkers' Union can be noted. The secretary stated that 'if a good leader like Kapoorchand Gupta (devoid of any corruption charges) wants to work for betterment of society as a whole without any vested interest, there will be others who always try to suppress people like them'. This statement is somewhat true. The case of Kapoorchand Gupta's murder (see Box 5.4) proves the statement. He was killed because he was a big threat not only to moneylenders but also to many others who were prevented from harassing vendors (through excessive rent extraction via bribes and interest rates).

Box 5.4 Obstacles to good leadership

Kapoorchand Gupta was an active crusader for vendors' rights at the workplace. A vendor himself, he tried to protect his fellow vendors by leading them to fight against all forms of exploitation: moneylenders, MCGM and police, and builders' and citizens' lobbies. All the stakeholders realised that with leaders like Gupta, their interests would be adversely affected, so he was brutally killed. Honest leaders like Gupta are considered a threat to the underground economy which thrives on the exploitation of street vendors and active unionisation is therefore not encouraged by the state. Thus the most important challenge for the unions to function is the presence of powerful stakeholders and their vested interests in urban and public space politics.

Source: Bhowmik & Saha (2013: xxiii).

Third, some union leaders among key respondents shared concerns about loopholes in trade unions by saying that some union leaders (not only in one city but across India) consider trade union activity as a profession of their own. They take money from vendors. Vendors also revealed some instances. In some places in Mumbai and Kolkata, especially Powai market and Andheri (Mumbai) and Garia market (Kolkata), unions charge money with the assurance of providing licence. This exercise is still continuing even after the Act. The amount of money was more before the Act was passed. Unions, however, charge a lower amount as vendors have yet to receive licence. Vendors feel that this will continue until they receive licence from the authority concerned.

Lastly, union leaders feel that there is less enthusiasm among members after the passing of the Act. Like other programmes implemented by the Government of India (e.g. MGNREGA), there is a possibility of high corruption at the time of licence distribution.

Nevertheless, the role of unions should be even more concerning than before at the time of execution. On the contrary, vendors in Mumbai reported that there is a persistent fear of losing *power* over street vendors as they [vendors] are now in a position to communicate directly with the state for addressing their issues and problems as a part of an apex body.

Status of women in trade unions

Most of the union leaders who were interviewed confirmed that only 10–15 per cent of the total members are women. Also, they highlighted the fact that the women vendors are less visible and it is difficult to organise them due to social constraints, thus making it obvious that most vulnerable vendors, i.e. women vendors who needed to be protected the most, are not yet organised or are less organised. Furthermore, the majority of trade unions' executive committee does not represent the substantial number of women vendors and women do not hold decision-making positions in the trade unions. SEWA is an exception to this, with almost 8,000 women vendors as its members and also almost all the trade committee members are women. But, such cases are limited to some cities like Ahmedabad, Delhi, Indore, etc., rather than all the cities.

Conclusion

Unionisation is perhaps the most effective way to guard against the increased vulnerability of workers arising from pressures of globalisation (Dasgupta 2002). Organising enables people to raise their voices against what is wrong, assembles both financial and emotional resources and empowers workers politically and economically. Kusakabe's study (2006) of street vendor associations in Asian countries shows that membership in organisations boosts self-confidence among the vendors and gives them the sense of being recognised by the society. In all, it gives them representation security so that they are free to express their views about their work and working conditions and enables them to bargain over their rights at work (ibid.). The study has highlighted many aspects of the collective bargaining process. Collective bargaining is an end in itself and also a means to other ends. It plays a major role in uniting vendors to fight against exploitation and also to secure their rights. There are several active unions and associations in the field sites of this study who are doing the job of mobilising vendors and organising collective protests against the civic authorities. The low rate of active union membership outlines the fact that awareness of their rights and responsibilities among vendors is generally lacking. Intermediaries take advantage of the lack of association among the vendors and exploit this to the maximum capacity.

It is hard to organise street vendors under one banner. First, there is no employer–employee relationship here, giving rise to confusion regarding identification of the parties involved in the bargaining process. Second, the self-employed street vendors are extremely heterogeneous in character. Vendors fall into many categories, whereas the degree of associability is higher among homogeneous groups of workers. Third, they are scattered and dispersed, which makes even organising difficult.

There are many strategies that unions have been taking up in order to provide credit and social security and also support at the time of emergency during eviction. But one can count such cases. It is also noticed that there is very less awareness among street vendors about the Act and its provisions. For most of the vendors, the Act means provision of licences. Some unions like Azad Hawkers' Union and Shahid Bhagat Singh Hawkers' Union (Maharashtra), sSTEP (Assam) and KSHU (West Bengal) have translated the Act into local languages and are organising awareness programmes but the turnout rate is very less. As mentioned earlier, unions facilitate for accessing credit and providing social security. The credit facility provided by the unions through cooperatives, however, is no longer imperative because there is a provision in the Act stating that vendors can avail the institutional loan facility directly from banks once they have licence. Post Act, the cooperative system can be modified in favour of the vendors. Now unions can facilitate loans from banks directly. Some other unions have already started strategically delivering loan facility through their own cooperatives (e.g. a newly formed cooperative under Azad Hawkers' Union) with the sole intention of benefitting vendors. However, this might escalate into lending business in future. While union leaders complain that the civic authorities are reluctant to speed up the process of legalisation, unions seem to be flaccid in pressurising authorities to take up the issues. After the Act, organisations should rather focus on monitoring the progress as well as coercing authorities to expedite the process of implementation.

Notes

1 The information on SEWA has been illustrated from http://www.sewa.org/aboutus/structure.asp, accessed on 12 May 2010.

2 To describe the function and the role of NASVI, the information has been illustrated from http://www.nasvinet.org/about.htm and it was accessed on 12 May 2010.

Chapter 6

Legislating street vending

Challenges and alternative development

Under a neoliberal regime when casualisation, informalisation and contractualisation have been taking place in the labour markets of the developing world, the informal sector is becoming the main source of livelihoods for the poor. It is a fact that street vendors are considered one of the most marginalised, poor and vulnerable group of workers in the urban informal economy. Their activity is broadly characterised by easy entry, strong social network, dominance of informal credit market and extensive rent seeking. All the hindrances that street vendors face and the issues that have emerged in this study point to a single broad theme – the denial of dignity. With the passing of Street Vendors (Protection of Livelihood and Regulation of Street Vending) Act, 2014, the hopes are that the activity would be regulated, protected and brought under the folds of legality. Not only will the livelihood of vendors be protected but also dignity and decency of work will be ensured to them. The concept of decent work is considered as most comprehensive measure of work which ensures workers' basic right – employment opportunities, rights at work, social protection and social dialogue. The meaning of decent work is contextual and varies from sector to sector and person to person. For instance, while decent work for children should be 'no work' at all, decent work for unemployed person will be providing employment in the first place and eventually other work-related benefits. Similarly the concept of decent work in its absolute term was not meaningful to street vendors before the Act was passed. Providing legal frame was first and foremost way of achieving decent work for street vendors. In spite of legal framework, it is difficult to examine whether the concept of decent work exists or not. After the Act, some basic characteristics of street vendors are enduring some structural changes. These are: entry to the activity will now become regulated to some extent, informal credit will be replaced by formal institutional credit and rent seeking will be substituted by revenue collection. These are the positive aspects or changes that one can aspire to have from this legality. However, in the process of legality, power relation, traditional market characteristics, bargaining power and livelihood strategy will also be restructured. The significance of the concept of decent work for street vendors in urban India along with the changing nature of informal market has been examined in this chapter. In the previous chapters we have examined the characteristics of street markets, associated politics and strategies which vendors practise to sustain at the market. This concluding chapter aims to explore the future of work and employment in the activity. This objective holds relevance especially after the Act. It is in this context that work and employment will be understood from the viewpoint of decent work. Before examining restructuring of informal market and working conditions, let us critically analyse the legal recognition of street vendors in India and assess the impact that the Act is likely to have on the restructuring of markets for vendors.

Legal recognition

The Street Vendors (Protection of Livelihood and Regulation of Street Vending) Act, 2014, is a step further in giving constitutional right to adequate means of livelihood to an emerging segment of the urban informal sector. This Act is comprehensive as it ensures livelihood security to the street vendors of the country. It is evident that the core of all struggles and disputes between the state and the street vendors was primarily over public space utilisation. All the aspects concerning public space utilisation are more or less addressed in the Act, and the responsibilities of the local authorities, TVCs and other stakeholders are clearly outlined. Undoubtedly the Act upholds street vendors' right to work and carry out their livelihood in the designated public places, at the same time regulating the activity so that welfare of all is ensured. Nevertheless, some provisions of the Act are clearly challenged in the current circumstances. Currently, the way in which the local administration deals with street vendors in cities across India shows corruption and vested interests involved, making the system volatile. Millions of rupees are accumulated through bribes and interest payment.

The challenge lies in replacing the existing system with a fair and just one. This may be the reason why some state machinery is reluctant to accept the Act or rather implement it.

Role of local authorities and the town vending committee (TVC)

Local authorities (the municipal corporation) are entrusted with power and responsibility to ensure that street vendors are protected under the law. The TVC is an implementing body of civic authorities at the city level. The members of TVC are representatives from the state government, the police, residents' associations, NGOs, MBOs and street vendors, and are bestowed with decision-making powers on all aspects of regulation and protection. Some of the clauses can be examined in the light of present evidence. Section 3 *(3)* of Chapter II of the Street Vendors Act 2014 mentions that 'no street vendor shall be evicted or as the case may be, relocated till the survey specified under Clause 3 *(1)* has been completed and the certificate of vending is issued to all street vendors' (GOI 2014: 3).

Section 18 *(1)* of Chapter IV points out that 'local authority on the recommendation of TVC declare the zones or a part of it to be a no-vending zone for any public purpose and relocate the street vendors vending in that area, in such manner as may be specified in the scheme' (ibid.: 5). This provision vests too much power (if not absolute) to the local authority (TVC shall recommend, but the chairperson of the TVC is also the municipal commissioner whose decision is taken to rule). Here the municipal corporation shall have the power to designate areas as 'no-vending' zones and relocate vendors elsewhere. However, the first schedule, Section 3(a) also points out that 'any existing natural markets, or a natural market as identified under the survey shall not be identified as no-vending zones' (ibid.: 12). This provision of the Act is commendable.

However, implementing the said two provisions of the Act would be difficult at the ground level. A case can be highlighted when in October and November 2013, the Municipal Corporation of Greater Mumbai (MCGM) had formed a two-member expert committee to conduct a survey of all existing street vendors in the three wards in Mumbai, namely, G-North, K-East and M-West.

In spite of complete assurances provided by the higher officials of the MCGM to the committee to conduct the survey without any interference, eviction was taking place in selected wards as well as other wards. This implied that lower officials were ignorant of the directive issued by the higher authorities or they were flouting the orders. From Chapter 3, it has also been shown that lower municipal officials are the main recipients of bribes from the vendors. The intention might be removal of street vendors from existing natural markets so that they are not recorded during the survey and hence the public places are declared as no-vending zones. Therefore a strong and independent monitoring mechanism might be put in place so that even the low-level officials of the civic authorities do not violate provisions of the law.

Section 18 *(3)* of Chapter IV states that 'no street vendor shall be relocated or evicted by the local authority from the place specified in the certificate of vending unless s/he has been given thirty day notice for the same in such manner as may be specified in the scheme' (ibid.: 5). This provision is nevertheless a noble attempt to restrict and put a check on the activities of the local authorities (mainly municipal officials) or police who randomly undertake eviction drives to harass vendors. But this provision is a challenge to the system that currently rests on malpractices such as bribe payments and associated harassments. The paradox is that these practices have formed institutions (informal) and operate in a well-organised manner. This might create an opportunity for other authorities or different ways to collect bribe.

Section 19 *(1)* and Section 19 *(2)* in Chapter IV of the Act states that if a street vendor fails to vacate the place specified in the certificate of vending after lapse of period as per notice, the local authority, in addition to evicting the vendor, may seize goods, a list of which is to be prepared and copies made to be issued to the vendor. The vendor may reclaim goods after paying requisite fees. In case of non-perishable goods, this reclamation may be made within two working days, whereas in case of perishable commodities, reclamation shall be done the same day (ibid.: 6). In light of these specifications, current practices might be compared. In many cases, goods that are confiscated by municipal officials (especially in case of perishable goods) are outright damaged or destroyed (such an incident was noticed in IIT Powai Market (Mumbai) in the month of November 2013). The reason might be: when eviction strikes at a particular location, vendors quickly respond by removing their stalls and hiding the wares. By the time one can make the seizer list of one vendor, others would run away. Hence to avoid this, authorities make sure that eviction strikes all of a sudden and that vendors do not have the time to save their goods from damage and destruction. If such practices continue, question remains as to who shall be responsible for damage and destruction caused to vendors' properties or goods, and the mechanism to claim compensation for damage done.

Vendor participation

Section 22 *(2) (d)* in Chapter VII states that in the formation of the TVC, street vendors' elected representatives would comprise not less than 40 per cent of the total membership, amongst whom one-third would be women vendors (ibid.: 7). This seems to be a vital step towards ensuring gender representation in the decision-making body in protecting the rights of women vendors who are worse off than their male counterparts. Section 7 of Chapter II states that the backward classes will be given priority in issuing certificates. Again, Section 22 *(1) (d)* in Chapter VII contains that, even in the forma-tion of TVC, due representation shall be given to persons belonging to socially backward groups. This is undoubtedly an important step to protect vendors belonging to Scheduled Castes, Scheduled Tribes and Other Backward Classes. However, the economically backward categories would as well be favoured in this issuance of vending cer-tificates as presently (as this study validates) vendors, irrespective of social groups, are found to suffer from low and erratic income.

Promotional measures

Section 31, Chapter X clearly states that 'the appropriate Govern-ment may, in consultation with the Town Vending Committee, local authority, planning authority and street vendors associations or unions, undertake promotional measures of making available credit, insurance and other welfare measures for the street vendors' (ibid.: 8). Nevertheless, what, how and to what extent these mea-sures shall be implemented by these stakeholders are not outlined. Unless the content and scope of the social security measures are outlined, it would be difficult for implementing authorities to put the same in practice.

Urban plan and street vending

The first schedule, Section (1) *(b)* of the Act upholds rights of commuters to use roads without any obstruction or impediment. However, this is a very necessary proposal for urban planning and should be taken up by the planners strictly. As we have seen, vendors do not always cause obstruction. In several cases, roads remain blocked due to wrongful car parking or shopkeepers' activities (displaying boards or hangers or cots and so forth). All such impediments must be removed by law and perpetrators severely penalised. The hawking zones need to be redesigned to cater to vendors' as well as buyers' requirements.

The Act did not consider vendors who are occupying railway land. In Section 1*(4)*, the Act clearly stated that 'the provision of this Act shall not apply to any land, premises and trains owned and controlled by the Railways under the Railway Act, 1989' (GOI 2014: 2). Vendors plying their business either in railway premises or on railway land are not considered in our study. Notwithstanding, a significant number of street vendors are seen operating on railway land. It is pertinent to ask what alternatives have been taken into consideration for these vendors who are so-called illegally occupying railway land then and now.

Informal markets: possible changes in market structure

The Street Vendors (Protection of Livelihood and Regulation of Street Vending) Act, 2014, has indeed impacted the activity and lives of street vendors. However, the question remains as to whether the Act provides any new direction to the informal market or remains same as before. Post Act, however, some inherent characteristics of this informal market have undergone structural changes. Let us discuss them in the following section.

Entry to the occupation

One of the important characteristics not only in street vending but also in the informal sector is easy entry to the occupation. The Act is about protecting the existing street vendors, not promoting the activity. Nonetheless, there is opportunity to the new entrants (vendors). But the total number of street vendors cannot exceed

2.5 per cent of the urban population in the city. As a result there is restriction in the market for entrants. Thus there will no free entry to the occupation. Street vending was found to be one of the easiest ways of livelihood in the urban economy for migrants. The Act clearly states that the TVC in each area, under their jurisdiction, will carry out surveys to count the total number of street vendors. After the survey is done, a certificate has to be issued, with an identity card, and a vending space will be allotted to the existing vendors. To obtain licence, a vendor needs to submit his/her residential proof in the city. Under this circumstance, migration in the occupation will be restricted and open only to the urban poor living in the city.

Kinship, ethnicity, religion, origin and localism are important factors for entering the activity. Need to mention that vendors earlier needed to have contacts with friends or relatives in the profession and same locality to set up their business. Now, social contacts are no longer the pre-requisites for entry to the occupation. Notwithstanding, contacts with civic authorities or somebody having contacts with them [civic authorities] are important. Competition among vendors will be enhanced as only one member of the household will be given the licence. Therefore, entry of the outsiders in the occupation will be limited.

Promoting licence raj and further rent seeking

The Act stipulates that the issue of identity card and business permits shall be the responsibility of civic officials. The way in which these licences are obtained may be enmeshed in rent payments and red-tapism. The application form for obtaining should be simple and hassle free. Otherwise the vendors will face difficulty in filling it up. In addition, this may give rise to another form of rent seeking while filling the forms. For instance, under MGNREGA those rural workers who are illiterate or functionally literate need to pay an additional amount to fill up their application form for opening savings accounts. One needs to pay bribes even for obtaining driving licence for auto rickshaw. Having seen the current attitude of civic authority and bribe extraction mechanism (Chapter 3), issuing licences will be dependent on the person concerned appointed by the civic authority, which might lead to another level of illegality.

Places for market

The market for street vendors is demand driven. They constructed their market in places where buyers naturally congregated in large numbers. These are known as natural markets. The Act states that hawking zones will be demarcated keeping natural markets in view. The zones might vary according to the place available in and around the existing natural markets. Notably the natural market is created by the vendors based on the demand of the consumers. The places provided by the civic authority subject to available places will not work out in case of the street markets. For instance, there was a designated place in Dadar (Mumbai) for hawkers and vendors started plying their business too. But vendors refused to continue their business from the designated place as there were hardly any customers to buy the products. According to the vendors, the market was not the market for consumers and later it became a wholesale market. The places for existing vendors will not be a problem but the place for new entrants will be dependent upon the civic authorities. There will no longer be choice-based markets for street vendors. Natural markets will be created and examined after approval of civic authorities.

Business for investors

Private and corporate investors like Faasos (an Indian fast-food chain that primarily sells wraps), ITC Limited and Reliance Industries Limited (RIL) are inducting their business plan either directly through vendors or convincing trade union leaders through their members in this retail sector. It is too early to comment but preliminary discussions show that these companies are labelling street vendors as micro-entrepreneurs and making business strategy/model for them and have started investing especially on food vendors. Vendors who sell cooked food, tea and coffee have larger share of the profit and they pay more bribes too as they require flame. Considering the profitability and certainty of the business (especially post Act), these private investors/companies are showing interest in investing especially in food retail. They [companies] are mainly using two business strategies. First, vendors will be provided credit and business support (in case of ITC). Second, readymade food wraps shall be provided to the vendors (in case of Faasos). Vendors will market the products.

Notably, some unions are in favour of these private investors in the vending and in consultation with these companies especially in Mumbai and Pune. The business opportunity provides definitely a new endeavour to the vendors but the basic question remains same as they [vendors] might lose their fundamental identity as self-employed. Providing credit at competitive rates to the vendors should not be a problem. But I believe that the idea of their interest in the street markets is not limited to investing in this micro-business. This can anyway happen with the help of different microcredit institutions. This raises a pertinent question, why do they enter this sector? One immediate response to this is profit and market sharing. Encouraging this sort of deregulation and allowing private investors in this activity, one can fear losing the inherent characteristics of these markets. The rent seeking from all the stakeholders, including the civic authorities and unions, might become part of profit sharing in this process. However, it is too early to comment on such development in street vending. One can undertake an in-depth research on these aspects of this new development.

Role of formal financial institutions

As mentioned, street vending is based on daily transaction. Due to its peculiar and heterogeneous nature, there are no direct schemes of formal financial institutions (apart from some of the SHG–bank linkages) targeted at vendors. In the absence of formal financial institutions in the street market, informal sources have become active players in the market, especially moneylenders, wholesalers, fellow vendors, friends, relatives and so on. Moneylenders and wholesalers are the main actors in this market. While moneylenders make different loan schemes for street vendors charging exorbitant rates of interest on loans to vendors, wholesalers offer loan facilities along with the products that they sell to the vendors. Moneylenders charge interest rates as cash whereas wholesalers charge as kind. Nonetheless, the importance of formal financial institutions in the vending activity was realised long ago. In order to further expand formal credit to vendors, the Act spells out that representatives from nationalised banks should be part of an apex body of decision making at the TVC. Banks are encouraged now to make exclusive credit facility and different schemes for street vendors. Earlier, Canara Bank (especially active in Bengaluru) was the only bank that had direct intervention through a financial inclusion division with the urban poor, yet they did not have any exclusive schemes for street vendors. Their model of intervention was well received and followed by other banks as well. Currently, other banks are also coming forward and making loans schemes for street vendors. For instance, SBI is the part of TVC in Guwahati, Mumbai and Delhi.

Profit-sharing stakeholders

Bribe payment was a common feature of street vending activity. Vendors are bound to pay a share of their income as bribe to civic authorities, mainly to police and municipal officials and intermediaries. After the Act was passed, although incidences of eviction after bribe payments have reduced in all the cities, incidences of bribe payments have not decreased significantly. In Mumbai, for instance, although survey of street vendors is over, issuing licences has not begun as yet. According to the union leaders, street vendors did not stop paying bribes to the civic authorities. Vendors prefer to operate their business without any hassle paying least heed to what leaders say.

Post Act, changes in union roles and activities are likely to bring in positive outcomes. The cooperative system can be modified in favour of the vendors. Now unions can facilitate loans from banks directly. Some unions have started strategically delivering loan facility through their own cooperatives (e.g. a newly formed cooperative under Azad Hawkers' Union) with the sole intention of benefitting vendors. However, this might escalate into lending business in future. While union leaders complain that the civic authorities are reluctant to speed up the process of legalisation, union seems to be flaccid in pressurising authorities to take up the issues. After the Act, organisations should rather focus on monitoring the progress as well as coercing authorities to expedite the process of implementation. On the other hand, some unions are in favour of these private investors in vending. Therefore with weak role of unions, basic inherent characteristics of street vending might change or rent seeking from all the stakeholders, including the civic authorities, might also transform into profit sharing.

Informal markets, state and alternatives

I have tried to bring the debate surrounding over the views put forward by De Soto (1989) and Portes (1994). The central discussion is revolved around the role of the state and politics that have performed in the process of development. On one hand, De Soto (1989) believes that the state has restricted or hampered the natural development process. On the other hand, Portes (1994) argues that state intervention is necessary for promoting development. There are two clear alternatives towards development. De Soto argued that people choose informal path for development to avoid the complex nature of regulatory governance. De Soto (1989) emphasised least government. Portes (1994), on the other hand, discusses a system of well-defined and well-designed rules and regulations that would secure property rights which will lead to a well-functioning market economy. Portes (1994) believes in stronger government. Marjit and Kar (2009) and RoyChowdhury (2007) have interestingly brought up the politics of the state that helps the informal sector to grow. According to them, it is the state that consciously wants this alternative path to grow. People do not choose the alternative; they are in fact compelled to choose and create their own alternatives. Brown (2006) identified social relationships that help to perpetuate this activity. In absence of (proper) legal framework, vendors exercise strong economic and social bargaining with various actors (state and non-state) to exist in the public space. As the state tries to restrict the growth of informality by not creating legal institutions, workers construct for themselves informal institutions through mutual bargaining, which naturally lead to growth in informality. This is a paradox of development.

In the present context, street vendors prefer not to operate outside formal rules. They do so because they have no alternatives. Some are forced to pay bribes and some of them prefer to pay. This is because they believe paying bribes is the only strategy to avoid harassment while plying trade and to survive. Vendors can be said to be extra-legal entities or outside legal boundaries as they operate or rather help forming an informal market institution of bribe payments. There are different actors involved in the process of bribes (vendors, police and civic authorities). The vendors perceive the bribes as an alternative arrangement that is the cost of being employed. Therefore, being less aware of exploitation in the hands of both formal and informal institutions, they understand that it is 'necessary and inevitable' as part of their daily lives. Extra-legality is characterised by political negotiations between vendors, civic authorities and others. It has been shown how each unit of bribes gets subdivided and distributed in a number of people in a well-coordinated and intricate manner.

De Soto (1989) pointed out that the main characteristic of the informal sector is due to the absence of laws and regulations, which is perhaps true in case of street vending. Implementation of laws, regulations and accountability requires the existence of 'property rights' or formal proofs of ownership or rights of use. Therefore the concept of property right is important in the context of street vending. De Soto (2000) remarked that property rights in the informal sector in the developing countries cannot be documented and permanently recorded in the legal framework by traditional techniques of registration. In his opinion, formalisation would create the rights, obligations and legal instruments that enable the owners to link the government and private entrepreneurs. De Soto (1989, 2000) further states that the informal sector is the part of the economy that lacks the institutions required to provide security and allow businesses and governments to perform efficiently. He highlights two important characteristics. First, there is an absence of proper machinery to provide security for the business to flourish. Second, this sector restricts the government from functioning efficiently. Inefficiency and insecurity characterise the informal sector.

In the developing countries, rights over property and ownership arrangements are defined by informal agreements, and the government machinery cannot efficiently regulate them. The traditional methods applied to confer property rights are not applicable in such cases. In short, the existing market mechanisms are not fully equipped to absorb the informal arrangements. This study found that street vendors pay significant amounts as bribe to the police and municipal officials to survive at the marketplace. Sometimes the police appoint local strongmen to collect the rent amount. Street vendors find bribe payment as the second best solution and best alternative way to sustain. They enter into mutual relationship with local authorities to establish their rights over space use. In this way informal market institutions are being created or it is being promoted by different agents.

Hernando de Soto made state responsible for the emergence of informal arrangements whereas Marjit and Kar (2009) in their study argued that in the absence of proper social welfare and democratic state, informality perpetuates. It can be perceived that in case of self-employed informal workers, total deregulation and decentralisation are harmful and result in further marginalisation. When left to the market, vendors are victims of illegal and rampant bribes and associated harassments. The state needs to interfere. Leaving totally on the market forces might lead to market failure. State refers to central law making and law-implementing agency of the national government. De Soto talks of devolution of powers between the Centre and constituent federal governments or lower machineries of the state. However, from the preliminary investigation, we have found that federal governments are often divided in their approaches, which results in lacunae in law implementation. Let us take the example of West Bengal. In Post-Act situation, it has been revealed that the state of West Bengal needs to frame separate legal frameworks to further the Act that involves changing the associated laws in the district and municipal machinery (police and municipal acts) to be able to implement the provisions. At present many of the provisions of the district and municipal acts contradict and contravene the provisions of the Street Vendors' Act. In this case, it would take years to implement the Act which is also affected by Centre–State political and financial relations. However even after the Act, the basic question is, will the street vending activity continue as an extra-legal occupation? In the absence of proper state response and legal frame, multiple layers of informality and illegality are perpetuated in the street vending activity. It is likely that the current protective measures if not carefully implemented might make them further marginalised or street vendors might further choose or prefer to operate outside the legal law. The current scenario hints at growing concerns of state authorities on how licences shall be distributed, how TVC shall be formed and how decisions on vending activity be more inclusive with respect to vendors' participation. The legal frame does not seem enough to what is required. The Act has to be implemented in a systematic manner. States need to look into the matter with a benevolent attitude and avoid nexus between civic authorities of different state governments at nullifying the progresses made. The activity substitutes for social security and emerges as self-innovative and effective re-distributive strategy. Bromley and Mackie (2009) in their study argued that formalisation and policy-led gratification result in further marginalisation of the poorest. Measures should be taken to ensure that vendors are not marginalised but actually benefitted by the Act. It is a fact that laws and regulations concerning street vending, and associated promotional measures, need to be made simplified and easy to comprehend so that the organisations can easily disseminate the provisions of the Act.

Conditions of street vendors: from decent work perspectives

Earlier studies (Saha 2010, 2014a) stated that achieving decent work for street vendors is a distant vision but not impossible. Unions can play an important instrumental role in attaining it (ibid.). As the Street Vendors Act 2014 ensures the protection of livelihood of street vendors, the concept of decent work holds significance because it is considered as the most comprehensive measurement of well-being in work. Thus it is interesting to understand how and whether the Act shall pave the way for achievement of decent work. However, this calls for long-term research on the topic. Let us examine the current working conditions of street vendors from the viewpoint of decent work. The concept of decent work was introduced by the International Labour Organisation (ILO) in 1999 in a report by its Director-General at the 87th International Labour Conference. According to the report, the ILO intends to promote 'opportunities for women and men to obtain decent and productive work in conditions of freedom, equity, security and human dignity' (ILO 1999: 3). The four major pillars recommended by ILO (1999) to achieve the goal of decent work are: opportunities for employment and income, respect for rights at work, social protection and strong social dialogue. Taking these four strategies into consideration together, ILO has defined 'decent work' as:

> Productive work in which rights are protected, which generates an adequate income, with adequate social protection. It also means sufficient work, in the sense that all should have full access to income-earning opportunities. It marks the high road to economic and social development, a road in which employment, income and social protection can be achieved without compromising workers' rights and social standards. Tripartism and social dialogue are both objectives in their own right, guaranteeing participation and democratic process, and a means of achieving all the other strategic objectives of the ILO. The evolving global economy offers opportunities from which all can gain, but these have to be grounded in participatory social institutions if they are to confer legitimacy and sustainability on economic and social policies.

> (ILO 1999: 12)

From the above definition of 'decent work', it can be deduced that first and foremost, there must be enough prospects for gainful employment and the work must ensure adequate income. Second, workers must have the right to work and rights at work. Third, workers must have social protection coverage which should be achieved without compromising workers' rights and social standards. Fourth, there must be scope for strong social dialogue through which workers can have a voice for collective bargaining. Let us examine the conditions of street vendors from decent work perspective considering these four major indicators, namely, employment and income opportunities, rights at work, social protection and social dialogue.

Income and employment opportunities and rights at work

Street vendors play an important role in the urban informal economy by generating self-employment for a significant portion of the urban population as a whole and youth as a particular. It is also seen that the income is sufficient and most workers can sustain with it. This means work must be productive subject to adequate income generation. The study finds that about 32 per cent of street vendors' households have a per capita income below Rs 100 a day (as highlighted in Chapter 1). The NCEUS report (2007) categorised people with this daily income as 'poor and vulnerable'. One of the factors responsible for the vendors' low income is the regular payment of bribes. Their income could have been more if they did not have to pay these amounts. Large family size leads to an increase in household expenditures which leaves little for reinvestment in the business. Excessive competition due to limited space of activity leads to further fall in incomes. Vendors with higher incomes tend to pay higher bribes to avoid interventions and associated harassment. Rights to decent work standards are violated when vendors have to ply their trade subject to paying bribes to municipal authorities and the police. It was observed that the level of daily income increases once the vendors pay bribes. This is due to a reduction in incidences of harassment and intervention from the local police and municipal officials *on the days that bribes are paid*. The trend of data further reveals that low income exists not along caste and religion but with the gender distinctions (females, irrespective of whether they belong to upper or lower castes, earn low daily incomes). Female

vendors are using more time for the sale of their products as compared to their male counterparts. Rights at work aim at securing
their employment and income by giving basic rights at the workplace. Rights at work cover issues like discrimination at work, and
the right to form associations to secure common demands related
to the vendors' welfare. It also implies that vendors carry out their
profession free of fear and harassment like bribes or extortion. On
the other hand, this activity attracts rural workers and less educated
people. As mentioned in Chapter 2, some street vendors flourish
with their business, earn decent and employ vendors as wage workers and also have scope for further expansion. Vendors reported
that they would continue and it would be more dignified if they do
not face harassment from the state in terms of eviction and bribe
payment. Notably, they do not want their children to get into the
profession. Majority of the street vendors (especially women) take
up this activity because of supporting their children's education.
Therefore, the occupation can provide income and has capacity
to absorb unemployed ones and can provide business opportunity
to them. From this aspect, it can be said that gainful employment
can be achieved through the activity if these insecurities can be
addressed.

Working hours

Informal sector workers, especially the street vendors, operate in
hostile working environments and their work is characterised by
prolonged working hours. Roadside vending exposes them to accidents, and they are prone to diseases contracted through air and
noise pollution. Results show that about 75.3 per cent of vendors
work eight to twelve hours per day and 13.6 per cent of vendors
spend more than twelve hours per day, and most vendors work
for seven days a week. Interestingly, working hours have increased
by three to four hours a day as seen from the study conducted by
Bhowmik in 2001. Women are more vulnerable as their working
hours include not only the time they devote to their vending stalls
but also the time required to perform domestic chores. Long working hours are a clear indication of the decent work deficit (Bescond
et al. 2003) and the reality is that longer working hours do not
mean an increase in income. These hours of vending are devoted
not only to selling but also to procure materials, to set up a stall and
reach workplace from home. Moreover, due to a rise in competition,

vendors find it difficult to sell their wares quickly and therefore have to sit at their stalls for a long time to make enough sales.

Social security

There is a lack of comprehensive social security schemes for unorganised sector workers and especially schemes which directly address the vendors' needs. However, the need for state-sponsored social security is perceived to be among the primary needs of the vendors. A small percentage of vendors are availing JBY through the active involvement of trade unions. But vendors complain about paying Rs 169 (approximate) as their annual insurance premium. They are not satisfied with the present coverage of the scheme provided by the union. In the low outreach of social security measures, vendors borrow from moneylenders or wholesalers at high rates and consequently fall into a debt trap because these are non-income-generating loans. But as some of them reported, they use a part of the fund to meet their business requirement. When they invest in business, some income is generated which help them to pay the interest. The present social security measures are therefore inadequate.

Social security for formal sector workers is mainly protective, but this section of the self-employed urban working poor needs promotional as well as protective measures. Street vendors require basic security cover (nutrition, housing and education for children) in addition to socio-economic security. As mentioned earlier, vendors pay a significant portion of their income as bribes and, due to their informal nature of work, they also need to depend on informal credit providers. Data show that often they need to mainly borrow for social security purposes and others which are non-income-generating activity for which some street vendors fall into a debt trap. Once they are assured of a regular flow of income by legalising this activity, they can contribute and invest towards their health and insurance. During the field surveys, many vendors have expressed their willingness to invest in human capital such as children's education and family's health care, which means they can contribute and cover towards their own protective social security. It is only then that the decent work standard with respect to social protection can be achieved.

During the field visits undertaken for this study, few observations were made about their living conditions even though it was not a main objective of the study. Most of the vendors live in slum settlements with improper drainage and sewerage disposal facilities. Their homes are ill-ventilated with inadequate spaces for the number of family members. They do not even have access to pure drinking water. All these conditions increase their vulnerability to illnesses. The ration they are provided through fair-price shops is of low quality, forcing them to sell it in the neighbourhood rather than using it. Proper targeting is not done to benefit the poor. Borrowing large amounts for children's education implies that vendors are serious about educating their children so that they can opt for better occupations. It is seen as an investment in human capital and also security in old age for the vendors. Post Act, stakeholders such as private and public insurance companies are showing their interest to collaborate in providing different insurance schemes through various trade unions or NGOs. Different micro-finance institutions (MFIs) are coming up with various micro-insurance schemes along with various credit facilities for vendors.

Harassment at the workplace

Decent working standards are violated when vendors have to ply their trade amidst harassments by paying bribes to municipal authorities and the police. It is found that the level of daily income increases with an increase in the daily sale. This is because when vendors pay more bribes, there are fewer incidences of harassment and intervention from the local police and municipality, but only for that day. This may have a positive effect on the income. Nevertheless, harassment, eviction and insecurity at the workplace are common phenomena. The degree of eviction and raid has decreased but not stopped. Vendors in different cities (Bengaluru, Delhi, Mumbai, Kolkata and Guwahati) across the country are facing eviction even after the Act. One of the provisions in the Act is to count total numbers of street vendors in each place. Local authorities are making all possible ways in which they can evict them [vendors] so that the total number of vendors can be shown less than actual on paper.

Collective bargaining

During this study, vendors agreed that they normally bring their people from the villages and smaller towns and help them to enter this profession as it requires small investment and low level of education. Vendors prefer to make their ethnic group a majority because it brings solidarity that helps to organise joint protests or struggles. Unfortunately unionisation among vendors is found to be thin. Vendors perceive union activities to be mere wastage of time. Sometimes unionisation is also avoided because vendors want to avoid paying the membership fees. Trade unions are seen to work effectively in securing their rights to public space utilisation and access to low-cost credit. However, union membership among street vendors depends on types of products they sell, language, religion, caste and education. For instance, caste, religion and language of the leader tend to bring together vendors belonging to same social group. Vendors belonging to same social groups tend to affiliate together with same union. Similarly, vendors selling same types of commodities will affiliate to the same union. Unionisation among educated vendors is found to be more.

Dignity of work and street vending

From the view of decent work, one can say that street vendors have absolute decent work deficit. But in relative terms, many vendors are happy with their occupation as it helps sustaining their livelihood, sending money back home and supporting children's education. Another important issue that has come up is 'denial of dignity'. Dignity of an individual is defined as the quality or state of being worthy of honour or esteem or respect. ILO stresses upon 'enhancing dignity of the individual' through ensuring his/her rights at work. The dimensions of decent work paradigm itself maintain a direct relation between 'decency of work' and 'dignity of the individual'. It implies that 'when work is considered decent', it would at that time 'ensure dignity of the worker'. The importance of 'assuring dignity' is expressed in the Indian Constitution as well. According to the Directive Principles of State Policy, Article 39 (e), 'the state shall in particular direct its policy towards securing that the health and strength of its workers, men and women and the tender age of children are not abused and that citizens are not forced by economic necessity to enter avocations unsuited to their age and strength' (Bakshi 2006: 22). Further Article 39 (f) also stresses that 'children are given opportunities and facilities to develop in a healthy manner, in conditions of freedom and dignity and that their childhood and youth are protected from exploitation and against moral and material abandonment' (ibid.). Article 41 further points out that 'the state shall, within the limits of economic capacity and development, make effective provisions for securing the workers' rights to work, to education and to public assistance in cases of unemployment, old age, sickness and disablement and in other cases of undeserved want' (ibid.: 88). Article 42 also states that the 'state shall make provisions for securing just and humane conditions of work and for maternity relief' (ibid.). Article 43 mentions that the 'state shall endeavour to secure by suitable legislation or economic organisation or in any other way to all workers, agricultural, industrial or otherwise, work, a living wage, conditions of work and a decent standard of life, and full enjoyment of leisure and social and cultural opportunities and, in particular, the State shall endeavour to promote cottage industries on an individual or cooperative basis in rural areas' (GOI 2008a: 23). The importance of securing dignity of an individual by protecting his/her rights at work and overall working conditions is therefore not new in the Indian context.

One of the street vendors in this study said, 'there is no dignity in this profession, I do not want my children to become street vendors'. Other vendors have mentioned the absence of recognition, respect, certainty and security of employment and income as major issues. They also talk of low and erratic income, in addition to being treated as a 'nuisance' and facing frequent evictions (70 per cent of vendors say they suffer from threats of eviction, while the rate of eviction has gone up to three times in a year). The degree of harassment from the police and civic authorities that vendors face has increased. They end up paying high interest on their loans. All these factors point to a 'chronic absence of decent working conditions' in this profession. The children of street vendors have the right to a safe and secure childhood free from exploitation. Decent working conditions among vendors will ensure a safe childhood for their wards.

Vendors have mentioned that loans are often taken for social security purposes, one of the main reasons being children's education. Both male and female vendors borrow anywhere between Rs 1,000 and Rs 30,000 for their business and social security requirements. Mindful of the lack of dignity in this profession, the vendors want their children to be well educated so as to find better employment opportunities. The absence of state-sponsored social security options also points out to the fact that vendors have to find their own means to educate their children. Article 39(f) of the

Indian Constitution clearly states that 'the state shall try to give opportunities to all children to develop in a healthy manner and prevent their exploitation'.

Every person has a right to adequate income not only to survive but also to lead a life of dignity. A decent standard of living depends upon the fulfilment of basic needs of food, nutrition, health, education, housing and sanitation as well as protection from contingencies arising out of unemployment, old age, accidents and so on. Right to social security ensures every person the right to live a decent and a dignified life. Recognition of social security as a human right represents the essential bridge between need-based charity and right-based social justice (Standing 2002). Social security is the basic right of every worker in the country because each one contributes to its national income. Formal sector workers have the rights to adequate social security coverage; however, the informal sector workers, who contribute more than 60 per cent to the country's GDP, do not have sufficient access to social security.

Standing (2002) points out that the acute sense of insecurity is all pervasive, in that it affects workers of all classes, age groups and both sexes. He says that the social security component of decent work paradigm as outlined by the ILO (1999) regards, in addition to basic security, seven forms of 'work-related security related to the labour market'. These seven forms precisely refer to security with regard to employment (as against arbitrary dismissal from work), labour market security (as productive employment and work opportunities), job, work and skill reproduction security (which refer to the elimination of barriers for acquiring skills and access to widespread opportunities to gain skills, protection against accidents or illness which may lead to discontinuance of income), income security (through right to minimum wages) and lastly representation security (protection of collective voice in labour markets).

In the context of street vendors, who are self-employed workers in the urban informal sector, labour market security and work security hold utmost relevance, in addition to representation security. Fulfilment of basic needs through promotional social security measures along with these securities would help them to lead a dignified life and prevent them from becoming victims of the vicious circle of debt and deprivation. Bhowmik (2005) made an important comment that in a country where thieves and criminals move about freely, the street vendors who try to make an honest living by toiling hard day in and day out are treated with disrespect, although they are citizens of the country who make vital contributions to the urban economy.

Interviews with vendors revealed that the space they occupy was previously occupied by a vendor from his/her same village. It is given to the present occupation against a nominal amount or rent. Thus the space of vending, which is not even formally recognised, is sub-rented and used by generations of vendors. Although the vendors widely agree that there is absolutely no 'dignity' in this profession and actively discourage their children to pursue this trade in the future, they also bring along and encourage people from their villages or native places to take it up as their profession. When asked why this is so, one of them remarked, 'we did not have a choice so we became street vendors. People from our village who are uneducated, unskilled, poor and asset-less come to us for help. We have no other choice but to help them become vendors, however the case with our children is different. We are earning to give them a better life; they have a choice to join better occupations'. Denial of dignity mainly comes from the current status of street vendors. But the situation is different post Act. They are no longer unrecognised. This approach is the result of the lack of formal recognition of their activities. The important role they play in the urban economy could be easily judged from the backward and forward linkages. State governments' initiatives at recognising them and execution through local-level governance will help in assigning 'dignity' to their occupation. Therefore, the argument is not that the state should provide dignity but the state can secure and implement the Act at the ground level by which dignity would follow automatically.

Concluding remarks

Workers in the urban informal sector are said to be 'working class in embryo' (Sanyal 1991). These workers have distinct issues and requirements from the state which are altogether different from the needs of industrial workers. Here workers face the problem of employment. As workers are seen to generate sources of employment in the urban informal sector, staying unemployed is not a plausible idea for them. Instead, as Hart points out, they create or generate their own employment opportunities. Self-employed workers in the informal sector due to their entrepreneurial abilities are also said to have abilities to organise themselves into a separate political force even to the point of moving governments and bringing about political revolution (ibid.). Sanyal's (1991) interesting observation can be seen from the aspect of perpetuation of vending as an extra-legal activity. The economic value of space rises when vendors use it to generate income. If they would not have been there, these spaces either would have been left open or would have fetched much less money. This explains the rationale behind letting vendors operate through these extra-legal arrangements. Vendors mainly operate in 'natural markets' and they concentrate in areas like railway stations, parks, temples and bus stands. Although railway land is included in the Act, existing markets must be designated as 'natural markets' where street vendors find a large number of customers. Securing the vendors' right to use these areas, with suitable restrictions at a particular time of the day or night, could serve both the customers who benefit from their presence and the street vendors. In the areas considered in this study, the number of vendors depends on the time of the day or the season of the year. Some vendors sell only in the morning, afternoon or evening, while some sell only on weekends; others sell only during certain seasons. For instance, in some of the streets in Dadar (Mumbai) or Garia Hat (Kolkata), three different vendors were found to occupy and sit at the same place in the morning, afternoon and evening, respectively. The first step of vendors' existence in the urban economy will legally be recognised by a systematic and detailed documentation as outlined in the Act, as a result of which rights over public utilisation will be secured and livelihood protected.

Given the importance of street vendors in the urban informal sector, some NGOs, cooperatives and other MBOs have come forward with initiatives for providing social security and other basic requirements to street vendors. De Soto supports the idea of the organisations in promoting and paving the third path of development, which precludes government on one hand and market on the other. But organisations need a direction and uncontrolled power assigned to the MBOs may also lead to power usurpation and abuse. In view of the present economic situation, ever-shrinking formal sector job opportunities at the labour market and current employment strategy, the informal sector would be likely to expand. Since street vending is one of the easiest ways to get into the urban informal sector and the Government of India seems to be promoting vocational training and entrepreneurial skills, growth of street vendors will also be increasing in the years to come. One of the major findings of this study is that in places where trade unions are performing efficiently and effectively, street vendors are found to be in relatively better position. Thus, trade unions or other MBOs could be a good way to organise vendors. They could achieve a reasonably decent working life or at least a better working environment with the help of trade unions.

Rights over utilisation of public spaces must be exercised in a manner that protects the rights of both citizens and vendors. Securing rights over commercial places should also accompany the provision of basic services like sanitation, drinking water and solid waste disposal. Though there is such provision in the Act, how shall it be executed is the basic question. The state governments concerned could take up the issue not only as an urban planning strategy but also as a livelihood promotion strategy for a large section of urban poor. In order to protect the means of livelihood for this growing segment of the poor, the issue of legalisation needs to be taken up more seriously as this would secure their other rights such as access to formal credit and social security. It is evident that street vendors are micro-entrepreneurs (not a nuisance) and have the potential to run a successful enterprise even with limited resources. Realising their capacity, corporates are showing keen interest in their business initiatives. However, there are already many schemes under different state policy initiatives such as the National Urban Livelihoods Mission of MoHUPA which are directly related to street vendors. Moreover, the stakeholders who are involved (municipal corporations, district administration, state governments, MBOs, trade unions, nationalised banks, MFIs and others) should include street vendors in various programmes and policies. Most street vendors considered in this study assumed that because they had employment and could remit money back to their families, they were already in a much better position than they were or could have been. This will also make them believe that their work is already 'decent'. If the provisions of the Act are implemented in right spirit along with a strong monitoring mechanism in place, street vendors' work and life would genuinely improve. More importantly, progressive realisation from below [vendors and organisations] and well-coordinated regulation from the state [mainly civic body] are needed to make efficient formal institutions. Decency of work would be attained if promotional measures are taken up along with protective measures and thereby making it 'decent' in its true sense.

With this current development on street vending, issues related to new forms of illegality, informality, scope of corporate investment, access to formal institutional credit, policy implementation and so on have emerged which can be deliberated further in future research. These will however involve more in-depth research that is, perhaps, beyond the scope of this book.

Bibliography

Agarwala, Rina. 2013. *Informal Labor, Formal Politics, and Dignified Discontent in India*, Cambridge: Cambridge University Press.

Agnello, Francesca and Joanne Moller. 2004. 'Vendors, Purses: Women Microentrepreneurs and Their Business Needs, Phnom Penh, Cambodia', Report-March, Urban Sector Group, Phnom Penh.

Ahmed, Iftikhar. 2003. 'Decent Work and Human Development', *International Labour Review*, 142(2): 263–271.

Anjaria, Jonathan S. 2006. 'Street Hawkers and Public Space in Mumbai', *Economic and Political Weekly*, 41(21): 2140–2146.

Anker, Richard, Igor Chernyshev, Philippe Egger, Farhad Mehran and Joseph Ritter. 2003. 'Measuring Decent Work with Statistical Indicators', *International Labour Review*, 142(2): 147–177.

Bakshi, P. M. (ed.). 2006. *The Constitution of India*, Delhi: Universal Law Publishing Co. Pvt. Ltd.

Bardhan, Pranab. 1984. *The Political Economy of Underdevelopment in India*, New Delhi: Oxford University Press.

Basu, Durga Das (ed.). 1989. *Introduction to the Constitution of India*, New Delhi: Prentice Hall.

Bescond, David, Anne Châtaignier and Farhad Mehran. 2003. 'Seven Indicators to Measure Decent Work: An International Comparison', *International Labour Review*, 142(2): 179–211.

Bhaduri, Amit. 2005. *Development with Dignity: A Case for Full Employment*, New Delhi: National Book Trust.

Bhowmik, Sharit K. 2001. 'Hawkers and the Urban Informal Sector: A Study of Street Vending in Seven Cities', Available at: http://wiego.org/sites/wiego.org/files/publications/files/Bhowmik-Hawkers-URBAN-INFORMAL-SECTOR.pdf (Accessed in March 2010).

Bhowmik, Sharit K. 2005. 'Street Vendors in Asia: A Review', *Economic and Political Weekly*, 40(22–23): 2256–2264.

Bhowmik, Sharit K. 2006. 'Social Security for Street Vendors', *Seminar*, 568(December): 49–57.

Bhowmik, Sharit K. (ed.). 2010. *Street Vendors in the Global Urban Economy*, New Delhi: Routledge.

Bhowmik, Sharit K. (ed.). 2014. *The State of Labour: Global Financial Crisis and Its Impact on Labour*, pp. 158–180, London and New Delhi: Routledge.

Bhowmik, Sharit K. and Debdulal Saha. 2012. 'Street Vending in Ten Cities in India', Available at: http://www.streetnet.org.za/docs/research/2012/en/NASVIReport-Survey.pdf (Accessed in June 2012).

Bhowmik, Sharit K. and Debdulal Saha. 2013. *Financial Inclusion of the Marginalised: Street Vendors in the Urban Economy*, New Delhi: Springer.

Breman, Jan. 1980. *The Informal Sector in Research: Theory and Practice*, Rotterdam: Comparative Asian Studies Programme, Erasmus University.

Bromley, Ray. 1978. 'Introduction – The Urban Informal Sector: Why Is It Worth Discussing?' *World Development*, 6(9–10): 1033–1039.

Bromley, Rosemary D. F. and Peter K. Mackie. 2009. 'Displacement and the New Spaces for Informal Trade in the Latin American City Centre', *Urban Studies,* 46(7): 1485–1506.

Brown, Alison (ed.). 2006. *Contested Space: Street Trading, Public Space and Livelihoods in Developing Cities*, Warwickshire: Intermediate Technology Publications.

Brown, Alison, Michal Lyons and Ibrahima Dankoco. 2010. 'Street Traders and the Emerging Spaces for Urban Voice and Citizenship in African Cities', *Urban Studies,* 47(3): 666–683.

Bryman, Alan. 2009. *Social Research Methods* (3rd edition), Oxford: Oxford University Press.

Byres, Terence J. (ed.). 1994. *The State, Development Planning and Liberalisation in India*, New Delhi: Oxford University Press.

Castells, Manuel and Alejandro Portes. 1989. 'World Underneath: The Origins, Dynamics, and Effects of the Informal Economy', in Alejandro Portes, Manuel Castells and Lauren A. Benton (eds), *The Informal Economy: Studies in Advanced and Less Developed Countries*, pp. 11–37, Baltimore and London: Johns Hopkins University Press.

Charmes, Jacques. 1998. 'Women Working in the Informal Sector in Africa: New Methods and New Data', Paper Prepared for the UN Statistics Division, the Gender and Development Programme of the United Nations Development Programme (UNDP) and Women in Informal Employment: Globalizing and Organizing (WIEGO) Network.

Charmes, Jacques. 2000. 'Informal Sector, Poverty and Gender: A Review of Empirical Evidence', Paper Commissioned for World Development Report 2000/1. Washington DC: World Bank.

Charmes, Jacques. 2012. 'The Informal Economy Worldwide: Trends and Characteristics', *Margin – The Journal of Applied Economic Research*, 6(2): 103–132.

Chen, Martha Alter. 2007. 'Rethinking the Informal Economy: Linkages with the Formal Economy and the Formal Regulatory Environment', DESA Working Paper No. 46, Department of Economic and Social Affairs, New York: United Nations. Available at: www.un.org/esa/desa/papers/2007/wp46_2007.pdf (Accessed in March 2010).

Chen, Martha Alter, Renana Jhabvala, Ravi Kanbur and Carol Richards. 2007. 'Membership-Based Organizations of the Poor', in Martha Alter Chen, Renana Jhabvala, Ravi Kanbur and Carol Richards (eds), *Membership-Based Organizations of the Poor*, pp. 3–20, New York: Routledge.

Creswell, John W. 2009. *Research Design: Qualitative, Quantitative, and Mixed Methods Approaches* (3rd edition), Thousand Oaks, CA: Sage Publications.

Cross, John C. 1998a. 'Co-optation, Competition, and Resistance State and Street Vendors in Mexico City', *Latin American perspectives*, 25(2): 41–61.

Cross, John C. 1998b. *Informal Politics: Street Vendors and the State in Mexico City*, Stanford, CA: Stanford University Press.

Dasgupta, Sukti. 2002. *Organizing for Socio-Economic Security in India*, Geneva: International Labour Office.

De Neve, Geert. 2005. *The Everyday Politics of Labour: Working Lives in India's Informal Economy*, New Delhi: Social Science Press.

De Soto, Hernando. 1989. *The Other Path: The Economic Answer to Terrorism*, New York: Harper Collins.

De Soto, Hernando. 2000. *The Mystery of Capital: Why Triumphs in the West and Fails Everywhere Else*, New York: Basic Books.

Dixit, Avinash. 2004. *Lawlessness and Economics: Alternative Modes of Governance*, New Jersey, NJ: Princeton University Press.

Donovan, Michael G. 2002. 'Space Wars in Bogotá: The Recovery of Public Space and Its Impact on Street Vendors', Master's Thesis, Department of Urban Studies and Planning, Cambridge: Massachusetts Institute of Technology.

Edgar, L. Feige. 1997. 'Underground Activity and Institutional Change: Productive, Protective and Predatory Behavior in Transition Economies', in Joan M. Nelson, Charles Tilly and Lee Walker (eds), *Transforming Post-Communist Political Economies*, pp. 19–34, Washington, DC: National Academy Press.

Fakier, Khayat and Elen Ehmke (eds). 2014. *Socio-Economic Insecurity in Emerging Economies: Building New Spaces*, London and New York: Routledge Earthscan.

Fields, Gary S. 1975. 'Rural-Urban Migration, Urban Unemployment and Underemployment and Job Search Activity in LDCs', *Journal of Development Economics*, 2(2): 165–188.

Fields, Gary S. 1990. 'Labour Market Modelling and the Urban Informal Sector: Theory and Evidence', Cornell: Cornell University ILR School.

Fine, Ben. 1998. *Labour Market Theory: A Constructive Reassessment*, London: Routledge.

Gaiha, Raghav and Ganesh Thapa. 2007. 'Super Markets, Small Holders and Livelihoods Prospects in Selected Asian Countries', ASARC Working Papers 2007/12, Italy: International Fund for Agricultural Development.

Geertz, Clifford. 1978. 'The Bazaar Economy: Information and Search in Peasant Marketing', *American Economic Review*, 68(2): 28–32.

Ghai, Dharam. 2003. 'Decent Work: Concept and Indicators', *International Labour Review*, 142: 133–145.

Ginneken, Wouter van. 2003. 'Extending Social Security: Policies for Developing Countries', *International Labour Review*, 142: 277–294.

GOI (Government of India). 1969. 'Report on National Commission on Labour', Delhi: Ministry of Labour and Employment and Rehabilitation. Available at: https://casi.sas.upenn.edu/sites/casi.sas.upenn.edu/files/iit/National%20Commission%20on%20Labour%20Report.pdf (Accessed on 20 September 2014).

GOI (Government of India). 2002. 'Report on National Commission on Labour', New Delhi: Ministry of Labour and Employment. Available at: http://www.prsindia.org/uploads/media/1237548159/NLCII-report.pdf (Accessed on 20 September 2014).

GOI (Government of India). 2006. 'National Policy on Urban Street Vendors-2006', New Delhi: Ministry of Housing and Urban Poverty Alleviation (MoHUPA). Available at: http://mhupa.gov.in/w_new/sug_npusv.pdf (Accessed in April 2013).

GOI (Government of India). 2009. 'National Policy on Urban Street Vendors-2009', New Delhi: Ministry of Housing and Urban Poverty Alleviation (MoHUPA). Available at: http://mhupa.gov.in/w_new/Street Policy09.pdf (Accessed in April 2013).

GOI (Government of India). 2014. 'The Street Vendors (Protection of Livelihood and Regulation of Street Vending) Act 2014', New Delhi: GOI. Available at: http://www.indiacode.nic.in/acts2014/7%20of%202014.pdf (Accessed in April 2014).

Gopalakrishnan, Ramapriya. 2008. 'Freedom of Association and Collective Bargaining in Export Processing Zones: Role of the ILO Supervisory Mechanisms', Working Paper 1, Geneva: International Labour Organisation. Available at: http://www.ilo.org/wcmsp5/groups/public/@ed_norm/@normes/documents/publication/wcms_087917.pdf (Accessed in November 2011).

Granovetter, Mark. 1985. 'Economic Action and Social Structure: The Problem of Embeddedness', *American Journal of Sociology*, 91(3): 481–510.

Granovetter, Mark and Richard Swedberg (eds). 2001. *Sociology of Economic Life* (2nd edition), Oxford: Westview Press.

Guha-Khasnobis, Basudeb, Ravi Kanbur and Elinor Ostrom (eds). 2006. *Linking the Formal and Informal Economy: Concepts and Policies*, New York: Oxford University.

Guruswamy, Mohan, Kamal Sharma, Jeevan Prakash Mohanty and Thomas J. Korah. 2005. 'FDI in India's Retail Sector: More Bad than Good?' *Economic and Political Weekly*, 40(7): 619–623.

Harris, John R. and Michael P. Todaro. 1970. 'Migration, Unemployment and Development: A Two-Sector Analysis', *American Economic Review*, 60(1): 126–142.

Harriss-White, Barbara. 2003. *India Working: Essays on Society and Economy*, Cambridge, UK: Cambridge University Press.

Hart, Keith. 1973. 'Informal Income Opportunities and Urban Employment in Ghana', *Journal of Modern African Studies*, 11(1): 61–89.

Harvey, David. 1973. *Social Justice and the City*, London: Edward Arnold.

Harvey, David. 1978. 'Urban Process under Capitalism: A Framework for Analysis', *International Journal of Urban and Regional Research*, 2(1–4): 101–131.

ILO (International Labour Organization). 1972. 'Employment, Incomes and Equality: A Strategy for Increasing Productive Employment in Kenya', Geneva: International Labour Organization.

ILO (International Labour Organization). 1999. 'Report of the Director-General: Decent Work', Geneva: ILO. Available at: www2.ilo.org/public/english/standards/relm/ilc/ilc87/rep-i.htm (Accessed in March 2010).

Jhabvala, Renana. 2000. *The Role of Street Vendors in the Growing Urban Economies,* Ahmedabad: Self-Employed Women's Association.

Kannan, K. P. 2009. 'Dualism, Informality and Social Inequality: An Informal Economy Perspective of the Challenge of Inclusive Development in India', *Indian Journal of Labour Economics*, 52(1): 1–32.

Kusakabe, Kyoko. 2006. 'On the Borders of Legality: A Review of Studies on Street Vending in Phnom Penh, Cambodia', Informal Economy, Poverty and Employment, Cambodia Series, Number 4, Geneva: International Labour Organization. Available at http://www.ilo.org/public/english/region/asro/bangkok/library/download/pub06–21.pdf (Accessed in December 2012).

Lewis, W. Arthur. 1954. 'Economic Development with Unlimited Supplies of Labour', *Manchester School of Economic and Social Studies*, 22: 139–191.

Lubell, Harold. 1991. *Informal Sector in the 1980s and 1990s*, Paris: OECD.

Lynch, Kevin. 1981. *A Theory of Good City Form*, Cambridge, MA: MIT Press.

Maloney, William F. 2004. 'Informality Revisited', *World Development*, 32(7): 1159–1178.

Marjit, Sugata. 2009. 'A Contemporary perspective on Informal Labour Market: Theory, Policy and Indian Experience', *Economic and Political Weekly*, 44(14): 60–71.

Marjit, Sugata and Saibal Kar. 2009. 'A Contemporary Perspective on the Informal Labour Market: Theory, Policy and the Indian Experience', *Economic and Political Weekly*, 44(14): 60–71.

Marjit, Sugata, Vivekananda Mukherjee and Martin Kolmar. 2006. 'Poverty, Taxation and Governance', *Journal of International Trade and Economic Development*, 15(3): 325–333.

McGee, T. G. 1973. *Hawkers in Hong Kong: A Study of Planning and Policy in a Third World City*, Hong Kong: University of Hong Kong, Centre of Asian Studies.

Mitra, Arup. 2002. 'Training and Skill Formation for Decent Work in Informal Sector: Case Studies from South India', Geneva: International Labour Organisation.

Mitullah, Winnie V. 2004. 'A Review of Street Trade in Africa', Working Draft, May 2004, Nairobi, Institute for Development Studies, University of Nairobi, Paper Commissioned by Women in Informal Employment Globalising and Organising (WIEGO).

Morales, Alfonso and John C. Cross (eds). 2007. *Street Entrepreneurs: People, Place and Politics*, New York: Routledge.

Morris, Jeremy and Abel Polese (eds). 2013. *The Informal Post-Socialist Economy: Embedded Practices and Livelihoods*, New York and London: Routledge.

Moser, Caroline. O. N. 1978. 'Informal Sector or Petty Commodity Production: Dualism or Independence in Urban Development?' *World Development*, 6(9–10): 1041–1064.

Nattrass, Nicholi. 1987. 'Street Trading in Transkei – A Struggle against Poverty, Persecution and Prosecution', *World Development*, 15(7): 861–875.

NCEUS (National Commission for Enterprises in the Unorganized Sector). 2007. 'Report on Comprehensive Legislation for Minimum Conditions of Work and Social Security for Unorganised Workers', New Delhi: National Commission for Enterprises in the Unorganised Sector. Available at: http://nceus.gov.in/Report_Bill_July_2007.htm (Accessed in March 2010).

Neetha, N. 2009. 'Contours of Domestic Service: Characteristics, Work Relations and Regulations', *Indian Journal of Labour Economics*, 52(3): 489–506.

Papola, T. S. 1994. 'Structural Adjustment, Labour Market Flexibility and Employment', *Indian Journal of Labour Economics*, 37(1): 3–16.

Pena, Sergio. 1999. 'Informal Markets: Street Vendors in Mexico City', *Habitat International*, 23(3): 363–372.

Planning Commission, Government of India. 2008. 'Eleventh Five Year Plan 2007–2012: Urban Infrastructure, Housing, Basic Services and Poverty Alleviation', Available at: http://planningcommission.nic.in/plans/planrel/fiveyr/11th/11_v3/11v3_ch11.pdf (Accessed in February 2010).

Portes, Alejandro. 1994. 'The Informal Economy and Its Paradox', in Neil J. Smelser and Richard Swedberg (eds), *The Handbook of Economic Sociology* (1st edition), pp. 426–449, Princeton, NJ: Princeton University Press.

Portes, Alejandro, Manuel Castells and Lauren A. Benton (eds). 1989. *The Informal Economy: Studies in Advanced and Less Developed Countries*, Baltimore and London: Johns Hopkins University Press.

Ranis, Gustav and John C. H. Fei. 1961. 'A Theory of Economic Development', *American Economic Review*, 51(4): 533–565.

Roever, Sally. 2006. 'Enforcement and Compliance in Lima's Street Markets: The Origins and Consequences of Policy Incoherence towards Informal Traders', in Basudeb Guha-Khasnobis, Ravi Kanbur and Elinor Ostrom (eds), *Linking the Formal and Informal Economy: Concepts and Policies*, pp. 246–262, New York: Oxford University Press.

RoyChowdhury, Supriya. 2005. 'Labour Activism and Women in the Unorganised Sector: Garment Export Industry in Bangalore', *Economic and Political Weekly*, 40(22–23): 2250–2055.

RoyChowdhury, Supriya. 2007. 'Informality in Globalised Forms of Production', *Indian Journal of Labour Economics*, 50(40): 765–774.

Saha, Debdulal. 2010. 'Decent Work for the Street Vendors in Mumbai, India: A Distant Vision!' *Journal of Workplace Rights*, 14(2): 229–250.

Saha, Debdulal. 2011a. 'Working Life of Street Vendors in Mumbai', *Indian Journal of Labour Economics*, 54(2): 301–325.

Saha, Debdulal. 2011b. 'Collective Bargaining for Street Vendors in Mumbai: Toward Promotion of Decent Work', *Journal of Workplace Rights*, 15(3–4): 445–460.

Saha, Debdulal. 2014a. 'Decent Work for Urban Informal Economy: The Case of Street Vendors in Mumbai', in Sharit Bhowmik (ed.), *The State of Labour: Global Financial Crisis and Its Impact on Labour*, pp. 158–180, London and New Delhi: Routledge.

Saha, Debdulal. 2014b. 'Public Space and Livelihood Security in the Urban Economy: The Case of Street Vendors in Mumbai', in Khayat Fakier and Elen Ehmke (eds), *Socio-Economic Insecurity in Emerging Economies: Building New Spaces*, pp. 56–67, London and New York: Routledge Earthscan.

Saint-Paul, Gilles. 2000. *The Political Economy of Labour Market Institutions*, New York: Oxford University Press.

Sallaz, Jeffrey J. 2013. *Labor, Economy and Society*, Cambridge and Malden: Polity.

Sanyal, Bishwapriya. 1991. 'Organizing the Self-employed: The Politics of the Urban Informal Sector', *International Labour Review*, 130(1): 39–56.

Sen, Amartya K. 2000. 'Work and Rights', *International Labour Review,* 139(2): 119–128.

Sengupta, Arjun K., K. P. Kannan and G. Ravindran. 2008. 'India's Common People: Who Are They, How Many Are They and How Do They Live?' *Economic and Political Weekly*, 43(11): 49–63.

Sethuraman, S. V. 1976. 'Urban Informal Sector: Concept, Measurement and Policy', *International Labour Review,* 114(1): 69–81.

Sethuraman, S. V. 1998. 'Gender, Informality and Poverty: A Global Review – Gender Bias in Female Informal Employment and Incomes in Developing Countries', Geneva: International Labour Organisation.

Sharma, R. N. 1998. *Census Survey of Hawkers on BMC Lands*, Mumbai: Tata Institute of Social Sciences.

Skinner, Caroline. 1999. 'Local Government in Transition – A Gendered Analysis of Trends in Urban Policy and Practice Regarding Street Trading in Five South African Cities', CSDS Research Report No. 15. Durban: University of Natal.

Standing, Guy. 1999. *Global Labour Flexibility: Seeking Distributive Justice*, London: McMillan Press Ltd.

Standing, Guy. 2002. 'From People's Security Surveys to a Decent Work Index', *International Labour Review*, 141(4): 441–454.

Tiwari, Geetam. 2000. 'Encroachers or Services Providers?' *Seminar,* 491(July): 26–31.

Tokman, Victor. 1978. 'An Exploration into the Nature of the Informal-Formal Sector Relationship', *World Development*, 6: 1065–1075.

Tokman, Victor (ed.). 1992. *Beyond Regulation: The Informal Economy in Latin America*, Boulder, Colorado: Lynne Rienner Publishers.

Tokman, Victor E. and Emilio Klein (ed.). 1996. *Regulation and the Informal Economy: Microenterprises in Chile, Ecuador, and Jamaica*, Boulder, Colorado: Lynne Rienner Publishers.

Uzzi, Brian. 1997. 'Social Structure and Competition in Inter-Firm Networks: The Paradox of Embeddedness', *Administrative Science Quarterly*, 42(1): 35–67.

Vanamala, M. 2001. 'Informalisation and Feminisation of a Formal Sector Industry: A Case Study', *Economic and Political Weekly*, 36(26): 2378–2389.

Index

For Product Safety Concerns and Information please contact our EU
representative GPSR@taylorandfrancis.com
Taylor & Francis Verlag GmbH, Kaufingerstraße 24, 80331 München, Germany